The Gospels

A lawyer's Translation from the Original Greek

Malcolm Bishop QC, MA (Oxon)

Bencher of the Inner Temple; a former deputy High Court Judge and Recorder; Hon. Fellow and Hon. Standing Counsel, Regent's Park College, Oxford University

With introductions by Dr Brendan Devitt

The Gospels

A Lawyer's Translation from the Original Greek

Malcolm Bishop QC

Matador
Unit E2 Airfield Business Park,
Harrison Road, Market Harborough,
Leicestershire. LE16 7UL
Tel: 0116 2792299
Email: books@troubador.co.uk
Web: www.troubador.co.uk/matador
Twitter: @matadorbooks

ISBN 978 1803132 358

British Library Cataloguing in Publication Data.
A catalogue record for this book is available from the British Library.

Printed and bound by CPI Group (UK) Ltd, Croydon, CR0 4YY
Typeset in 11pt Century Gothic by Troubador Publishing Ltd, Leicester, UK

Matador is an imprint of Troubador Publishing Ltd

In Loving memory
Anthony Patrick Van der Woerd
1948 - 2019
Deeply loved by all who knew him

Just as the Father's loved me
so I've loved you
(John 15:9)

Dedicated to the Christian Martyrs of the Middle East and Africa

Hold fast to your belief that Jesus is the Messiah the Son of God

and that by believing you may have life in his name
(John 20:31)

FOUNDATION
FOR RELIEF AND
RECONCILIATION
IN THE MIDDLE EAST

www.acnuk.org
Tel: 02086 428668

All profits will be donated for the relief of the suffering church in the Middle East & Africa.

About This Book

Over the years I have frequently consulted my Greek New Testament for inspiration and comfort. In recent times I have embarked on a translation of some of the books of the New Testament, beginning with John. I have followed this up with Revelation, Mark and Matthew (which have been published by Matador separately), and finally with Luke, which completes the gospels, and is now included in this volume. Wherever possible I have adopted the strategy of preserving the use of the "present tense" where it occurs in the original Greek (in English, translators typically use a "past tense," often referred to as the "historic present," in order to make narratives conform to our English style of telling stories in the past tense.) This may sound strange at first, but as one becomes accustomed to this usage it gradually begins to sound not simply less odd, but entirely appropriate and fitting, both enhancing and making vivid, the lively, sometimes urgent nature of biblical storytelling.

I claim no particular expertise in biblical scholarship, but my training and experience as a lawyer may offer useful insights into the message of the gospels. I have spent all my adult life as an advocate. The aim of an advocate is to persuade. His tools are words. He uses them to make his case. He can deploy both the blunderbuss and the rapier, sometimes to overpower, sometimes to pierce the heart. The aim of the four Evangelists was to persuade that Jesus Christ is God's one and only son—God's complete self-expression in the form of a human being. To meet and know Jesus, therefore, is to encounter God and to receive his gift of everlasting life life. My hope and prayer is that, following a lifetime in the law and with God's accompanying grace, I might have succeeded—however inadequately—of shedding something of a forensic searchlight on the Good News that four of Jesus' earliest followers have bequeathed to humanity.

Malcolm Bishop QC
3, Hare Court,
The Temple,
London EC4Y 7 BJ

Epiphany 2022

About the Translator

Malcolm Bishop QC is a prominent British barrister and Queen's Counsel. He has practiced throughout England and Wales at every level, as well in the Caribbean. Before studying Law he read theology at Oxford where he learned Biblical Greek as part of his Honour Moderations.

Thanks

I owe my Greek teachers over the years an enormous debt of gratitude: the late Mr Warner, senior classics master at Ruabon Grammar School, for guiding me through my first faltering steps in Classical Greek; the Rev. Aubrey Argyle, for teaching me grammatical rigour at Oxford; and especially *Dr Brendan Devitt, who not only took me painstakingly through a Greek revision course, but also fired my enthusiasm to attempt my translations of the books of the New Testament. I have been greatly assisted by the helpful comments and insights of both theologians and lawyers, in particular Professor Fiddes FBA, the Rt.Hon Sir Malcolm Pill, the Hon. Arnold Nicholson QC, Rev Canon Edwin Urquart, and Dr Peter J Williams. However, I take responsibility for any errors or oversights. My thanks are also due to the German Bible Society for allowing me to use the 5th revised edition (2014) of its Greek New Testament.

I very much welcome comments:
malcolmbishop@3harecourt.com

** Dr Devitt is a graduate of Dublin and Oxford universities and teaches New Testament Greek and Biblical Hebrew to students, all over the world via Skype. He can be contacted at drbwd@gmail.com*

Contents

Matthew

Mark

Luke

John

Matthew

Introduction

The opening line of an old English nursery rhyme (sometimes referred to as the "Black Paternoster") preserves for us the order in which the gospels have come down to us: *Matthew, Mark, Luke and John/Bless the bed that I lie on*. Matthew's primacy reflects the stature and esteem in which the book was held in the early Church; it also reflects the belief (popular until the eighteenth century) that Matthew was the first gospel to be written, and therefore the most authoritative. A gospel that bore the name of one of Jesus's twelve apostles was naturally a highly prized possession. Matthew had been personally called by Jesus to be a disciple, had sat at his feet when he taught both publicly and privately, and had seen him perform miracles throughout his ministry. He was also among the first of Jesus's followers to be sent out on a mission to "the lost sheep of the house of Israel." More significantly, Matthew had been witness to Jesus's death and resurrection, and is listed in the Acts of the Apostles as being among those awaiting the coming of the Holy Spirit at Pentecost. In this light Matthew's gospel would have been perceived as having superior authority than the writings of Mark, and the Gentile physician, Luke, neither of whom belonged to Jesus's original core of twelve apostles. (Even the gospel of John, traditionally believed to have been written by a disciple who was even closer to Jesus than Matthew, does not seem to have usurped Matthew's primacy—perhaps because the latter was indeed the first to be written, as the Greek Church Father, Papias of Hierapolis [*fl.*60-150AD], suggests). However, when all four gospels were composed, copied, distributed among the various Christian communities, and later read and commented upon by theologians and bible scholars, it was evident that each of the evangelists had a particular and unique take on Jesus's life. Each emphasised different aspects and truths about his mission and identity. Mark lays stress on Jesus's powerful words and deeds, as Son of God; Luke (along with his companion volume, Acts), highlights how the message of salvation that was first preached in rural Galilee spread as far as Rome, the imperial capital. John, by contrast, takes us on more of an inner, mystical journey, that affords us glimpses and insights into Jesus's divine life, rooted in his relationship with his heavenly Father, and expressed in and through his flesh and blood existence as a human being.

Matthew's gospel also touches on many of these themes, but draws especial attention to Jesus's Jewish roots: in particular his attitude towards Jewish beliefs and traditions, religious leaders, the synagogue and temple cult, as well as with the prophetic writings, which Matthew claims Jesus brought to fulfilment in his life, death and resurrection. There are sound reasons for believing that Matthew wrote his gospel in some measure as a riposte to Jewish antagonism against Christians, possibly in Jerusalem, or groups further afield, in places such as Antioch or Rome, where diaspora Jews would have encountered Christians proclaiming the good news of Christ for the first time. We see this tension, in particular, in Matthew's account of Jesus's denunciation of the Jewish leaders as hypocrites, and in Matthew's claim that the priestly establishment in Jerusalem made up lies about the disciples stealing Jesus's body. At Jesus's trial moreover Matthew reports that the Jews cried out, "his blood be upon us," which implies a collective rejection of Jesus (though at another level it may reflect Matthew's desire that this cry might eventually become a genuine plea for atonement and salvation). For these, and other reasons, it has been suggested (notably since the holocaust) that Matthew's gospel has "anti-Semitic" tendencies. Through the centuries, it is maintained, Christian antipathy towards Jews, in the shape of racism, pogroms, expulsions, murders and executions, were inspired by the kind of words that Matthew put in the mouth of Jesus. Thus as the Jews hated Christ, it is posited, so Christians responded in kind. While we must accept that Christians have periodically adopted murderous and hostile attitudes towards Jews, it is wrong to suggest that Matthew's gospel is culpable in this regard. Matthew, like Jesus, was himself a Jew. He wrote as Jew, interpreted scripture as a Jew, and like all Jews held out hope that someday God's Messiah would come to redeem and deliver Israel from its enemies. It was just that Matthew conceived that these promises had been realised in the person of Jesus of Nazareth. That Matthew believed Jewish hopes and expectations had come to a climax in Jesus did not imply the annulment of Judaism, so much as its fulfilment. Some theologians and biblical scholars however continue to accuse Matthew of being "supercessionist," meaning that Matthew thought that the coming of Christ rendered Judaism a defunct religion. This, however, is surely incorrect. As a Jew, Matthew wanted his fellow Jews and co-religionists to recognise in Jesus the climax of all that the prophets had spoken about regarding Israel's salvation. That Matthew highlights, among other things, the tension and conflict between Jesus and the religious establishment, only serves to show the nature of the "in-house" debate that was going on within the Jewish community regarding the status of Jesus. Matthew belonged to and was part of the Jewish community that had to grapple with the implications of Jesus's career. He can hardly be called "anti-Semitic" for weighing in on the debate, or even for criticising or disagreeing with his co-religionists. As a Jew, Matthew believed that he had a strong case for arguing that Jesus was in fact God's long awaited Messiah. He is concerned that his fellow Jews will miss out on God's blessing if they ignore the gospel proclaimed by Jesus. So he set out to prove to his fellow Jews, and perhaps also to show interested Gentile converts, that Jesus is God's chosen one, the saviour and redeemer of Israel—and also of the wider world. He sets out to prove this in a number of ways, predominantly by viewing Jesus's life and ministry through the lens of the Hebrew scriptures. If Jesus is the Messiah, Matthew suggests, then there will be scriptural evidence to back up this claim. It should be possible, in other words, to see the promises of redemption and salvation in the bible outworked or fulfilled in the person of Christ. So at the very start of his gospel Matthew compiles a genealogy that traces Jesus's ancestry back to Abraham via king David, through whose lineage the

Messiah was expected to come. He points out, for example, that Isaiah foretold that a saviour would be born of a virgin and would be known as Immanuel, "God with us." In the rest of his gospel Matthew shows how Jesus mediated, or more precisely, became God's presence among his people. At the close of his gospel, in the very last verse, Matthew underscores this point by informing his readers that God, through the person of his Messiah, would always be among his people, even till the end of time. God would no more be separate from them, because he had definitively redeemed them through the Messiah's sacrificial death.

Matthew explores this notion further by highlighting how in his life, death and resurrection, Jesus took upon himself the role of historic Israel, by undergoing the same experiences that it went through in its journey with God. Thus when Joseph and Mary return from exile in Egypt, after fleeing king Herod, Matthew says that a prophecy in Hosea was fulfilled which states, "Out of Israel I called my son." Although in the first instance this refers to historic Israel, fleeing pharaoh in Egypt, Matthew sees it as having a deeper significance in pointing to the call of Jesus to serve God as his viceroy or emissary. Whereas Israel largely failed in this mission, Matthew contends that Jesus succeeded. Hence when Jesus is tempted in the desert by Satan for forty days, he triumphs in the very arena where Israel failed during its forty-year moral and spiritual examination in the wilderness. For Matthew, Jesus is the obedient Son of God, living selflessly and obediently in ways that pleased God, in contrast with the disobedient and rebellious children of Israel. But for Matthew, Jesus is also the new Moses. In three lengthy chapters detailing Christ's Sermon on the Mount, a Moses-like Jesus proclaims the values and ethics of God's kingdom. Here we encounter a radical reinterpretation of the Jewish Torah in which Jesus transcends strict or literal observances of Mosaic Law, to make explicit the underlying principle of love that should really be animating our relationships with God and other people. So whereas adultery was legally defined as having sexual relations with somebody else's wife or husband, Jesus would argue that this particular sin is committed at a much earlier stage, at the point where one begins to look lustfully at another person. Likewise, says Jesus, everybody will be familiar with the commandment that prohibits murder; but if our hearts burn with anger towards another individual then, according to Jesus, we are as guilty as if we had killed them. Jesus also warns how easily religious ritual, which is meant to focus our attention on God, can become a bind and suffocate us with its shallowness and superficiality, such that we imagine our rote prayers impress God, because they are long, drawn out. The Law also permits us to seek redress when others violate our rights. Moses speaks of "an eye for an eye, and a tooth for a tooth." But Jesus says, if anybody takes advantage of you, turn the other cheek, go out of your way to do them good, instead of seeking compensation. In each case Jesus elevates his interpretation of scripture above that of the fathers, and even the literal text of scripture itself: "You have heard that it was said...but I say to you." Nothing could be more challenging and confrontational than for Jesus to suggest that his own word carries greater weight than Mosaic Law. Yet Jesus also said that he had not come to "abolish the Law and the prophets, but to fulfil them." If then his attitude towards the Judaism of his day seems to be one of iconoclasm, it was only insofar as he sought to rescue people buried beneath layers of man made rules and traditions. This, of course, was nothing less than the prophets did, and the reason why so many people thought that Jesus himself was a prophet, in the style of an Elijah or Jeremiah.

But Matthew's Jewish Jesus is more than just a prophet. Symbolically, he reconstitutes the twelve tribes of Israel in the guise of his twelve apostles (a sure sign that God's promised kingdom was finally at hand), and sends them out to preach the gospel to Israel. Here he fulfils Isaiah's prophecy that Messiah would give sight to the blind, cleanse lepers, raise the dead and preach good news to the poor. Matthew identifies Jesus as God's chosen servant, an important figure in the second half of the book of Isaiah. Often referred to as the "suffering servant," this individual is sometimes linked with Israel in its capacity as God's witness or representative, but more intriguingly with a messianic figure who is destined to rule the nations—but not before he suffers at the hands of his own people, for whom also he dies as an atonement for their sins. In his account of the last supper, Matthew interprets this sacrificial death as the sealing of a "covenant" (or "new covenant," in some manuscripts), symbolised by bread and wine (Christ's "body" and "blood"). Yet Matthew's emphasis on God's "chosen servant" also concerns his role in bringing "justice" to the Gentiles, and in causing them to "hope" in God's "name"—something that was not on the agenda of the Jewish authorities, who, in the spirit of Ezra and Nehemiah, sought to separate themselves from the uncircumcised.

This sheds light on later chapters, where several of Jesus's parables spell out the judgment that awaits Israel and its spiritual leaders. In the parable about the tenants, Jesus warns that those who were entrusted with the task of producing a harvest from the vine, will suffer the death penalty for abusing servants, and later for murdering the son of the vineyard owner, all of whom were sent to gather fruit. Thus Jesus warns that the vineyard will be let out to others (i.e. the Gentiles) who, by contrast, will produce fruit in its season. To emphasise the precarious position of the Jews, Matthew writes two substantial chapters in which Jesus decries the failed spiritual leadership and hypocrisy of the scribes and Pharisees, and also that of the priestly establishment, whose temple, Jesus predicts, faces complete annihilation as judgment from God. This underscores Matthew's wider concern to show that the old way of accessing and worshipping God is coming to an end. In his passion narrative he speaks of the curtain of the temple (i.e. the holy of holies) being rent in two, symbolising that everybody, through the Messiah's death, could enter God's presence. There was no further need therefore for the high priest to enter the sanctuary (once a year), to offer atonement for sins, either for his own, or for those of the people. Coupled with Jesus's prediction about the destruction of the temple, Matthew affirms what he had earlier said about the Gentiles receiving "justice" and "hope." For Jesus was now the locus of God's presence. In his life, death and resurrected life, he had become, and had shown himself to be,

"God with us." At the close of the gospel, Jesus commands his followers to make disciples of "all nations, baptising them in the name of the Father, and of the Son, and of the Holy Spirit." Thus the gospel that starts out with a highly Jewish-centred understanding of Christ and his mission ends with an apostolic commission to bring the good news about the saviour to the pagan, Gentile world. It is significant then that Jesus admonishes his followers to teach the nations "all that *I* have commanded you." It is not Mosaic Law or temple rituals that the Gentiles must observe, but the Law of Love, which Christ preached in his Sermon on the Mount.

Dr Brendan Devitt

Chapter One

The Genealogy of Jesus Messiah vv1–17

The book of the genealogy of Jesus Messiah, the son of David, the son of Abraham: Abraham fathered Isaac, and Isaac fathered Jacob, and Jacob fathered Judah and his brothers, and Judah fathered Perez and Zerah by Tamar, and Perez fathered Hezron, and Hezron fathered Ram, and Ram fathered Amminadab, and Amminadab fathered Nahshon, and Nahshon fathered Salmon, and Salmon fathered Boaz by Rahab, and Boaz fathered Obed by Ruth, and Obed fathered Jesse, and Jesse fathered David, the king. And David fathered Solomon by Uriah's wife, and Solomon fathered Rehoboam, and Rehoboam fathered Abijah, and Abijah fathered Asa, and Asa fathered Jehoshaphat, and Jehoshaphat fathered Joram, and Joram fathered Uzziah, and Uzziah fathered Jotham, and Jotham fathered Ahaz, and Ahaz fathered Hezekiah, and Hezekiah fathered Manasseh, and Manasseh fathered Amos, and Amos fathered Josiah, and Josiah fathered Jechoniah and his brothers, at the time of the exile to Babylon. After the exile to Babylon Jechoniah fathered Shealtiel, and Shealtiel fathered Zerubbabel, and Zerubbabel fathered Abiud, and Abiud fathered Eliakim, and Eliakim fathered Azor, and Azor fathered Zadok, and Zadok fathered Achim, and Achim fathered Eliud, and Eliud fathered Eleazar, and Eleazar fathered Matthan, and Matthan fathered Jacob, and Jacob fathered Joseph, Mary's husband, of whom Jesus was born, who is called Messiah. Therefore all the generations from Abraham to David were fourteen generations, and from David to the exile to Babylon fourteen generations, and from the exile to Babylon to the Messiah fourteen generations.

Joseph obeys the angel vv18–25

This is the account of how the birth of Jesus the Messiah came about. Mary, his mother, was engaged to be married to Joseph, but before they came together she was found to be pregnant by the Holy Spirit. But because her husband, Joseph, was a just man and did not want to disgrace her publically, he planned to divorce her discreetly. But as he was thinking about this, behold an angel of the Lord appeared to him in a dream, saying, Joseph, son of David, don't be afraid to accept Mary as your wife, because what is conceived in her is from the Holy Spirit. She will give birth to a son, and you shall name him Jesus, because he will save his people from their sins. All this took place to fulfil what the Lord had said through the prophet, ***Behold, the virgin will conceive and give birth to a son. They will call him Immanuel, which means, God with us.*** When Joseph woke up he did what the angel of the Lord had told him, and took Mary as his wife, but he did not consummate the marriage until she had given birth to a son, whom he called Jesus.

Chapter Two

Visitors from the East vv1—12

Following the birth of Jesus in Bethlehem, Judaea, during the reign of King Herod, there came astrologers from the East to Jerusalem, saying, Where is the one born king of the Jews? We saw his star at its rising, and have come to worship him. When King Herod heard this he was gravely concerned, as was all Jerusalem. So he summoned together the chief priests and legal experts, and asked them where the Messiah should be born. In Bethlehem, Judaea, they told him. For this is what the prophet wrote: ***And you, Bethlehem, in the land of Judah**, **you are by no means least among Judah's princes, for a ruler will emerge from you who will shepherd my people, Israel.*** Then Herod invited the astrologers to meet him secretly, and he found out from them the precise time that the star appeared. Then he despatched them to

Bethlehem, saying, When you get there, search for the child with utmost care. When you've found him, let me know so that I too can come and worship him. So the astrologers listened to what the king had to say and went on their way to Bethlehem. And the star, which they had seen in the East, went in front of them until it eventually stood over the place where the child was. When they saw the star they were ecstatic with joy, and having entered the house they saw the child with Mary his mother, so fell to their knees and worshipped him. Then they opened their treasure boxes and presented him with gifts—gold, incense and myrrh. Then after being warned in a dream not to return to Herod, they returned to their homeland by a different route.

Refugees in Egypt vv13—18

After they had left, an angel of the Lord appeared to Joseph in a dream and said, Up you get and take the child and his mother and escape to Egypt, and stay there until I tell you. So Joseph got up and taking the child and his mother with him by night, he left for Egypt where he remained until Herod's death. This fulfilled the Lord's word through the mouth of the prophet: ***Out of Egypt I called my son.*** When Herod realised that the astrologers had tricked him he was beside himself with fury. He sent and killed all of the male children aged two and under in Bethlehem and the surrounding area. He based this on calculations he received from the astrologers. This fulfilled Jeremiah's prediction: ***In Ramah a voice was heard, weeping and great lamentation, Rachel weeping for her children. And she would not take comfort, because they were no more.***

The exiles return to Nazareth vv19—23

But when Herod died, behold an angel of the Lord came in a dream to Joseph in Egypt. Get up, he said, take the child and his mother and go to the land of Israel, for those who were seeking the child's life are dead. So up he got and took the child and his mother, and went to the land of Israel. But when he heard that Archelaus was reigning over Judaea in place of his father Herod, he was afraid to go there, and after being warned in a dream he left for the region of Galilee. So he went and lived in a city called Nazareth, so that what the prophets had foretold might come to pass: ***He shall be called a Nazarene.***

Chapter Three

The Baptist proclaims his mission vv1—12

At that time John the Baptist comes preaching in the Judean desert, saying, Repent, for the Kingdom of heaven is at hand. For this is the one that was spoken about by Isaiah the prophet, saying, ***A voice of one shouting in the desert, Make ready the way of the Lord, make straight paths for him.*** John wore clothes of camel's hair with a leather belt around his waist, and his food was locusts and wild honey. So people began flocking to him from Jerusalem and all Judaea, and the whole region around the Jordan. And they were being baptised by him in the Jordan confessing their sins. But when he saw many of the Pharisees and Sadducees coming to be baptised by him he said to them, You brood of vipers! Who warned you about the coming wrath? Bear fruit that shows you've repented. And don't presume to say to yourselves, We've

Abraham as our Father. For I say this to you, God's able to raise up children to Abraham from these stones. Already the axe is at the root of the trees, and every tree that doesn't produce good fruit will be cut down and thrown into the fire. I baptise you with water for repentance, but the one who succeeds me is more powerful than I am—I'm unworthy to carry his sandals. He'll baptise you with the Holy Spirit and with fire. His winnowing fork is in his hand, and he'll clean out the threshing floor. He'll gather the wheat into the barn and will burn up the chaff with unquenchable fire.

The baptism of Jesus Messiah vv13—17

Then Jesus comes from Galilee to the Jordan to be baptised by John. But John was trying to dissuade him, I need to be baptised by you and yet you come to me! Jesus replied, Let it be so for now—it's only fitting that we should fulfil all righteousness. So John relented. And when Jesus was baptised, immediately after he came out of the water, the heavens were opened and he saw the Spirit of God coming down on him like a dove. And a voice from heaven said, This is my well-loved Son—I take great delight in him.

Chapter Four

Jesus tempted in the desert vv1–11

Then Jesus was led by the Spirit into the desert to be tempted by the devil. When he had fasted forty days and forty nights he was hungry. And the tempter came and said to him, If you're the Son of God, order these stones to become bread. He replied, It's written: ***Man can't live by bread only, but by every word that comes out of God's mouth.*** Then the devil brings him to the holy city and stood him on the pinnacle of the temple and says to him, If you're the Son of God throw yourself down, because it's written, ***He will order his angels concerning you, and they will carry you in their hands, in case you dash your foot against a stone.*** Jesus said, Again it's written: ***You shall not test the Lord your God.*** So again the devil takes him to a very high mountain and shows him all the earth's kingdoms and their glory. And he said to him, I'll give you all this if you fall down and worship me. Be off with you Satan, says Jesus, for it's written: ***You shall worship the Lord your God and serve only him.*** Then the devil leaves him, and suddenly angels came and began to serve him.

Jesus starts his ministry vv12–17

When Jesus heard that John had been arrested he went off to Galilee. Then after he left Nazareth he went to live in Capernaum by the sea, in the district of Zebulun and Naphtali. This was in order that the message spoken through the prophet Isaiah might be fulfilled: ***Land of Zebulun and land of Naphtali—the coastal route, beyond the Jordan, Galilee of the Gentiles. The people sitting in darkness have seen a great light, and on those living in the region and shadow of death, light has dawned on them.*** From then on Jesus began to preach, saying, Repent for the kingdom of heaven is near!

The first disciples called vv18–22

As he was strolling by the Sea of Galilee, he spotted two brothers, Simon (known as Peter) and his brother Andrew, casting a net into the sea, for they were fishermen. So he says to them, Come, follow me, and I'll make you fish for men. Instantly they left their nets and followed him. And moving on he saw two other brothers, James, Zebedee's son and his brother John, they were mending their nets in the boat with their father Zebedee, and he called them. Straightaway they quit the boat, and their father, and followed him.

Preaching to a large crowd vv23–25

So he was going all over Galilee, teaching in their synagogues, and proclaiming the good news of the kingdom, and healing people with every kind of disease and illness. And his fame spread throughout all Syria. And they brought to him all who were sick with a variety of diseases and pains, including those oppressed by demons, as well as epileptics and paralytics—and he healed them. And great crowds followed him from Galilee and the Decapolis, from Jerusalem, Judaea and from the other side of the Jordan.

Chapter Five

Blessings from a mountain top vv1–12

When he saw the crowds, Jesus went up the mountainside, and when he had sat down his disciples came to him and he began to teach them. Happy are those who own their spiritual poverty—for the kingdom of heaven is theirs. Happy are those who mourn—they'll be comforted. Happy are the humble—for the earth will be given to them. Happy are those hungry and thirsty for justice—they'll receive it in full measure. Happy are those who show mercy—mercy will be shown to them. Happy are those pure in thought—they'll see God. Happy are the peace brokers—for they'll be known as God's children. Happy are those who suffer persecution in the cause of what is right—the kingdom of heaven is theirs. Happy are you when others insult and persecute you and say all sorts of bad things against you falsely, because of me. Be happy and rejoice! You'll have a great reward in heaven! Remember, they persecuted the prophets who preceded you in exactly the same way.

The salt of the earth vv13–16

You're the earth's salt; but if it loses its taste how will its saltiness be restored? It's now good for nothing, except to be thrown away and trampled under foot by people. You're the world's light. A city built on a hill cannot be hidden. Nor does anyone light a lamp and cover it up, but rather puts it on a stand and it lightens everything in the house. Let your light shine in this way before everybody, so that they may see the good you do and praise your Father in heaven.

Jesus Messiah fulfils the law vv17–20

Don't think that I've come to abolish the law and the prophets. I've not come to abolish them, but to fulfil them. I'm telling you the truth: until heaven and earth are gone, not one dot or dash will disappear from the law until everything's accomplished. Therefore anyone who undermines the least of these commandments, and teaches others to do the same, will be called the least in the kingdom of heaven. But whoever practices and teaches them, will be regarded as great in the kingdom of heaven. For I tell you, unless you surpass the Pharisees and the legal experts in righteousness, you'll never enter the kingdom of heaven.

Teaching about murder vv21–26

You've heard what was said to people long ago, ***Don't murder***, and anyone who commits murder is liable to judgment. But what I say is this: anyone who's angry with his brother will be subject to judgment. And whoever says to his brother, You idiot, will be subject to the court, and whoever says, You fool, will be at risk of hell fire. So if then you're in the process of bringing your gift to the altar and remember that your brother has a grudge against you—leave your gift before the altar and first go and be reconciled with your brother, and then come back and offer your gift. Settle matters quickly with your opponent, while you're going to court with him, lest your opponent deliver you to the judge, and the judge to the guard, and you be flung into prison. Truly I tell you, you won't get out of there until you've paid the last penny.

Teaching about sexual wrongdoing vv27–30

You've heard that it was said to the men of old, ***Don't commit adultery.*** But I tell you whoever looks at a woman lustfully has already committed adultery with her in his heart. So if your right eye causes you to sin, gouge it out and throw it away—it's better for you to lose one part of your body, than to have your whole body thrown into hell. And if your right hand makes you sin, cut it off and throw it away, it's better to lose one body part than for your whole body to be cast into hell.

Teaching about divorce vv31—32

It's been said, ***Anyone who divorces his wife must give her a certificate of divorce.*** But I tell you, anyone who divorces his wife, except for sexual immorality, makes her an adulteress. And anyone who marries a divorced woman commits adultery.

Teaching about oaths vv33—37

And you've heard said to people long ago, ***Don't break your oath, but perform the vows***

you've made to the Lord. But I tell you, don't swear at all, either by heaven, for it's God's throne, or by the earth, for it's his footstool for his feet—or by Jerusalem, for it's the city of the Great King. Nor should you swear by your head, for you can't make a single hair white or black. All you need to say is a simple, Yes or No. Anything more comes from the evil one.

Teaching about revenge vv38–42

You've heard it said, ***Eye for eye, tooth for tooth;*** but I say, don't resist an evil person. If anyone slaps you on the right cheek, turn your other cheek to him too. And if anyone wants to sue you and take your shirt, hand over your coat as well. And if anyone forces you to go one mile, then go two miles with him. Give to the person who asks you, and don't turn down the person who wants to borrow from you.

Teaching about love vv43–48

You've heard it said, ***Love your neighbour*** and hate your enemy. But I say, love your enemies, pray for those who persecute you. In this way you'll be sons of your Father in heaven. For he makes his sun to shine on both the evil and the good, and sends rain on the just and the unjust. If you love only those who love you, what good is that? Don't tax collectors do the same? And if you only greet your relatives, what more are you doing than others? Even pagans do that—don't they? Be perfect therefore, just as your Father in heaven is perfect.

Chapter Six

Giving to the poor vv1—4

Don't make a show of your piety in front of others, for then you'll have no reward from your Father in heaven. So whenever you give to the poor don't announce it with the blast of a trumpet, as the hypocrites do—in the synagogues and in the streets—in order to be praised by others. In truth, they have their reward in full. But when you give to the poor don't let your left hand know what your right hand's doing, so that your giving will be in secret. Then your Father who sees in secret will reward you.

Teaching about prayer vv5—15

And whenever you pray don't be like the hypocrites. They love to pray standing in the synagogues and at street corners to be seen by all. Truly I tell you, they have their reward. But when you pray go into your room, shut the door and pray to your Father who is hidden. Then your Father, who sees in secret, will reward you. And when you pray don't keep on babbling like pagans—they think they'll be heard because they use lots of words. Don't be like them, your Father knows what you need before you ask him. Pray then like this: Our Father in heaven—all honour to your name! May your kingdom come. May your will be done on earth, as in heaven. Give us our food for today. Forgive our wrongdoing, just as we've forgiven those who've wronged us. Don't lead us into trials that overpower us, but deliver us from the evil one. For if you forgive those who wrong you, then your heavenly Father will also forgive you. But if you don't forgive others their wrongdoings your Father won't forgive you your sins.

Fasting vv16–18

Whenever you fast don't be like the long-faced hypocrites. They disfigure their countenance so others can tell that they're fasting. Seriously, I tell you, they've had their reward. But when you fast, spruce up your appearance—scrub your face so that others can't tell that you're fasting, except your Father who is hidden. And your Father, who sees in secret, will reward you.

Possessions vv19–24

Don't stockpile riches on earth where moths and worms devour, and where thieves break in and steal. But store up for yourselves treasures in heaven, where neither moths nor worms destroy and where thieves don't break in and steal. For wherever your treasure is, that's where your heart will be. The lamp of the body is the eye. If your eyes are healthy your whole body will be radiant with light; but if your eye is evil your whole body will be plunged into darkness—and what a darkness that will be! Nobody can serve two masters. He'll either hate one and love the other, or he'll be devoted to one and despise the other. You can't serve God and money.

No need to worry vv25–34

So I tell you, don't worry about your life—what to eat or drink, or about your body, what you will wear. Isn't life more important than food or the body more than clothing? Look at the birds of the air, they don't sow, reap or gather into barns, and yet your heavenly Father feeds them. Aren't you much more valuable than they? And which one of you can, by worrying, add a single inch to his height? And why do you worry about clothing? Think about the lilies in the fields, how they grow. They don't work or spin, and yet not even Solomon in all his splendour clothed himself like one of these. So if that's the way God clothes the grass in the fields, which is here today and tomorrow thrown onto the fire, won't he much more clothe you—O you with little faith! Stop worrying, saying, What shall we eat? What shall we drink? What shall we wear? The Gentiles are obsessed with such things. But your heavenly Father knows that you need them all. So, first seek God's kingdom and his righteousness, and all these things will be given to you. Stop worrying about tomorrow—tomorrow will have its own worries. Today has enough trouble of its own.

Chapter Seven

Judging others vv1—6

Don't judge, or you'll be judged. For as you judge, so you too will be judged—measure for measure. And why do you look at the speck in your brother's eye, but overlook the plank in your own? And how can you say to your brother, Let me take out the speck from your eye when there's a plank in your own? Hypocrite! First take out the plank in your own eye, and then you'll be able to see clearly to take out the speck in your brother's eye. Don't give what's holy to dogs, or throw your pearls in front of pigs, or they'll trample them under their feet, and turn on you and tear you to pieces.

Just ask vv7—12

Ask, and it'll be given to you; seek, and you'll find; knock, and it'll be opened to you. For all who ask receive, and whoever seeks finds, and for everyone who knocks it'll be opened. Which of you will give his son a stone if he asks for bread, or a snake if he asks for fish? If you then, though evil, know how to give good gifts to your children, how much more will your Father in heaven give good gifts to those who ask him? So in everything you do, treat others as you would have them treat you; this sums up the Law and the Prophets.

The wide and narrow gate vv13—14

Go in through the narrow gate. For the way is broad and the road wide that leads to destruction, and many are entering through it. So too the gate is narrow and the route is difficult that leads to life—and few find it.

Prophets true and false vv15–20

Watch out for false prophets: they come to you dressed as sheep but inwardly are ravenous wolves. You'll recognise them by their fruits. Do people pick grapes from thorn bushes or figs from thistles? So every healthy tree bears good fruit, but the unhealthy tree can't bear good fruit. Every tree that doesn't bear good fruit is cut down and thrown into the fire. So you'll know them by their fruits.

Discipleship vv21–28

Not everyone who says to me, Lord, Lord, will enter the kingdom of heaven, but he who does my heavenly Father's will. On that day many will say to me, Lord, we prophesied in your name, didn't we? And didn't we drive out demons in your name, and in your name perform many mighty deeds? Then I will tell them plainly, I never knew you—be gone, evildoers! So everyone who hears my words and puts them into practice is like the wise man that built his house upon rock. When it rained and the waters rose and the winds blew and lashed that house, it didn't collapse because it was built on rock. But everyone who hears my words but does not act on them is like the foolish man who built his house on sand and when it rained, and the waters rose, and the winds blew and beat against that house, it collapsed with a great crash. And when Jesus finished speaking the crowd was amazed at his teaching, because he taught them with authority, not like their scribes.

Chapter Eight

A healed leaper vv1–4

As he came down from the mountain large crowds followed him. And behold a leper came up to him, and falls before him, saying, Lord, if you want to you can make me clean. Jesus reached out his hand and touched him, saying, I do want to—be clean! Immediately his leprosy was cleansed. Jesus says to him, Be sure you tell no one, but go and show yourself to the priest, and offer the gift Moses commanded as evidence for them.

A centurion's faith vv5–13

When Jesus entered Capernaum a centurion came up to him, pleading with him and saying, Lord, my servant is at home lying paralyzed and suffering great anguish. Jesus says, I'll come and heal him. The centurion said, Lord, I'm not worthy that you should come under my roof. Just speak a word and my servant will be cured. For I myself am a man under authority, with soldiers under me. So I can say to this one, Go! and he goes; and to that one, Come! and he comes. And I say to my slave, Do this, and he does it. When Jesus heard this he was astonished and said to those following him, Really—I'm telling you—I haven't found such faith, not even in Israel! I tell you this; many will come from the East and West and take their place at the table with Abraham, Isaac and Jacob in the kingdom of heaven. But the heirs of the kingdom will be hurled into outer darkness, where there'll be weeping and gnashing of teeth. Then Jesus said to the centurion, Go! As you believe so will it happen for you. And instantly his servant recovered.

Jesus heals many vv14–17

When Jesus entered Peter's house he saw his mother in law lying ill with a fever. He touched her hand and straightaway the fever left her and she got up and began to serve him. That evening they brought to him many who were demon-possessed, and with a word he cast out the spirits and healed all the sick. This was done to fulfil the word of Isaiah the prophet, who said: He took our illnesses and bore our diseases.

The cost of discipleship vv18–22

And when Jesus saw the crowd around him, he gave instructions to cross to the other side. A legal expert approached and said to him, Teacher, I will follow you wherever you go. Jesus says to him, Foxes have holes and the birds of the air nests, but the Son of Man has nowhere to rest his head. Another of his disciples said to him, Lord, let me go and bury my father first. Jesus says to him, Follow me, leave the dead to bury their own dead.

A storm calmed vv23–27

And when Jesus got into the boat his disciples followed him. Suddenly a great storm arose on the sea, so that the boat began to be flooded by the waves—but he was asleep. And they went and woke him saying, Save us, Lord, we're drowning! And he says to them, Why are you such cowards, men of little faith? Then he got up and rebuked the winds and the sea, and a great calm prevailed. And the men were astonished saying, What sort of person is this? Even the winds and sea obey him.

Demons expelled vv28–34

When he came to the other side, into the region of the Gadarenes, two men who were demon possessed met him as they came out of the tombs. They were so violent that nobody could pass that way. And the demons cried out saying, What have you to do with us, Son of God? Have you come here to torment us before the time? Now some pigs were feeding some distance away. The demons were begging him saying, If you're going to expel us, send us into the herd of pigs. So he said to them, Go! So they came out and entered into the pigs, and behold the whole herd rushed down the steep bank into the sea, and perished in the waters. The herdsmen fled into the city and there told everything, especially what had happened to the demon possessed men. And behold, the entire city came out to meet Jesus and they implored him to get out of their region.

Chapter Nine

Healing and forgiveness vv1—8

Jesus then got into a boat and crossed to the other side and came to his own town. And behold they were bringing to him a paralyzed man lying on a stretcher. When Jesus saw their faith he said to the paralytic, Be brave, son, your sins are forgiven! At this some of the lawyers said among themselves, This man is blaspheming. Jesus, knowing their thoughts, said, Why do you have evil thoughts in your hearts? What's easier to say, Your sins are forgiven, or, Stand up and walk? But so that you may know that the Son of Man has power on earth to forgive sins (he says to the cripple), Up you get! Take your stretcher, and go to your home. So up he got and went to his home. When the crowds saw this they were awestruck, and glorified God who had given such authority to men.

Matthew called to discipleship vv9–13

And when Jesus passed on from there, he saw a man called Matthew, sitting at the tax office, and he says to him, Follow me! So he got up and followed him. Later, when Jesus was sitting at table in Matthew's house, behold many tax collectors and sinners came and were sitting with Jesus and his disciples. When the Pharisees saw this they began to say to his disciples, Why does your teacher eat with tax collectors and sinners? When he heard this he said, The healthy don't need a doctor, only the sick. Go and learn the meaning of this, ***It's mercy I want, not sacrifice.*** For I haven't come to call the righteous, but sinners.

Teaching about fasting vv14–17

Then John's disciples come to him, saying, Why do we and the Pharisees fast but your disciples don't? Can the wedding guests mourn, asked Jesus, as long as the bridegroom is with them? There'll be a time when the bridegroom is taken from them, then they'll fast. Nobody puts a new patch on old clothing, because the patch comes away from the garment and it becomes worse than before. So also new wine is not put into old wineskins. If it is, the skins burst and the wine's spilled and the skins are ruined. New wine goes into fresh skins, to preserve them both.

A dead girl raised, a sick woman healed vv18–26

As he was saying all this, behold, a ruler came and knelt before him saying, My daughter's just died; but come and lay your hands on her and she'll live. Jesus got up, and together with his disciples, followed the man. And behold a woman who had suffered for twelve years with a haemorrhage came up behind him and touched the fringe of his robe, for she kept telling herself, If I only touch the fringe of his garment I'll be cured. Jesus turned around and said to her, Have courage, daughter, your faith has cured you! At that very moment the woman was healed. And when Jesus came to the ruler's house, and saw the flute players and the crowd making a commotion, he said, Be off with you! The girl's not dead, only sleeping. And they laughed at him. When the crowd had been sent away he went in and took the girl by the hand and she got up. And news of this swept through that whole region.

Two blind men healed vv27—31

And as Jesus passed on from there two blind men followed him, crying out and saying, Have mercy on us, Son of David! And when he had come to the house the blind men came to him and Jesus says to them, Do you believe that I'm able to do this? They say to him, Yes, Lord. Then he touched their eyes saying, Because of your faith—so be it! And their eyes were opened. And Jesus sternly warned them, Make sure you don't tell anybody. And after they had left they spread the news throughout the region.

A mute man healed vv32-34

As they were heading off, behold, they brought a mute man to him who was demon possessed. Once the demon had been cast out, the mute man began to speak, and the crowds were dumbstruck. Never, they said, have we seen the likes in Israel. But the Pharisees said, By the ruler of demons he is casting out demons.

Harvest and labourers vv35-38

And Jesus went around all the cities and villages, teaching in their synagogues and proclaiming the gospel of the kingdom of God, and healing all and every illness and frailty. And when he saw the crowds he was filled with compassion for them, because they were hassled and destitute, like sheep without a shepherd. Then he says to his disciples, The harvest is great, but the labourers are few. Ask therefore the Lord of the harvest to send out workers into his harvest.

Chapter Ten

The Twelve called and sent out vv1–15

Jesus called his twelve disciples and gave them authority to drive out unclean spirits and to cure every disease and illness. The names of the twelve apostles are as follows: Simon, known as Peter, and his brother Andrew; James, Zebedee's son and his brother John; Philip and Bartholomew; Thomas, and Matthew the tax collector; James, Alpheus's son; and Thaddeus, Simon the Zealot, and Judas Iscariot, who betrayed him. These twelve Jesus sent out after he had commanded them, saying, Avoid Gentile areas, don't set foot in any Samaritan town, but go to the lost sheep of the house of Israel. As you go, proclaim this message, The kingdom of heaven is near! Heal the sick, raise the dead, cleanse lepers, drive out demons. You've received freely, so give freely. Don't take gold, silver, or copper in your money belts—no bag for your journey, or two tunics or spare sandals or a walking stick—for the worker deserves his keep. Whatever town or village you come to, seek out someone who's trustworthy and stay there until you leave. As you enter the house give it your greeting, and if the house is worthy let your peace rest upon it. But if it's unworthy, take back your peace. If someone won't welcome you or listen to what you have to say, shake the dust off your feet as you leave that town. I'm telling you, it'll be more tolerable for Sodom and Gomorrah on judgment day than for that town.

Warnings vv16–42

Behold, I'm sending you like sheep among wolves. So be as wise as serpents and as innocent as doves. Watch out! People will hand you over to the courts and flog you in their synagogues. And you'll be brought before governors and kings on my account, to give testimony to them and to the Gentiles. Don't worry about what to say, or how to say it, for what you're to say will be given to you then. For it won't be you speaking, but your Father speaking through you. Brother will hand over brother to death, and a father his child, and children will rise up against their parents and have them put to death. Everyone will hate you because of my name. But whoever's faithful to the end will be saved. If they persecute you in one town, flee to another. For the truth is, you won't complete a journey through the towns of Israel before the Son of Man comes. A student is not above his teacher; nor a servant above his master. It's enough that students become like their teachers and servants like their masters. If they've called the head of the house Beelzebub, how much more the members of his household! So don't be afraid of them; for there's nothing hidden that won't be revealed, or concealed that won't be disclosed. What I tell you in the darkness, proclaim in the light. And what you hear whispered to you, shout from the rooftops. Don't fear those who can kill the body but can't kill the soul. But rather fear the one who can destroy both body and soul in hell! Aren't two sparrows sold for a penny? And yet not one of them will fall to the ground without your Father's consent! For even the hairs of your head are numbered. So don't be afraid, you're worth much more than many sparrows! Therefore whoever will acknowledge me before men, I'll also acknowledge before my Father in heaven. But whoever disowns me before others, I'll disown him before my Father in heaven. Don't think I've come to bring peace on earth; I've not come to bring peace, but a sword.

I've come to turn ***a man against his father, a daughter against her mother, a daughter-in-law against her mother-in-law, and a man's enemies will be from his own household.*** Anyone who loves their father or mother more than me is unworthy of me; anyone who loves their son or daughter more than me is unworthy of me. And anyone who doesn't take his cross and follow me is unworthy of me. Whoever saves his life will lose it; whoever loses his life because of me will find it. Whoever receives you receives me. And whoever receives me, receives the one who sent me. Whoever welcomes a prophet, because he's a prophet, will receive a prophet's reward, and whoever welcomes a good person, because he's a good person, will receive a good person's reward. And whoever gives the most insignificant of my followers a cup of cold water, because he's my follower, I assure you he won't miss out on a reward.

Chapter Eleven

The Baptist's questions answered vv1–6

After Jesus had finished instructing his disciples, he went on from there to teach and to preach in all their towns. Meanwhile, in prison, John heard about what the Messiah was doing, and sent his disciples to ask, Are you the one who's to come, or should we look for someone else? Jesus answered, Go, tell John what you hear and see: the blind receive sight, the crippled walk, lepers are cleansed, the deaf hear, the dead are raised, and the poor are brought good news—and happy is the one who isn't offended by me.

Nobody greater than John the Baptist vv7–19

As John's disciples left, Jesus began to speak about him to the crowds. What did you go into the desert to look at? A reed shaken by the wind? What did you go out to see, a man dressed in expensive clothes? No! You'll find those who wear flashy clothing in kings' palaces. So what did you go out to see? A prophet? Yes indeed, and much more than a prophet. This is the one about whom it's written, ***Behold, I send my messenger ahead of you. He will prepare your way before you.*** Truly, I tell you, no one born of a woman is greater than John the Baptist; yet the least in the kingdom of heaven is greater than he. From the time of John the Baptist until now the kingdom of heaven has endured violence, and violent persons are taking it by force. For all the prophets and the law prophesied until John. And if you're willing to accept it, he's Elijah who is to come. You've got ears—so listen up! To what shall I compare this generation? They're like children sitting in the market place shouting to their friends, We played the flute for you but you didn't dance; we sang a lament but you didn't mourn. For John came neither eating or drinking and they say, He's got a demon. The Son of Man came eating and drinking and they say, Look at him! A glutton and a drunkard, a friend of tax collectors and sinners! But wisdom's vindicated by its deeds.

Judgment on unrepentant towns vv20–24

Then Jesus began to denounce the towns in which his mighty deeds had been done, because they did not repent. Woe to you Chorazin! Woe to you Bethsaida! For if the mighty works which were performed among you were done in Tyre and Sidon, they would've repented ages ago, in sackcloth and ashes. Nevertheless, I tell you it'll be more bearable for Tyre and Sidon on judgment day than for you. And as for you, Capernaum, will you be exalted to heaven? No! You'll be flung down to Hades. For if the mighty works you experienced had been done in Sodom, it would've remained until now. Nevertheless, I say to you it'll be more bearable for Sodom on judgment day than for you.

The prayer of Jesus Messiah to his Father vv25–30

At that moment Jesus said, I praise you Father, Lord of heaven and earth, because you've hidden these matters from the wise and clever and revealed them to little children. Yes, Father, for this is what you were only too pleased to do. My Father's handed everything over to me. Nobody knows the Son except the Father, and nobody knows the Father except the Son, and to whomever the Son chooses to reveal him. Come to me, all you who are weary and burdened, and I'll give you rest. Take my yoke upon you and learn from me, for I'm gentle and humble of heart, and you'll find rest for your souls, for my yoke's easy and my burden's light.

Chapter Twelve

Questions about the sabbath vv1–8

At that time Jesus walked though the grain fields on the sabbath. His disciples were hungry and began to pluck some of the heads of grain and eat them. But when the Pharisees saw this they said to him, Look, your disciples are breaking the sabbath. He answered them, Haven't you read what David and his companions did when they were hungry? He entered the house of God and ate the consecrated bread that was unlawful for him to eat (and those that were with him), but only the priests? Or haven't you read in the law that on the sabbath the priests in the temple break the law and yet are guiltless? I tell you, something greater than the temple is here! But if you'd known what this means, ***I want mercy not sacrifice***, you wouldn't have condemned the guiltless. For the Son of Man is Lord of the sabbath.

Jesus heals on the sabbath vv9–14

So leaving that place he entered their synagogue, and behold there was a man there with a withered hand. And they asked him, saying, Is it lawful to heal on the sabbath? They said this to accuse him. He said to them, Who among you if he'd only one sheep and it should fall into a pit on the Sabbath, wouldn't grab it and pull it out? How much more valuable is a man than a sheep! So it's lawful to do good on the sabbath. Then he says to the man, Stretch out your hand. He did so, and it was restored, as sound as the other one. But the Pharisees went out and plotted how they might destroy him.

A prophecy fulfilled vv15–21

But Jesus knew this, and so he withdrew from there. And a large crowd followed him, and he healed all of them. But he sternly warned them that they should not make him known. He did this to fulfil what the prophet Isaiah had written: ***Here is my servant, the one I have chosen, my beloved in whom my soul delights. I will bestow my Spirit upon him. And he will proclaim justice to the nations. He will not bicker nor cry out, nor will anyone hear his voice in the streets. He***

will neither break a bruised reed nor snuff out a smouldering wick, until through triumph he brings justice. And the nations will put their hope in his name.

Demons and Pharisees vv22–32

Then a blind and dumb demoniac was brought to him, and he healed him so that the mute could both speak and see. All the people were amazed, and they were saying, Could this be David's son? But when the Pharisees got wind of this they said, This man only casts out demons through Beelzebub, the ruler of demons! But knowing their thoughts he said to them, Every kingdom divided against itself is brought to ruin, and every town or house divided against itself will not stand. If Satan drives out Satan, he is divided against himself, so how then will his kingdom endure? But if it's through Beelzebub that I drive out demons, by whom do your sons drive them out? Therefore they'll be your judges. But if it's by God's Spirit that I cast out demons, then the kingdom of God has come upon you. Or how can anyone go into a strong man's house and steal his belongings unless he first ties up the strong man? Then he can ransack his house. You are either for me or against me. And whoever doesn't gather with me, scatters. So I tell you, every sin and blasphemy of people will be forgiven; but blasphemy of the Spirit won't be forgiven. So also whoever speaks a word against the Son of Man will be forgiven. But whoever speaks against the Holy Spirit won't be forgiven, either in this age or the age to come.

Rebuking the faithless vv33–37

Either make the tree good and its fruit good; or make the tree bad and its fruit bad—for from its fruit a tree is known. You brood of snakes! How can you speak good things when you're evil? For the mouth speaks what's in the depths of the heart. A good person, out of his good treasure brings out good things, but a wicked person brings out of his treasure evil things. And I tell you; on the Day of Judgment people will give account of every careless word they speak. For by your words you will be justified, or by your words you will be condemned.

Jonah's experience vv38–42

Then some of the Pharisees and lawyers answered him, and said, Teacher, we'd like to see a sign from you. He said to them, An evil and adulterous generation seeks a sign. But it won't be given a sign, except the sign of the prophet Jonah. For just as Jonah spent three days and three nights in the belly of the great fish, so the Son of Man will be three days and three nights in the bowels of the earth. The men of Nineveh will be raised at the judgment with this generation, and condemn it—because they repented at Jonah's preaching. And behold something greater than Jonah is here. The queen of the South will be raised in the judgment with this generation and condemn it; for she came from the ends of the earth to hear the wisdom of Solomon, and behold something greater than Solomon is here.

Evil spirits itinerary vv43–45

When the unclean spirit has left a person it wanders through waterless places looking for rest, but doesn't find any. Then it says, I'll return to the house I came from. And when it arrives to find the house empty, swept and put in order, it goes and fetches seven other spirits more evil than itself, and they go in and live there, and the condition of the person becomes worse than it was at first. So it'll be with this evil generation.

Jesus's family go looking for him vv46–50

As he was still speaking to the people, suddenly his mother and brothers were stood outside, asking to speak to him. But he replied to the one who had given him the message, Who is my mother? And who are my brothers? And he stretched out his hand towards his disciples, and said, Here's my mother and my brothers! Whoever does the will of my Father in heaven is my brother and sister and mother.

Chapter Thirteen

The parable of the sower vv1–9

That same day Jesus went out of the house and sat beside the sea. And great crowds gathered around him, so that he got into a boat and sat down. And the whole crowd were stood on the beach. And behold, he told them many things using parables, saying, A sower went out to sow. And as he sowed, some seeds fell along the path, and the birds came and devoured them. Other seeds fell on rocky ground, where there wasn't a lot of soil, and they sprang up straightaway, because they'd no depth of soil, but when the sun rose they were scorched, and because they'd no root they withered away. Other seeds fell among thorns, and the thorns grew up and choked them. Other seeds fell on good ground and produced grain, some a hundredfold, some sixty and some thirty. You've got ears—use them!

Why speak in parables? vv10–17

Then the disciples approached him and asked, Why speak to them in parables? He answered, The mysteries of the kingdom of heaven have been given to you, not to them. For to whoever has even more will be given to him, and he will have abundance. But the one who doesn't have anything, even what he has will be taken away from him. That's the reason I speak to them in parables, because seeing they don't see, and hearing they neither hear nor understand. For them the prophecy of Isaiah is fulfilled that says: ***You will indeed see but never comprehend, see but never discern. Because this people's heart has become dull and they can barely hear with their ears, and they have closed their eyes, lest they should see with their eyes, hear with their ears, understand with their heart, and turn and I would heal them.*** But your eyes are blessed, because they see, and your ears, because they hear. For in truth, I tell you, many prophets and righteous persons yearned to see what you see, and to hear what you hear, but didn't hear it.

The meaning of the parable of the sower vv18–23

Listen, this is what the parable of the sower means. When anyone hears the word of the kingdom, but doesn't understand it, the evil one comes and snatches away what has been sown in his heart. That's what's been sown along the path. As for what was sown on rocky ground, that's someone who hears the word and immediately accepts it joyfully, but he's rootless and so he lasts for a little while, and when there's hardship and persecution because of the word, immediately he falls away. As for what was sown among thorns; this is the one who hears the word, but frets about worldly concerns, so that the lure of wealth chokes the word and it becomes fruitless. As for the one sown on good soil, this is the one who both hears and understands the word. So then he bears fruit and yields a hundredfold, or sixty or thirty.

The parable of the weeds and wheat vv24–30

He put another parable to them, saying, The kingdom of heaven is like someone who sowed good seed in his field. But when everyone was asleep, his enemy came and sowed weeds among the wheat, and left. When the plants sprang up and bore grain, so did the weeds. The owner's servants came and said to him, Sir, didn't you sow good seed in your field? So why has it got weeds? And he said to them, An enemy has done this. Then the servants say to him, Do you want us to go and gather them up? No, he says, in case when you gather the weeds you also uproot the wheat with them. Let both grow together until the harvest. When harvest comes I'll tell the harvesters, First gather the weeds; tie them in bundles to be burned; then gather my wheat and put it into my barn.

Parables about mustard seeds and leaven
vv31—33

He then told another parable. The kingdom of heaven is like a mustard seed that a man sowed in his field. It's the smallest of all seeds, but when it's grown it's bigger than all the plants of the garden, and becomes a tree, so allowing the birds of the air to nest in its branches. He spoke yet another parable to them. The kingdom of heaven resembles leaven that a woman took and hid in three measures of flour, until it was all leavened.

The parable of the weeds explained vv34—43

Jesus said all this to the crowds by means of parables, and told them nothing except in a parable, so that what the prophet had said might be fulfilled, saying, ***I will open my mouth in parables. I will proclaim what has been kept secret from the foundation of the world.*** Then he left the crowds and went indoors. His disciples approached him saying, Explain to us the parable of the weeds in the field. He answered, saying, The person who sows the good seed is the Son of Man, and the field is the world, and the good seed, the sons of the kingdom, and the weeds are the sons of the evil one, and the enemy who sowed them is the devil, and the harvest represents the end of the age, and the harvesters are the angels. So just as the weeds are gathered and burned in the fire, so it'll be at the end of the age. The Son of Man will send his angels, and they will weed out of his kingdom everything which causes sin, and all who do evil. They will throw them into the blazing furnace, where there will be weeping and gnashing of teeth. Then the righteous will shine like the sun in the kingdom of their Father. You've got ears—use them!

Parables of hidden treasure and a pearl vv44–46

The kingdom of heaven resembles treasure hidden in a field, that a man found and hid. Then with joy he goes and sells all he has and buys that field. Again, the kingdom resembles a merchant looking for fine pearls. When he found one of great value, he went and sold all that he had and bought it.

The parable of the net vv47–50

Again, the kingdom of heaven is like a net thrown into the sea that collected all kinds of fish. When full, men dragged it ashore and sat down, and sorted the good into containers and threw out the bad. That's what it will be like at the end of the age. The angels will come and separate the evil from the righteous, and throw them into the blazing furnace. There there will be weeping and gnashing of teeth.

These parables explained vv51–52

Have you understood all this, he asked? We have, they replied. So you see, he said to them, every scribe who has been trained for the kingdom of heaven is like a master of a house, who brings out from his treasure both old and new.

Jesus rejected at Nazareth vv53–58

Once he had finished these parables, Jesus left. When he came to his hometown he began teaching them in their synagogue, so that they were amazed, and said, Where did he get this wisdom and these powers? Isn't this the carpenter's son? Isn't Mary his mother? Aren't James, Joseph, Simon and Judas his brothers? Aren't all his sisters here with us? Where did this man get all these things? And they took offence at him. But Jesus said to them, A prophet is not dishonoured, except in his own town and among his own kin. So he didn't do many mighty works there, because of their unbelief.

Chapter Fourteen

John the Baptist beheaded vv1—12

At that time Herod the Tetrarch heard about the fame of Jesus, and said to his servants, This must be John the Baptist! He's been raised from the dead! That's why these miraculous powers are at work in him. For Herod had arrested John, bound him and put him in jail on account of Herodias, his brother Philip's wife. Because John kept telling him, It's unlawful for you to have her. Although he wanted to put him to death, he feared the crowd, who held John to be a prophet.

But on Herod's birthday, Herodias' daughter danced in front of the gathering, and pleased Herod, so much so that he vowed under oath to give her whatever she asked. Prompted by her mother, she says, Give to me here the head of John the Baptist on a plate. And the king was saddened; but because of his oaths to his guests, he sent and had John beheaded in the jail. So his head was brought on a plate, and given to the young girl who gave it to her mother. His disciples then came and took the body and buried it, and they went and told Jesus.

Feeding five thousand vv13–21

When Jesus heard this, he left in a boat for a remote place, in private. But when the crowds heard about it, they followed him on foot from the towns. When he disembarked, he saw a large crowd and had pity on them and healed their sick. When evening came his disciples approached him, saying, This is a desolate place, and it's late. Send the crowds away to the villages, so they can buy food for themselves. But Jesus said, There's no need for them to go away—you give them something to eat. But they say, We've only five loaves here and two fish. Then he said, Bring them here to me. So he ordered the crowds to sit down on the grass, and after he took the five loaves and two fish, he looked up to heaven, said a blessing, broke the loaves and gave them to the disciples, and the disciples gave them to the crowds. And they all ate their fill. And they took up twelve baskets full of the leftovers. And those who ate were about five thousand, besides women and children.

Walking on water vv22—36

Straightaway Jesus made his disciples get into a boat and go ahead of him to the other side, while he sent the crowds away. And after dismissing the crowds, he went up to the mountainside on his own, to pray. When evening came, he was there alone. Meanwhile the boat, already far from the land, was being tossed by the waves, because the wind was against it. Shortly before dawn Jesus went out to them, walking on the sea. When the disciples saw him walking on the sea they were terrified, saying, It's a ghost! And they cried out in fear. Immediately he spoke to them, saying, Be brave! It's me! Don't be frightened! Lord, if it's you, Peter replied, order me to come to you on the water. Come on then! said Jesus. So Peter got out of the boat, and began to walk on the water towards Jesus. But when he realised the strength of the wind, he got scared, and began to sink, and shouted, Lord, save me! Straightaway Jesus reached out his hand, grabbed him, and says, What little faith you have! Why did you doubt? And as they got back into the boat the wind died. Then those in the boat worshipped him, saying, Truly, you are the Son of God.

So when they crossed over, they came to the Gennesaret region. When those there recognised Jesus they sent word to all the surrounding countryside, and they brought all their sick to him. And they begged him only to be allowed to touch the fringe of his cloak, and all who touched it were healed.

Chapter Fifteen

Breaking with tradition vv1–9

Then the Pharisees and legal experts from Jerusalem come to see Jesus, saying, Why do your disciples break with the tradition of the elders? For they don't wash their hands before they eat! And for what reason, he answered them, do you disobey God's commandment for the sake of your tradition? For God said, Honour your father and mother, and whoever dishonours them will be put to death. But you say, If someone tells his father or mother, whatever gift you would have got from me belongs to God, then there's no need to honour his father. So for the sake of your tradition you ignore God's word. Hypocrites! How well did Isaiah prophesy about you when he says, ***This people honour me with their lips, but as for their heart—it's far from me. In vain they worship me, teaching human precepts, as if they were Torah.***

Impurity Defined vv10–20

Then he called the crowd to him and said, Hear and understand. It's not what goes into a person's mouth that defiles him; but what comes out, that's what defiles him. Then the disciples came to him, and say, Do you know that when the Pharisees heard this saying they were scandalised? He replied, Every plant not planted by my heavenly Father will be uprooted. Let them be; they're blind guides. If the blind lead the blind both will fall into a ditch. Peter said to him, Explain this parable to us. Jesus said, Do you still lack understanding? Don't you see that what goes into the mouth passes through the stomach, and exits through the sewer? But what comes out of the mouth comes from the heart, and this is what defiles a person. Because out of the heart come evil thoughts, murder, adultery, sexual immorality, theft, false testimony, slander. These are what defile a person—not eating with unwashed hands.

Healing through faith vv21–28

And Jesus left that area and went to the district of Tyre and Sidon. And who should come up to him, but a Canaanite woman from that region crying out, saying, Have pity on me, Lord, Son of David, my daughter is demon possessed. But he said nothing, and his disciples came and were imploring him, saying, Get rid of her, because she's shouting after us. He replied, I was only sent to the lost sheep of the house of Israel. But she came and kneeling before him says, Lord, help me! He answered, It's not right to take the children's bread and toss it to the dogs. True, Lord, she said, but even the dogs eat the crumbs that fall from the master's table. Then Jesus replied, Woman, great is your faith! As you wish—so may it be! And at that very hour her daughter was healed.

Many healed vv29–31

And Jesus went on from there, and passed along the Sea of Galilee. And he went up into the mountain and sat down there. And large crowds came to him bringing with them the lame, the blind, the crippled, the mute and many others, and they laid them down at his feet, and he healed them. The crowd were amazed when they saw the mute speaking, the crippled restored, the lame walking, and the blind seeing. And they glorified the God of Israel.

The hungry fed vv32–39

Then Jesus called his disciples to him, and said, I feel compassion for the crowd because they've been with me three days now and have nothing to eat. I can't send them away hungry in case they collapse on their way. And his disciples say to him, Where can we get enough bread to feed so many in such a remote spot? Jesus says to them, How many loaves have you got? They said, Seven and a few small fish. So he instructed the crowd to sit on the ground. And taking the seven loaves and the fish, he gave thanks and broke them and began to give them to the disciples, and the disciples to the crowds. And they all ate and were satisfied. And they collected seven baskets full of the leftovers. Those who ate numbered four thousand, not counting women and children. After sending the crowds away, he got into a boat and came to the regions of Magadan.

Chapter Sixteen

Request for a sign rejected vv1—4

The Pharisees and Sadducees came to Jesus to test him. They asked him to show them a sign from heaven. He replied saying, When evening comes you say, It's going to be fair because the sky is red; and in the morning it's going to be stormy because the sky is red and gloomy. You know how to interpret the weather, but not the signs of the times. An evil and adulterous generation wants a sign, but none will be given it except Jonah's sign. He then left them and went off.

Beware the teaching of the Pharisees and Sadducees vv5–12

The disciples arrived at the other side, but had forgotten to bring bread. Watch out, Jesus warned them, be on your guard against the yeast of the Pharisees and Sadducees. So they began to debate the matter among themselves, saying, It's because we brought no bread. When he became aware of this Jesus said to them, Why are you arguing among yourselves–men of little faith—that you have no bread? Are you still ignorant? Don't you remember the five loaves for the five thousand, and how many baskets you filled? Or the seven loaves for the four thousand, and how many baskets you collected? Why can't you grasp that I wasn't speaking to you about bread? Be on your guard against the yeast of the Pharisees and Sadducees! Then it dawned on them that he was not referring to the yeast used in bread, but about the teaching of the Pharisees and Sadducees.

Peter's confession vv13—20

Now when Jesus came to the region of Caesarea Phillippi, he asked his disciples, saying, Who do people say that the Son of Man is? They answered, Some say John the Baptist, others Elijah, and yet others Jeremiah or one of the prophets. And he says to them, But who do you say that I am? Simon Peter said, You're the Messiah, the Son of the living God! You're blessed Simon, son of John, Jesus said to him, because it wasn't flesh and blood that revealed this to you, but my Father in heaven. I tell you, You're Peter, and I'll build my church on this rock, and the gates of Hades won't overpower it. And I'll give you the keys to the kingdom of heaven, and whatever you permit on earth will already have been permitted in heaven, and whatever you allow on earth will already have been sanctioned in heaven. Then he instructed his disciples to tell nobody that he was the Messiah.

Jesus shares his fate vv21—28

From then on, Jesus began to explain to his disciples that he must go to Jerusalem and suffer greatly at the hands of the elders, ruling priests and legal experts, and that he must be killed, and on the third day be raised. Peter took him aside and started to rebuke him saying, No Lord! Don't say that, this must never happen to you! But Jesus turned, faced him and said, Get behind me, Satan! You're a stumbling block, because you're not thinking like God but like men. Then Jesus said to his disciples, If anyone wants to follow me he must deny himself, take up his cross and follow me; for whoever wants to save his life will lose it, but anyone who loses his life for my sake will find it. For what good would it do anyone if he should gain the whole world,but forfeit his life? Or what can anyone give in exchange for his life? For the Son of Man is about to come in the glory of his Father with his angels, and then he'll repay each person according to what he's done. Truly, I tell you, there are some standing here who will not taste death until they see the Son of Man coming in his kingdom.

Chapter Seventeen

Jesus's transfiguration vv1–13

Six days later Jesus takes Peter, James and John his brother, and leads them up a high mountain on their own. And he was transfigured in front of them: his face shone like the sun and his clothes became white as light. Suddenly Moses and Elijah appeared speaking with Jesus. Peter said to Jesus, Lord, it's great for us to be here! If you want I'll make three shelters—one each: for you, Moses and Elijah. While he was still speaking, behold a bright cloud overshadowed them, and a voice comes from out of the cloud saying, This is my son, the one I love—I'm well pleased with him—listen to what he says! When the disciples heard this they fell on their faces and were scared witless. But Jesus came to them, touched them and said, Get up, don't be afraid. When they looked up, they saw nobody except Jesus himself, alone. And as they were coming down from the mountain, Jesus instructed them saying, Tell nobody about the vision until the Son of Man has been raised from the dead. So the disciples then asked him, Why is it that the scribes say that Elijah must come first? He replied, Elijah is coming and he'll restore everything. But I'm telling you that Elijah has already come, but they didn't recognise him. Instead they treated him as they pleased. In the same way, the Son of Man is about to suffer at their hands. Then the disciples realised that he had been speaking to them about John the Baptist.

An epileptic boy healed vv14–23

And when they came to the crowd, a man came and knelt in front of Jesus and said, Lord, take pity on my son, he's an epileptic and suffers terribly. For he often falls into both fire and water. I did bring him to your disciples, but they couldn't cure him. Jesus answered, saying, Faithless and crooked generation! How long must I be with you? How long do I have to tolerate you? Bring him here to me. Jesus rebuked the demon and it came out of him, and the boy was cured instantly. Then the disciples came to Jesus privately and said, Why couldn't we cast it out? Jesus says to them, Because your faith is so little. I tell you the truth, if you've faith the size of a mustard seed you can say to this mountain, Move from here to there, and it'll move! Nothing will be impossible for you. When they were still together in Galilee Jesus said to them, The Son of Man is about to be delivered into the hands of men. They will kill him, and he will be raised on the third day. And they were deeply upset.

How to pay the Temple tax vv24–27

When they arrived at Capernaum the temple tax collectors approached Peter and said, Doesn't your teacher pay the two-drachma tax? Yes, he answers. When he went into the house Jesus spoke to Peter first, saying, What do you think, Simon, from whom do earthly kings collect tolls and taxes: from their children or from strangers? And he answered, From strangers. So the sons are exempt, said Jesus. But in case we cause offence, go to the sea and cast a hook, and take the first fish that comes up. And when you have opened its mouth, you'll find a two-drachma coin, give it to them as my tax and yours.

Chapter Eighteen

Who is the greatest vv1—9

At that time the disciples came to Jesus, asking, Who's the greatest in the kingdom of heaven? Calling to himself a child, he set it among them and said, Really, unless you change and become like little children, you'll never enter the kingdom of heaven. Whoever humbles himself like this child is the greatest in the kingdom of heaven. And whoever welcomes a child like this in my name, welcomes me. But should anyone cause one of these these little ones to sin, it would be better for him if a huge millstone were hung round his neck and he were drowned in the depths of the sea. Woe to the world for its temptations to sin! Temptations are bound to come; but woe to the person through whom they come! If your hand or foot makes you sin, cut it off and throw it away. It's better for you to enter in to life crippled or lame, than to have two hands or two feet, and to be thrown into the hell of fire. And if your eye makes you sin, gouge it out. It's better to enter into life with one eye, than to have two eyes and be thrown into the hell of fire.

A lost sheep vv10–14

See that you don't despise one of these little ones. For I'm telling you their angels in heaven always see the face of my Father in heaven. What do you think? If someone owns a hundred sheep and one goes missing, won't he leave the ninety-nine on the mountains and look for the one that went astray? And if he finds it, truly I tell you, he rejoices over it more than over the ninety-nine that didn't go astray. So it's not the will of your Father in heaven that one of these little ones should perish.

Lessons in forgiveness vv15–20

If your brother sins against you, go and tell him his fault between you and him alone, and if he listens to you, you have won over your brother. But if he doesn't listen, take one or two others with you so that, ***By the mouth of two or three***

witnesses every word may be confirmed. And if he ignores them, report it to the church. And if he doesn't listen even to the church, then treat him as a Gentile and tax collector. In truth, I tell you, whatever you bind on earth shall be what's already been bound in heaven; and whatever you loose on earth shall be what's already been loosed in heaven. Again I tell you, if two of you agree on earth about anything they ask, my Father in heaven will do it for them. For where two or three are gathered together in my name, there I am among them.

The unforgiving servant vv21–35

Peter then came up and said to him, Lord, how often when my brother sins against me must I forgive him? Seven times? Jesus says to him, I don't say to you seven times, but seventy times seven. Therefore the kingdom of heaven is like a king who wished to settle an account with his servants. As he began to settle it, one of them was brought to him who owed him ten thousand talents. And because he could not pay, his master ordered him to be sold, and his wife and children and all he had, so that payment could be made. The servant then fell on his knees and implores him saying, Be patient with me and

I'll pay you everything! Moved with pity, that servant's master released him and forgave him the debt. But when that same servant went out, he found one of his fellow servants who owed him a hundred denarii, and seizing him he began to choke him, saying, Pay what you owe! So his fellow servant fell down and pleaded with him, Have patience and I'll pay you. But he refused, and he went and put him in prison until he should pay the debt. His fellow servants, on seeing what had happened, were greatly distressed and they went and reported to their master all that had taken place. Then his master summoned him and said, You wicked servant! You pleaded with me and I forgave you all that debt. Shouldn't you have had mercy on your fellow servant, as I had mercy on you? In anger his master handed him over to the jailers, until he should pay all that he owed. This is what my heavenly Father will do to each of you, if you do not forgive your brother from your heart.

Chapter Nineteen

Is divorce permitted? vv1—12

So when Jesus finished saying all this, he left Galilee and came to the Judean regions on the other side of the Jordan. Large crowds followed him and he healed them there. And some Pharisees came to him to test him, asking, Is it lawful for a husband to divorce his wife for any reason? Haven't you heard, Jesus replied, that from the beginning, ***He made them male and female?*** That's why, ***A man will leave his father and mother and be united with his wife, and the two will become one flesh.*** So they're no longer two, but one flesh. So let no one separate what God's joined together. Why then, they ask him, did Moses order that a husband give his wife a divorce certificate and send her away? Jesus answers them, Moses let you divorce your wives because of your hard hearts. This wasn't how it was in the beginning. So I tell you, whoever divorces his wife, except for sexual immorality, commits adultery. His disciples say to him, If that's what marriage is like then better not get married at all! But he answered them, Not everyone can receive this teaching, except those to whom it has been granted. For there's eunuchs who have been eunuchs from their mother's womb, and there's eunuchs who were made eunuchs by others, and still others who made themselves eunuchs for the kingdom of heaven's sake. Whoever is able to accept this—let them accept it.

Children blessed vv13–15

Then children were brought to him so that he might lay his hands on them and pray. But the disciples scolded those who brought them. Jesus said, Let the children come to me—don't try to stop them, for to such belongs the kingdom of heaven. And after he had placed his hands on them he left.

The rich young ruler tested vv16–27

And behold a young man came to Jesus and said, Teacher, what good deed must I do to have eternal life? He answered him, Why do you ask me about what's good? There's only one who's good. But if you want to enter into life, keep the commandments. He asks him, Which ones? Jesus said, ***Don't murder, Don't commit adultery, Don't steal, Don't give false evidence, Honour your father and mother, and love your neighbour as yourself***. The young man says to him, I've kept all these! So what do I lack? Jesus said to him, If you want to be perfect, go and sell all your possessions and give to the poor, and you'll have treasure in heaven—and come, follow me! When the young man heard this he went away in sadness, because he had many possessions. Jesus said to his disciples, In truth I tell you, it's difficult for a rich person to enter the kingdom of heaven; indeed I tell you it's easier for a camel to go through a needle's eye than for a rich person to enter the kingdom of God. When they heard this the disciples were stunned, saying, Who then can be saved? Jesus looked them in the eye, and said, People can't do this—it's impossible; but with God everything's possible. Peter responded, saying to him, Look, we've left everything and followed you—what's in it for us? Jesus said to them, I tell you the truth in the new age, when the Son of Man sits on his glorious throne, you who've followed me will also sit on twelve thrones judging the twelve tribes of Israel. And everyone who has left homes, or brothers or sisters or father or mother or children or fields, for the sake of my name, will inherit eternal life. But many who are first will be last, and the last first.

Chapter Twenty

A fair wage? vv1–16

For the kingdom of heaven's like this: a vineyard owner went out in the early morning to hire workers for his vineyard. And after agreeing with the workers to pay them the standard daily rate, he sent them to his vineyard. And going out at about nine o'clock, he saw others standing idly in the market place. He said to them, Off you go as well and work in my vineyard, and I'll pay you what's right. So off they went. Again he went out about noon and then around three o'clock, and did the same thing. At about five o'clock he found others standing around and he says to them, Why are you standing around idle all day? They say to him, Because nobody hired us. He says to them, Off you go too and work in my vineyard. When evening came the vineyard owner says to his foreman, Call the workers and pay them their wages, beginning with the last and then going on to the first. So those hired about five o'clock came and each received the daily rate; but when those hired first came they expected to receive more, but they also received the same pay. When they took it they began to complain to the vineyard owner saying, This lot has only worked an hour, yet you've treated them the same as us, though we've had to withstand the scorching heat of the day! But he answered one of them and said, Friend, I'm not being unfair to you. Didn't you agree with me to work for the standard rate? Take what you've earned and be gone. Am I not permitted do what I like with my own money? Or is it that you despise my generosity? So the last will be first and the first last.

Jesus tells his disciples what will happen to him
vv17—19

As he was going up to Jerusalem, Jesus took aside the twelve, and along the way says to them, Look, we're going up to Jerusalem, and the Son of Man will be handed over to the chief priests and scribes. And they'll condemn him to death, and hand him over to the Gentiles to be mocked, flogged, and crucified, and on the third day he will be raised up.

Jesus speaks to a mother vv20–28

Then the mother of Zebedee approached Jesus and kneeling down asks him for something. He said to her, What do you want? Let one of these two sons of mine, she says, sit at your right hand and the other on your left in your kingdom. Jesus replied, Neither of you know what you're asking. Can any of you drink the cup I'm going to drink? We can, they reply. Jesus says to them, You will indeed drink from my cup, but as for sitting on my right hand and on my left, it's not up to me, but it's for those for whom it's been prepared by my Father. When the ten heard this they became angry with the two brothers. But Jesus called them and said, You know that the rulers of the Gentiles lord it over them, and their rulers in turn exercise authority over them; but it'll not be like that among you. Whoever wants to be great among you must become your servant, and whoever wants to be first among you must be your slave. For the Son of Man didn't come to be served but to serve, and to give his life as a ransom for many.

Two blind men vv29–34

As they were leaving Jericho, a large crowd followed him. And sitting by the roadside were two blind men. When they heard that Jesus was passing by, they cried out, saying, Pity us Lord, Son of David! The crowd reproved them and told them to shut up, but they shouted out all the louder, Pity us Lord, Son of David! Jesus stopped and called them, saying, What do you want me to do for you? Let our eyes be opened, Lord, they answer. Moved with compassion, Jesus touched their eyes, and straightaway they regained their sight, and followed him.

Chapter Twenty-One

The coming king vv1–11

Now as they approached Jerusalem and came to Bethphage, at the Mount of Olives, Jesus sent two disciples, saying to them, Go to the village ahead of you, and straightaway you'll see a donkey tied, and a colt with her. Untie them and bring them to me. And if anybody says anything to you, say, The Lord needs them; then he'll send them at once. This happened to fulfill what was spoken through the prophet, saying, ***Tell the daughter of Zion, Behold, your king comes to you, humble, mounted on a donkey, and on a colt, the foal of a donkey.*** So the disciples went and did as Jesus told them. They brought the donkey and colt, put their cloaks on them, and he sat on them. A very large crowd spread their cloaks on the road, while others cut down branches from the trees, and were spreading them on the road. The crowds moving ahead of him, and those following, were shouting, ***Hosanna*** to the Son of David! ***Blessed is the one who comes in the name of the Lord! Hosanna*** in the highest! And when he entered Jerusalem the entire city was in turmoil, saying, Who's this? The crowds kept repeating, This is the prophet Jesus, from Nazareth in Galilee.

Jesus in the temple vv12—17

And Jesus went into the temple and drove out all those selling and buying there. He overturned the tables of the moneychangers and the seats of those selling doves. It's written, he says to them, ***My house shall be called a house of prayer,*** but you've made it a den for thieves. The blind and the crippled came to him in the temple, and he healed them. But when the chief priests and the scribes saw the marvelous works he performed, and the children shouting in the temple, Hosanna to the Son of David! they were angry and they said to him, Can you hear what they're saying? Yes, Jesus says to them, and have you never read, ***Out of the mouths of infants and nursing babies you have drawn out praise***? So he left them and went out of the city, and came to Bethphage where he spent the night.

The barren fig tree vv18–22

In the early morning, as he was returning to the city, Jesus felt hungry, and when he saw a fig tree at the roadside he went over to it but found nothing on it except leaves. And he says to it, Nevermore bear fruit! At once the tree withered. When the disciples saw this they were amazed, saying, How did the fig tree wither so quickly? Jesus answered them, The truth is, if you've faith and don't doubt, not only will you be able to do what was done to the fig tree, you'll be able to say to this mountain, Up! Get yourself into the sea! and it will happen. And whatever you ask in prayer, you'll receive if you believe.

Questioning the authority of Jesus vv23—27

When he entered the temple, the ruling priests and the elders approached him as he was teaching. By what authority are you doing these things? they asked. Who gave you this authority? Jesus answered them, saying, I'll ask you one question as well, and if you answer me, then I'll tell you by what authority I do these things. John's baptism: where did it come from; heaven or men? They began debating among themselves, If we say, From heaven, he'll say to us, Then why didn't you believe him? But if we say, From men, we have the crowd to fear, for all hold John to be a prophet. We don't know, they said to Jesus. He also said to them, Neither will I tell you by what authority I'm doing these things.

Two sons vv28—32

What do you think? A certain man had two sons. And when he approached the first he said, Come on, boy, go and work in the vineyard today. He answered, No, I won't. But later he changed his mind and went. When he approached the other he said the same. He answered, I will, sir. But he didn't go. Which of the two did as his Father wished? They say, The first. The truth is, says Jesus, tax collectors and prostitutes are entering the kingdom of God ahead of you! For John came to show you the way of righteousness, but you didn't believe him—however tax collectors and prostitutes did believe him. And even though you saw it, you didn't afterwards change your minds and believe him.

Sinful tenants vv33–46

Here's another parable. A landowner planted a vineyard, built a fence around it, dug a winepress, and built a watchtower. Then he rented it to winegrowers and went away. Come harvest, he sent his servants to the winegrowers to collect his share of the crop. But the winegrowers seized the servants, and beat one, killed another and stoned a third. Then he sent other servants, more this time, and they did the same to them. Finally, he sent his son, saying, They'll respect my son, surely. But when the winegrowers saw the son they said to each other, This is the heir—come on, let's kill him and we'll have his inheritance. So they seized him, threw him out of the vineyard and killed him. So what'll the owner of the vineyard do to those tenants when he comes back? They say to him, He'll bring those wretches to a gruesome end, and give the vineyard to other tenants, who'll give him his share of the crop at harvest time. Jesus says to them, haven't you ever read the scriptures? ***The stone the builders rejected has become the cornerstone. This is the Lord's doing and is marvelous in*** our sight. Therefore I tell you, the kingdom of God will be taken from you and given to those who produce its fruit. Anyone who falls on this stone will be broken to pieces; and anyone on whom it falls will be crushed.

When the chief priests and the Pharisees heard his parables, they realized that he was speaking about them. Although they wanted to arrest him, they feared the mob because they believed that he was a prophet.

Chapter Twenty-Two

Guests at a wedding vv1–14

So again Jesus spoke to them in parables, saying, The kingdom of heaven is like a king who prepared a wedding banquet for his son, and sent out his servants to summon those invited to the feast. But they wouldn't come. So he sent different servants, saying, Tell those invited, Look, I've prepared my banquet, my oxen and fattened calves have been slaughtered, and it's all ready. Come to the wedding feast! But they took no notice: one went off to his farm, another to his business, while the rest seized his servants and treated them shamefully and killed them. The king was furious, and sent his soldiers and destroyed those murderers, and burned their city. Then he says to his servants, The wedding banquet is ready, but those invited were unworthy. So head out on to the roads, and invite anyone you find to come to the banquet. The servants went out and brought in everyone they could find, both evil and good. So the wedding hall was packed with guests. When the king came in to have a good look at the guests, he noticed there a man not wearing a wedding outfit, so he says to him, Friend, how did you get in without a wedding outfit? The man was speechless. Then the king said to his staff, Tie him up, hand and foot, and throw him into outer darkness, where there'll be wailing and gnashing of teeth. For many are called, but few chosen.

Taxes for Caesar vv15–22

Then the Pharisees went and plotted to trap him in his speech. So they send their own followers to him along with the Herodians, saying, Teacher, we know that you've integrity and teach God's way truthfully and defer to nobody, and you're not swayed by appearances. So tell us, what's your opinion? Is it right to pay tax to Caesar, yes or no? But Jesus saw through their evil purpose. He said, Why are you testing me, you hypocrites? Show me the coin used for the tax. So they brought a denarius to him. He says to them, Whose image and inscription is this? Caesar's, they reply. Then give to Caesar what's Caesar's, and to God what belongs to God. When they heard this they were stunned, so they left him and went away.

Marriage and resurrection vv23–33

That same day Sadducees (who say that there is no resurrection) came to him and said, Teacher, Moses said that, ***If a man dies with no children, his brother must marry his widow and raise children for his brother***. So let's say there were seven brothers. The first one married her and died, and since he'd no children, he left his widow to his brother. Then the second died, the third, and so on, to the seventh. Eventually, the woman died as well. In the resurrection then, whose wife will she be, since they'd all been married to her? Jesus answered, You err, because you don't know the scriptures nor God's power, because in the resurrection they won't marry nor be given in marriage—they'll be like the angels in heaven. And as far as the resurrection of the dead is concerned, haven't you read what God said, ***I am the God of Abraham, Isaac and Jacob***? He's not the God of the dead, but of the living! And when the crowd heard this, they were taken aback at his teaching.

The greatest commandment vv34–40

When the Pharisees heard that Jesus had silenced the Sadducees, they met together, and one of them, a legal expert, asked him a question to test him. Teacher, which is the greatest commandment in the law? He said to him, ***You shall love the Lord your God with all your heart, and with all your soul and with all your mind***. This is the first and greatest commandment. And the second's just like it, ***You shall love your neighbour as yourself***. Everything in the law and the prophets hinge on these two commandments.

Whose son is the Messiah? vv41—46

While the Pharisees were gathered together, Jesus asked them, saying, What do you think of the Messiah? Whose son is he? David's, they reply. He says to them, Why then does David, speaking by the Spirit, call him Lord, saying, ***The Lord said to my Lord, Sit on my right, until I put your enemies under your feet?*** If David calls him Lord, how can he be his son? Nobody said a word to him in reply. And from then on, no one dared to ask him any more questions.

Chapter Twenty-Three

Hypocrisy and a lament over Jerusalem vv1–39

Then Jesus spoke to the crowds and to his disciples, saying, The scribes and the Pharisees sit on Moses' seat. So you must do, and continue to pay heed to, whatever they tell you. But don't do what they do, for they preach but don't practice. They tie up heavy and burdensome loads and put them on others' shoulders, while being unwilling to lift a finger to move them. They do everything to be seen by others. They enlarge their phylacteries and lengthen the tassels on their clothing. They love the place of honour at banquets and the best seat in the synagogue, and being saluted in the market place, and to be called, Rabbi, by others. But you shouldn't be called, Rabbi, because you've one teacher, and you are all brothers. And don't call anyone on earth, Father, for you've one Father who's in heaven. On no account either should you be called, Teacher, because the Messiah is your one and only teacher. And the greatest among you will be your servant. Whoever exalts himself will be humbled, and whoever humbles himself will be exalted. But woe to you scribes and Pharisees—hypocrites! You shut the door of the kingdom of heaven in people's faces. You don't go in yourselves, and neither do you allow those who are entering to go in. Woe to you scribes and Pharisees, hypocrites! You travel over land and sea to make a single convert, but when he becomes one you make him twice as much a child of hell as yourselves. Woe to you, blind guides! You say if anyone swears by the temple it means nothing, but if anyone swears by the gold that's in the temple he's oath bound. Blind fools! For what's more important, the gold or the temple, which sanctifies the gold? You also say if anyone swears by the altar that means nothing, but if anyone swears by the gift on the altar he's oath bound. Blind men! For what's more important, the gift or the altar that makes the gift sacred? So anyone who swears by the altar swears not only by it, but also by everything on it. And anyone who swears by the temple, swears by it and by the one who dwells there. And anyone who swears by heaven, swears by God's throne and by the one who sits on it. Woe to you, scribes and Pharisees—hypocrites! You tithe mint and dill and cumin, but have neglected the greater matters of the law—justice, mercy, and faithfulness. You should have done these things without neglecting the others. Blind guides! You strain out a gnat but swallow a camel! Woe to you, scribes and Pharisees—hypocrites! You clean the cup and dish on the outside, but inside they are full of greed and self-indulgence. You blind Pharisee! Clean the inside of the cup and dish first, so that the outside may be clean as well. Woe to you, scribes and Pharisees—hypocrites! You are like whitewashed tombs that look exquisite on the outside, but inside are full of dead men's bones and everything filthy. So on the outside you appear righteous to people, but on the inside you are full of hypocrisy and lawlessness. Woe to you, scribes and Pharisees! You build the tombs of the prophets and adorn the monuments of the righteous and claim, If we'd lived in our fathers' time we wouldn't have joined them in shedding the blood of the prophets. So then you incriminate yourselves, because you are the descendants of those who murdered the prophets! Carry on and finish what your ancestors started! You snakes, children of vipers! How will you avoid the judgment of hell? Therefore, behold, I'm sending you prophets, wise people and scribes. You will kill and crucify some, others you will flog in your synagogue and chase them from town to town, so that you will be responsible for all the righteous blood being shed on earth, from the blood of righteous Abel to the blood of Zechariah, Berekiah's son, that you murdered between the temple and the altar. I'm telling you bluntly, all this will befall this generation. Jerusalem, Jerusalem, that kills the prophets and stones those sent to her! How often have I longed to gather together your children, as a hen gathers her young chickens under her wings, but you were unwilling. See, your house is left desolate! I'm telling you, you won't see me from now on until you say: ***Blessed is he who comes in the Lord's name.***

Chapter Twenty-Four

The destruction of the temple and the end of the age vv1—51

Then Jesus left the temple and was walking away. His disciples came to him to point out the temple buildings. He said to them, You see all these, don't you? I tell you the truth: not a single stone will be left on another. All will be thrown down. When Jesus was sitting on the Mount of Olives his disciples approached him privately, saying, Tell us, when will all these things happen, and what'll be the sign of your coming and of the end of the age? Jesus answered them, Take care no one misleads you. Many will come using my name and saying, I'm the Messiah, and will mislead many. You'll hear about wars and rumours of wars, but don't panic—this must happen—but the end is not yet. Nation will be raised against nation and kingdom against kingdom. There'll be famines and earthquakes in various places. All these things are just the beginning of the birth pangs. Then they'll hand you over to be persecuted and they'll kill you, and you will be hated by all nations because of me. Then many will fall away and betray and hate one another. And many false prophets will be raised up and lead many astray. Because lawlessness will increase, the love of many will grow cold. But whoever stands fast to the end will be saved. And then this gospel of the kingdom will be proclaimed to the whole world as a testimony to all nations, and then the end will come. So whenever you see ***the abomination that causes desolation,*** standing in the holy place (as the prophet Daniel foretold—let the reader understand), then those in Judaea should flee to the mountains. No one on the housetop should go down to take anything out of the house. Whoever happens to be in the fields shouldn't return to get his cloak. And there'll be woe for pregnant women and nursing mothers at that time. Pray that your escape won't be in winter or on the sabbath. For there'll be great distress such as has not been experienced since the world's creation, and such as will never be experienced again. No one would survive if those days weren't shortened, but they will be shortened; for the sake of the chosen ones. Then if anyone says to you, Look, here's the Messiah! Or, There he is! Don't believe them. Because false messiahs and false prophets will be raised up, and they'll perform great signs and wonders to lead astray, if that were possible, even the elect. So watch out! I've told you in advance! If they say to you, He's out there in the wilderness! Don't go out, or, He's here in the inner rooms, don't believe it. For just as lightning flashes in the east and is visible as far as the west, so will be the Son of Man's coming. For vultures will gather wherever there's a corpse. Immediately after the tribulation of those days, the sun will be darkened and the moon will not give its light, and the stars will be falling from heaven and the powers of the heavens will be shaken. And then sign of the Son of Man will appear in heaven and all the earth's tribes will mourn, and they'll see the Son of Man coming on the clouds of heaven with power and great glory. And he'll send his angels with a loud trumpet call, and they'll gather his chosen ones from the four winds, from one end of heaven to the other. Learn the lesson of the fig tree; as soon as its branch becomes tender and it sprouts its leaves, you know summer's on its way. In the same way, when you see all these things, you know he's near, at the gates. Truly I tell you, this generation won't pass away until all these things happen. Heaven and earth will pass away, but my words won't pass away. No one knows that day and hour—not even the angels in heaven or the Son, but only the Father. The coming of the Son of Man will be just like the days of Noah. For as people were eating and drinking, marrying and giving in marriage, right up until the time Noah entered the ark, they were unaware, until the flood came and swept everyone away. So will be the coming of the Son of Man. Two men will be in a field, one will be taken and the other left. Two women will be grinding at the mill, one will be taken, the other left. So be vigilant, because you don't know when your Lord is coming. But know this, if the householder had known what part of the night the thief was coming, he would've stayed awake and wouldn't have allowed his house to be broken into. So be ready, because the Son of Man is coming when you least expect him. Who then is the loyal and wise servant that his master has put in charge of his household, to feed them at the right time? Happy will be the servant whose master will find him so doing when he returns home. In truth I tell you, he'll put him in charge of all his possessions. But if in the case of a wicked servant, who says to himself, My master's held up, so he starts to assault his fellow servants and eats and drinks with drunkards, the master will come unexpectedly, and cut him in two and put him with the hypocrites, where there'll be weeping and gnashing of teeth.

Chapter Twenty-Five

Virgins wise and otherwise vv1—13

So the kingdom of heaven will be like ten virgins who took their lamps and went out to meet the bridegroom. Five were stupid and five sensible. Because when the stupid ones took their lamps they didn't take any oil with them; but the wise ones took flasks of oil with their lamps. As the bridegroom was delayed, they all became drowsy. But at midnight there was a cry, Here's the bridegroom! Come out to meet him! The virgins got up and prepared their lamps. The stupid ones said to the sensible ones, Give us some of your oil, because our lamps are going out. The sensible ones replied, saying, We don't have enough for us and for you. Go to the suppliers and buy your own. And while they were going to buy it, the bridegroom came. Those who were ready went with him to the marriage feast; then the door was locked. Later the other virgins come saying, Lord, Lord open to us! He answered, Truly, I tell you, I don't know you. Watch therefore, because you don't know the day or the hour.

Talents used and wasted vv14–30

It'll be like this: a man was setting out on a journey, and summoned his servants and entrusted his property to them. He gave five talents to one, to another two, and to another one, according to his ability. And he departed. The one with five talents immediately traded with them, and made five more. Similarly, the man with two talents made two more. But he who had received the one talent went off, dug a hole in the ground and hid his master's money. After a long time the master of those servants comes and settles accounts with them. The one with five talents came up bringing five more, saying, Master you gave me five talents, I've made five more. His master said to him, Well done! You're a good and loyal servant. You've been loyal over a little, so I'll put you in charge of more. Enter into your master's joy. Then the one with two talents came up and said, Master, you gave me two talents, look, I've made two more. His master said to him, Well done! You're a good and loyal servant. You've been loyal over a little, so I'll put you in charge of more. Enter into your Master's joy. But the one who had received the one talent came forward, and said, Lord, I knew you were a harsh man, reaping where you didn't sow and harvesting where you hadn't scattered any seed. So I was afraid and I went and hid your talent in the ground. Here's what's yours, take it. But his master answered him, You wicked and lazy servant! You know I reap where I haven't sown, and harvest where I haven't scattered seed. So you should've invested my money with the bankers, so that when I returned I would get back what was mine with interest. Take the talent from him, and give it to the one with ten talents. So to everyone who has, more will be given, and they'll have abundance. But as for the one who has nothing, even what he has will be taken away from him. And cast out the worthless servant too into outer darkness, where there'll be weeping and grinding of teeth.

The Day of Judgment vv31—46

Whenever the Son of Man comes in his glory, together with all the angels, he will sit on his glorious throne. All the nations will be gathered before him, and he will separate them from each other, as a shepherd separates the sheep from the goats. And he will place the sheep on his right, and the goats on the left. Then the king will say to those on his right, Come, you who are blessed by my Father, receive the kingdom prepared for you from the creation of the world. For I was hungry and you fed me, thirsty and you gave me drink, a stranger and you welcomed me, naked and you dressed me, sick and you visited me, in prison and you came to me. Then the righteous will answer saying, Lord, when did we see you hungry and feed you, or thirsty and give you drink? And when did we see you a stranger and welcome you, or naked and clothe you? And when did we see you sick, or in prison and visit you? And the king will say, truly I tell you, as you did it to the least of my brothers, you did it to me. Then he'll say to those on his left, Away from me, you cursed, into the eternal fire prepared for the devil and his angels! For I was hungry and you didn't feed me, thirsty and you didn't give me a drink, I was a stranger and you didn't welcome me, naked and you didn't clothe me, sick and in prison and you didn't visit me. Then they'll also answer saying, Lord, when did we see you hungry or thirsty, or a stranger or naked, or sick or in prison, and didn't help you? Then he'll answer them saying, Truly I tell you, inasmuch as you didn't do it to the least of these my brothers, you didn't do it to me. So these will go to eternal punishment, but the righteous into eternal life.

Chapter Twenty-Six

The plot to kill Jesus vv1–5

When Jesus had finished saying all this, he said to his disciples, You're aware that it will be Passover in two days, and the Son of Man will be handed over to be crucified. Then the chief priests and the elders of the people got together in the lodgings of Caiaphas, the high priest, and plotted together to arrest Jesus secretly and kill him. But they were saying, Not during the feast, or there'll be uproar among the people.

Anointing for burial vv6–13

Now when Jesus was at Bethany at the home of Simon the leper, a woman came up to him with an alabaster flask of expensive ointment, and poured it on his head as he reclined at supper. And when his disciples saw it, they were indignant, saying, What a waste! This could've been sold and the proceeds given to the poor. But Jesus, aware of this, said to them, Why give this woman grief? She's done something beautiful to me. You've got the poor with you always, but you won't always have me. By pouring this ointment on me she's prepared my body for burial. In truth, I tell you, wherever this gospel's proclaimed throughout the world, what she's done will also be told in memory of her.

Judas betrays Jesus vv14–25

Judas Iscariot, one of the twelve, went to the chief priests and said, What'll you give me if I hand him over to you? They paid him thirty pieces of silver. From then on he began to look for an opportunity to betray him. So on the first day of Unleavened Bread the disciples came to Jesus, saying, Where do you want us to prepare the Passover for you to eat? He said, Go into the city, to you know who, and say to him, The teacher says, My time's come; I'll keep the Passover at your house with my disciples. The disciples did as Jesus instructed them, and prepared the Passover. Come evening, he was sitting at table with the twelve, and as they were eating, he said, Truly, I tell you, one of you is going to betray me. They were devastated, and began to say in turn, Surely not me, Lord, is it? He answered, It's the one who dipped his hand in the dish with me—he's the one. The Son of Man goes, as it's written about him—but woe to that man by whom the Son of Man is betrayed! Better he'd not been born. Then Judas (who would betray him) said to him, Surely it's not me is it, Rabbi? You said it, Jesus replies.

The Lord's supper vv26–29

Now while they were eating, Jesus took bread and after blessing it, broke it and gave it to his disciples, saying, Take, eat, this is my body. And after taking a cup, he gave thanks, and gave it to them, saying, Drink it, all of you, for this is my blood of the covenant, poured out for many for the forgiveness of sins. I tell you, I'm not going to drink this fruit of the vine until the time I'll drink it again with you in my Father's kingdom. So when they had sung a hymn, they went to the Mount of Olives.

Jesus predicts Peter's denial vv31–35

Then Jesus says to them, You'll all desert me tonight, for it's written, ***I will strike the shepherd, and the flock of sheep will be scattered.*** But after I'm raised, I'll go ahead of you to Galilee. Peter said to him, Even if everybody else deserts you, I won't. Jesus said to him, Listen, I'll tell you, this very night, before the rooster crows, you'll deny me three times. Peter says to him, Even if I have to die with you, I won't deny you! And all the other disciples said the same.

Jesus prays in the garden vv36—46

Then Jesus goes with them to a place known as Gethsemane, and he says to his disciples, Sit here while I go and pray over there. He took Peter and the two sons of Zebedee, and became grief-stricken and distressed. Then he says to them, My sorrow is deathly; stay here and watch with me. He went a little further and fell on his face, praying and saying, My Father, if possible, take this cup from me; nevertheless, not as I will—but as you will. So he returns to the disciples and finds them sleeping, and says to Peter, Couldn't you all watch an hour with me? Watch and pray, so that you don't enter into temptation. The spirit's willing, but the flesh is weak. He went away a second time and prayed, saying, My Father, if this cup can't pass unless I drink it, your will be done. He returned again and found them sleeping, because their eyes were heavy. So he left them and he went off and prayed for the third time, using the same words. Then he comes back to the disciples and says to them, Still sleeping and resting? Behold, the hour has come! The Son of Man is delivered into the hands of sinners. Up—let's go! My betrayer's close by.

The arrest of Jesus vv47–56

As he was speaking, behold, Judas, one of the twelve, came with a large crowd with swords and clubs. They were sent from the chief priests and elders of the people. Now the betrayer had given them a signal, Whoever I kiss—he's the one—take him! Straightway he came up to Jesus, and said, Greetings, Rabbi! And he kissed him. Jesus said to him, Friend, Do what you've come for. Then they came, laid hands on Jesus and seized him. One of those with Jesus reached out his hand, drew his sword and struck a servant of the high priest, and cut off his ear. Then Jesus says to him, Put your sword back into its sheath! For all who take up the sword will perish by the sword. Don't you think I can't appeal to my Father, and immediately he'll send me more than twelve legions of angels? But how, then, should the scriptures be fulfilled, that this is how it must be? At that moment Jesus said to the crowds, Have you come out with swords and clubs to arrest me, as if I was a robber? I used to sit teaching in the temple day after day, and you never arrested me. But all this has happened, so that what the prophets wrote might be fulfilled. Then all the disciples left him and ran away.

Jesus examined before Caiaphas vv57–68

And those who had seized Jesus led him to Caiaphas, the high priest, where the scribes and elders had gathered. And Peter was following him at a distance, as far as the courtyard of the high priest. He went inside, and sat with the guards to see what would happen. Now the chief priests and the whole council were looking for false testimony against Jesus, so that they might put him to death. But they found none, although many false witnesses came forward. Eventually, two showed up and said, This fellow was saying I can destroy God's temple and rebuild it in three days. And the high priest got up, and said, Have you no answer? What are these men testifying against you? But Jesus was silent. Then the high priest said to him, I put you on oath, by the living God, tell us, are you the Messiah, the Son of God? Jesus says to him, You said it. But I tell you, from now on you'll see ***the Son of Man sitting on the right hand of power and coming on the clouds of heaven.*** At this, the high priest ripped his clothes, and said, He's blasphemed, what other witnesses do we need?—now you've heard the blasphemy! What's your verdict? He deserves death, they answered. Then they spat in his face and struck him. Some slapped him, saying, Prophesy to us, Messiah, who struck you?

Peter denies Jesus vv69–75

Now Peter was sitting outside in the courtyard. And a servant girl came up to him, and says, You were with that Jesus, the Galilean, weren't you? But he denied it before everyone, saying, I've no idea what you're talking about. And when he went out into the porch another servant girl saw him, and says to those who were there, This one was with Jesus from Nazareth. And again he denied it with an oath, I don't know the man! After a little while the bystanders came up and said to Peter, For sure you're one of them, because your accent betrays you. Then he began to curse and swear an oath saying, I don't know the man! Immediately the rooster crowed. Then Peter remembered what Jesus had said, Before the rooster crows you'll deny me three times. And he went out and wept bitterly.

Chapter Twenty-Seven

Jesus sent to Pilate vv1–2

When morning came, the chief priests and elders of the people plotted against Jesus, to put him to death. And they bound and led him away, and handed him over to Pilate, the governor.

Death of Judas vv3–10

Then when Judas, his betrayer, saw that Jesus was condemned, he was afflicted with remorse, and returned the thirty pieces of silver to the chief priests and the elders, saying, I've sinned by betraying innocent blood. They said, What's that got to do with us? You sort it out. So he flung the money into the temple sanctuary and left, then went off and hanged himself. But when the chief priests took the money, they said, We can't put it into the treasury because it's blood money. So after deliberating, they bought the potter's field with the money, as a burial ground for strangers. That's why that field is called, Field of Blood, to this day. Then what Jeremiah the prophet said was fulfilled, ***And they took the thirty pieces of silver, the value of him set by some of the children of Israel. And they used them to buy the potter's field, as the Lord ordered me.***

Jesus before Pilate vv11–14

So Jesus was stood before the governor, and the governor asked him, Are you the King of the Jews? Jesus said, You say this. But when accused by the chief priests and the elders, he said nothing. Then Pilate says to him, Don't you hear how many charges they're bringing against you? But he did not answer him even a single word, so that the governor was greatly taken aback.

Jesus or Barabbas? vv15–23

Now it had been the custom at the feast for the governor to release to the crowd any prisoner they wanted. And they had, at that time, a notorious prisoner called Barabbas. So when they had gathered, Pilate said to them, Who do you want me to release for you: Barabbas or Jesus, called Messiah? For he knew that they had handed him over out of jealousy. And while he was sitting on the judgement seat his wife sent word to him, Don't have anything to do with that just man, because I've suffered a lot dreaming about him today. Then the chief priests and the elders persuaded the crowd that they should plead for Barabbas, and that Jesus should be destroyed. So the governor said to them again, Which of the two do you want me to release for you? And they said, Barabbas! Pilate then says to them, So what do you want me to do with Jesus, called Messiah? All of them say, Let him be crucified! And he replied, Why? What evil has he done? But they started to shout all the more, Let him be crucified!

Pilate washes his hands of Jesus vv24–26

So when Pilate realised that he was not getting anywhere, and that a riot might start, he took water and washed his hands in front of the crowd, saying, I'm innocent of this man's blood—deal with it yourselves. And all the people responded, Let his blood be upon us and upon our children!

So he released Barabbas for them and had Jesus flogged; then he handed him over to be crucified.

The soldiers mock Jesus vv27–31

Then the soldiers of the governor took Jesus into the governor's headquarters, and they mustered the entire battalion before him. And they stripped him and put a scarlet robe on him. And they twisted together a crown of thorns and put it on his head, and put a reed in his right hand, and kneeling before him they mocked him, saying, Hail! King of the Jews! And they spat on him, and took the reed and struck him on the head. And when they had mocked him they stripped him of the robe, and put his own clothes on him, and led him away to crucify him.

The crucifixion of Jesus the Messiah vv32–44

And as they went out, they found a man called Simon, from Cyrene, whom they forced to carry his cross. And when they came to a place called Golgotha (which means, the Place of a Skull), they gave him wine mixed with gall to drink, but when he tasted it, he refused to swallow it. And after they had crucified him, they throw dice to divide his clothes between them. Then they sit down, and were guarding him there. And they put the charge above his head, which read, This is Jesus, the King of the Jews. Then they crucify two robbers with him, one on the right and the other on the left. And passers by were blaspheming him, wagging their heads, saying, You who'd destroy the temple and rebuild it in three days—save yourself! If you're the Son of God, come down from the cross! The chief priests with the scribes and the elders also joined in, and were mocking him, saying, He saved others, but can't save himself! If he's the King of Israel, let him come down from the cross now, and we'll believe him. He trusts in God—let him rescue him now—if he wants to. For he said, I'm the Son of God. And the robbers crucified with him were also cursing him in the same way.

The death of Jesus Messiah vv45–56

Now there was darkness over all the earth, from noon until three o'clock. And about three o'clock, Jesus loudly cried out, *Eli, Eli, lema sabachthani?* That is, ***My God, my God, why have you abandoned me?*** One of the bystanders, when he heard this, kept saying,

He's calling Elijah! And someone immediately ran and took a sponge and filled it with sour wine, and put it on a reed, and gave it to him to drink. But others were saying, Wait! Let's see if Elijah comes to save him. And again, Jesus cried out loudly, and gave up his spirit. And behold, the temple curtain was rent in two, from the top to the bottom. And the earth trembled, and the rocks were split. The tombs were opened, and many bodies of holy people who had died, were raised, they came out of the tombs after his resurrection, and went into the holy city and appeared to many. Then the centurion, and those who were with him guarding Jesus, saw the earthquake and what had happened. They were terrified, saying, This really was God's Son! There also were many women there, watching from a distance. They had followed him from Galilee, serving him. Among them were Mary Magdalene, and Mary, the mother of James and Joseph, and the mother of the sons of Zebedee.

The burial of Jesus Messiah vv57–61

When evening came, Joseph, a rich man from Arimathea, who had also become a disciple of Jesus, came to Pilate and asked for Jesus's body. So Pilate ordered it to be given to him. And Joseph took the body and wrapped it in a clean linen shroud, and laid it in his own new tomb, that he had cut out of the rock. And he rolled a great stone to the entrance of the tomb, and went away. Mary Magdalene and the other Mary were there, sitting opposite the tomb.

Guarding the tomb vv62–66

The next day, that is, after the day of Preparation, the chief priests and the Pharisees assembled before Pilate saying, Sir, we remember what that deceiver said while he was still alive, After three days I will rise. So order that the tomb be made secure, until the third day, in case his disciples come and steal him and tell the people that he has risen from the dead. In this case, the last deception would be worse than the first. Then Pilate said to them, You have a detachment of soldiers, go and make it as secure as you can. So they went and secured the tomb by sealing the stone and placing a guard.

Chapter Twenty-Eight

The resurrection of Jesus the Messiah vv1–10

After the Sabbath, at dawn, Mary Magdalene and the other Mary, went to see the tomb. And behold, there was a mighty earthquake, because an angel of the Lord had come down from heaven and rolled back the stone, and was sitting on it. His appearance was like lightning, and his clothing white as snow. For fear of him, the guards trembled and were as dead men. But the angel answered and said to the women, Don't be afraid! I know you're looking for Jesus, who's been crucified. He's not here! He's risen, just as he said. Come, see the place where he lay. Then hurry and tell his disciples that he's risen from the dead, and behold, he's going ahead of you to Galilee—you'll see him there. See, I've told you. So they fled the tomb in fear and great joy, and ran to tell his disciples. And behold, Jesus met them and said, Good morning! And they came up and grabbed hold of his feet and worshipped him. Then Jesus says to them, Don't be afraid! Go and tell my brothers to go to Galilee, and there they'll see me.

The guards report to the chief priests vv11–15

As they were on their way, behold some guards went and told the chief priests everything that had happened. And when they had met and conferred with the elders, they gave a sufficient sum of money to the soldiers, saying, Tell the people, His disciples came and stole him while we were asleep. And if the governor hears of it, we'll reassure him and keep you out of trouble. So they took the money and did as they were instructed, and this story has been spread among the Jews to this day.

Make disciples of all nations vv16–20

So the disciples went to Galilee, to the mountain where Jesus had directed them. And when they saw him they worshipped him, but some were hesitant. And Jesus came and spoke to them, saying, All authority in heaven and on earth has been given to me. Go then and make disciples of all nations, baptizing them in the name of the Father and of the Son and of the Holy Spirit, teaching them to observe all that I have commanded you. And behold, I am always with you—to the very end of the age!

Amen.

Mark

Introduction

Each of the four evangelists invites us to meet the person of Jesus Christ. Yet no one gospel says everything that could be said about him. At the end of John's gospel the author says that Jesus did so many things that the world itself could not contain the books that could be written about him. If so, then how would the gospel writers decide what to include or exclude in their narratives? How best for them to summarise what Jesus was about—his deeds, his teaching, etc? Where, moreover, should they begin and end their respective stories?

That we have four instead of one gospel narrative is testimony to the fact that none of the evangelists had a monopoly on the story about Jesus. However, it is equally clear that Matthew, Mark, Luke and John agreed about most things concerning Christ: his identity, character, message, mission, miracles, death and resurrection. All alike identify his person and ministry as the fulfilment of messianic prophecies contained in the Hebrew Scriptures (or the Old Testament, so called). Nevertheless, each of the evangelists sought to emphasise Christ's significance in different ways. Matthew lends weight to Jesus' Jewish roots, in particular how he realised God's promises to Israel found in their bible. Mark, for his part, focuses heavily on Jesus' ministry of teaching, healing and exorcism in the light of God's coming kingdom. Luke (along with his second volume, Acts of the Apostles) draws attention to how the message of Christ first took root in Galilee and later spread to Judaea, Samaria, and then to Rome itself, the imperial capital. John follows the same basic outline as the other three evangelists, but takes us on more of an inward journey into the mystery of Christ, notably with regard to how the man Jesus was both human and divine, and what this means for us in terms of our experience of God.

Here, though, I want to say a few words about Mark's gospel, which you hold in your hand. What background information might help and inform your reading of this book? Most commentators would want to say something about the identity of the author, the people for whom he originally wrote, the date in which his gospel was written, and what type of sources the author might have used in order to compose his narrative. They will also want to say something about the overall theme (or themes) of Mark's gospel. However, there is no consensus about any of these issues. Mark is generally believed to be the earliest written gospel, produced sometime before 70AD. The author is traditionally identified with John Mark, an associate of Paul, who is supposed to have turned the apostle Peter's reminiscences about Jesus into the volume we now know as Mark's gospel (this at least is the view of Papias, a second century bishop from Hierapolis, in what is now modern day Turkey). Beyond this we know little or nothing about the author or composition of Mark, and even less about the people for whom his gospel was originally written (often believed to be the early gentile Christian community in Rome). Some scholars question whether Mark was in fact the first gospel to be written. Some favour Matthew, others point out that material in John contains some of the oldest traditions or eyewitness accounts about Jesus. The reality is we know far less about the origins of the gospels than scholars are wont to suggest.

All these historical and critical issues, important though they are, fade into the background when set against Mark's real concern. While he may have little or nothing to tell us about himself, or his readers, he has a lot to say about Jesus. When we read Mark therefore it is Christ we encounter rather than the author or his addressees. Everything is subordinated to the concern of making known the good news about Jesus.

But what does Mark tell us about the Messiah, Jesus Christ? What did he do and teach?

Mark wastes no time in addressing these issues. Right at the outset of his gospel he proclaims that Jesus was the Messiah, the Son of God. Towards the end of his gospel, a Roman centurion, charged with overseeing Jesus' execution, makes the same acclamation. In the chapters in between Mark has a lot to say about Jesus being God's Son, and what exactly this means in terms of Jewish messianism. Notable, in this connection, is the opening of Mark where two Old Testament prophets announce God's imminent visitation among his people. John the Baptist, we learn, is chosen to "prepare the way of the Lord" (Malachi) and to "make his paths straight" (Isaiah). However, as soon as we begin to read Mark's story we discover that the prophets are in fact referring to Jesus of Nazareth. Thus when God finally and definitively visits his people with salvation and deliverance, says Mark, it is through the person of his Son. Jesus stands in the place of God. He acts and speaks on his behalf in a way that the prophets did not. At his baptism God identifies Jesus as his "beloved Son" in whom he takes great pleasure and delight. Demons, moreover, acknowledge that he is the "Holy One of God." Before religious leaders Jesus declares that he is "Lord of the Sabbath," and thus free to do whatever he likes on the seventh day. In further contradiction of Mosaic Law Jesus pronounces all foods clean. He demands that his followers be prepared to die for him, and asserts that his words will never pass away, even though the heavens and the earth will one day cease to be. In the transfiguration story God enjoins Peter, James and John to pay heed to Jesus, his Son, rather than Moses and Elijah, who represent the Old Covenant. Time and again in Mark we see that Jesus says and does things that properly belong to God. He heals sickness and disease, cures the deaf, mute and blind, forgives sin, cleanses the impure, miraculously feeds thousands in the wilderness, shepherds his flock, raises the dead, walks on water, has control over the forces of nature, including power to overcome his own death, and subsequently baptise his followers with the Holy Spirit (the prophet Joel says it is God alone who will pour out his Spirit on all flesh). In Mark's apocalyptic thirteenth chapter Jesus identifies himself as the one at the centre of cosmic history and the purposes of God for the world. At his trial he identifies himself with the "Son of Man" figure in the book of Daniel, a royal, heavenly person who sits on God's right hand, one who will come to earth on the clouds of heaven, flanked by legions of angels, to execute divine justice and reign eternally on earth. Thus when one individual runs up to Jesus and calls him "good teacher," Jesus alerts him to the implications of making such a statement: "only God is good." Yet, given all that we outlined above, it is difficult to deny that Jesus was also good, and that divine goodness inhered and was reflected in his life. To meet Jesus was to meet God at work, active among his people, bringing them healing and deliverance, as Malachi and Isaiah prophesied that he would. It is important, in all of this, to remember that Jesus was charged with blasphemy, for which he received the sentence of death. His co-religionists knew only too well what his claims implied—namely that he had a status above men and angels, and the right to co-rule the world with God. Through his Son, Christians later came to believe, God had turned his face toward humanity.

It was once fashionable among some scholars to argue that Mark's gospel centred on the theme of the "messianic secret." This is the idea that Mark deliberately created sayings in his gospel in which Jesus commanded his followers, and those healed of sickness or freed from demonic possession, to keep silent about the fact that he was the Messiah (i.e. God's envoy, representative). This was a ploy on Mark's part, it was argued, to explain the fact that Jesus was never really accepted as Messiah during his lifetime. However, by suggesting that Jesus purposely concealed his messianic identity, Mark was said to have deflected attention from the apparent failure of Jesus' ministry. This theory is no longer in fashion, for reasons that need not concern us here. But there is perhaps a "secret" of sorts in Mark's gospel that we should think about. We know, for instance, that in his parables Jesus demanded that his audience wrestle with his teaching, and come to understand it, so as to prove whether they were for or against God's kingdom. For most people, Jesus suggests, the parables would have the effect of blinding them to the truth, confirming them in their unbelief (cf. Isaiah). Parables were thus for "outsiders." Only those granted insight into "the secret of the kingdom of God" would grasp the meaning and significance of Jesus' message.

For Mark, the "secret" or "mystery" is centred on Jesus' identity. He is God's Son; but in a unique and startling way. When the prophets foretold that God would himself come down among his people and bring them final deliverance, it was not suspected that this would be in the shape of a crucified Galilean peasant. But this is what the first Jewish believers discovered: God fulfilled all his promises to save, heal and forgive his people in the person of Jesus of Nazareth. The apostle Paul put it this way writing to Christians in Corinth: "All the promises of God find their Yes in him." This is precisely the angle that Mark takes in his gospel. Broadcasting God's imminent arrival, as announced in the prophets and the preaching of John the Baptist, he shows how God's Son, the man Christ Jesus, did everything expected of Yahweh in the last days.

But not everybody discerned this. A pagan Roman centurion, at the foot of the cross, recognised the divine in the crucified Messiah, while the most religious people of the day saw only a blasphemer and a heretic. However, if we take Mark's cue, posted at the very outset of his gospel, then we will recognise God in Christ, drawing his own to himself, even at the expense of his own life: "For the Son of Man came not to be served but to serve, and to give his life a ransom for many." Here Mark anticipates themes that will be more fully explored in John, particularly regarding Christ's relationship with God, and how, as his Son, Jesus makes God fully known through his sacrificial death and resurrection. What Mark invites us to do as readers (or listeners), is to be aware of the multitude of different ways in which God comes to us in our humanity—whatever our circumstances. For Jesus reaches out to lepers, the demon possessed and unclean, the sick, the poor, the rich, religious leaders, prostitutes, gentiles, old people, young people, the fearful, the bereaved, the wise and ignorant, hypocrites, a breed of people known collectively as "sinners," as well those who hated him. No sector of society is outside the bounds of God's providential love and concern—not even the dead. As we read through Mark we glimpse the human face of God in the suffering servant, the crucified one who knew pain and rejection in his own life. Matthew will come to speak of "God with us," John of the pre-existent "Word" become "flesh." Already we see here the beginnings of a new way of thinking about God. In Mark we see how Jesus gets tied up with the meaning of the word God, but also how God in turn is definitively revealed in the words and deeds of Jesus of Nazareth, his Son. This is indeed a mystery, something that only makes sense when it becomes a part of lived experience, accessible through faith. Yet Mark raises an important question that lies at the very heart of his gospel: who is this man Jesus that he can wipe out people's sins and come back from the dead? By what authority, and for what reason, should he be sat at God's right hand and be delegated the task of judging the world—something that God alone can do? Mark expresses this mystery in terms of Father-Son language. There is only one God, to be sure. But whoever can act on God's behalf and shock with the immediacy of the divine presence in his own life must be God's Son—someone sent from the heart of God himself.

Dr Brendan Devitt

Chapter One

The Baptist's cry vv1-8

This is how the good news of Jesus Christ, the Son of God, begins: As the prophet Isaiah wrote: ***Look, I send my messenger before you. He will prepare your way. The voice of one shouting in the wilderness, Prepare the way of the Lord, make his paths straight!*** John the Baptist appeared in the desert preaching a baptism of repentance, for the forgiveness of sins. All Judea—Jerusalem included—was flocking to him and were being baptised by him in the River Jordan, confessing their sins. And John wore camel's hair with a leather belt around his waist. He ate locusts and wild honey. He proclaimed, Somebody more powerful than I am is on his way. I'm not fit to bend down and untie his sandals. I baptised you with water—he will baptise you in the Holy Spirit.

Jesus is baptised vv9-11

In those days Jesus came from Nazareth in Galilee and was baptised by John in the Jordan. As he came out of the water he saw the sky being ripped apart and the Spirit coming down like a dove. A voice came from heaven: You're my Son, the one I love so much. I'm well pleased with you!

Jesus in the desert vv12-13

Then the Holy Spirit drives him into the desert. He was there forty days being tempted by Satan. Wild animals were with him, and angels were serving him.

Repent and believe vv14-15

After John was arrested Jesus headed for Galilee, proclaiming God's good news and saying, The time has fully come! The Kingdom of God is near! Repent and believe the gospel!

Jesus calls his first followers vv16-20

As he was walking beside the Sea of Galilee, Jesus saw Simon and his brother Andrew casting their nets into the sea, for they were fishermen. Jesus said to them, Come on—follow me! Straightaway they abandoned their nets and went after him. A little further on he saw James, the son of Zebedee and his brother John—they were in their boat repairing their nets. Immediately he called them. So they left their father, Zebedee, in the boat along with his helpers.

A demonic spirit cast out vv21-28

So they arrive at Capernaum, and immediately on the sabbath he went into the synagogue and began to teach. And they were astounded at his teaching because he was teaching them with authority, unlike the lawyers. In the synagogue was a man with an unclean spirit. He screamed, What business is it of yours, Jesus from Nazareth! Have you come here to destroy us? I know who you are. You're God's holy one! But Jesus cut him short, Silence! Come out of him! The evil spirit shrieked and convulsed the man, then left him. Everyone was dumbstruck.

They were debating among themselves, What's this? A new teaching—with such authority! He even orders the unclean spirits and they obey him! Word of this got out so his fame spread throughout the region of Galilee.

Healing the sick in body and mind vv29-34

On leaving the synagogue he immediately went to Simon and Andrew's house, together with James and John. Simon's mother in law was in bed with a fever, so they tell him. He went to her, and took her by the hand and lifted her up, and straightaway the fever was gone and up she got and cooked a meal for them. Come evening, at sunset, they brought to him all the sick and those possessed by demons. The whole city was gathered around the door. He cured many with various diseases and expelled many demons. But he would not let the demons utter a word, because they knew him.

Prayer in the desert vv35-39

At the crack of dawn, while it was still dark, he got up and went to a remote spot and prayed. But Simon and those who were with him tracked him down. They found him and say, Everybody's looking for you! Come on, he says to them—let's go elsewhere, to the next towns, so I can preach there too—that's what I came out for. So he went preaching in synagogues all over Galilee, as well as casting out demons.

A leper cured vv40-45

A man with leprosy comes to him, and pleads with him on his knees saying, If you want to, you can cure me. Moved with pity Jesus stretched out his hand, touched him and says, Of course I want to—be cured! Instantly the leprosy vanished and he was healed. He gave him a strict warning and sent him away. On no account, he says, tell anyone. But show yourself to the priest and make the offering for cleansing prescribed by Moses to prove that you're well. Instead he went out telling all and spreading the word. So Jesus could no longer go openly into a town, but stayed outside in desert places. But still they kept coming to him from all directions.

Chapter Two

A paralytic healed and forgiven vv1-12

Within a few days of his return to Capernaum the word got around that he was at home. Because so many came the house was full to the rafters. There was no room even about the door. And he began teaching the word to them. So four men arrive carrying a paralysed man. When they could not get him anywhere near Jesus, because of the crowd, they tear off the roof and lower the cripple lying on his mat. When Jesus saw their faith he says to the paralytic, My son, your sins are forgiven! Now some lawyers who happened to be present started discussing among themselves, What's he saying? This is blasphemy! Only God can forgive sins! Immediately Jesus sensed what they were arguing about and says to them, What are you muttering about? Tell me, which is easier, to say to the paralysed man, Your sins are forgiven, or, Take that mat of yours and start walking? So that you know that the Son of Man has authority on earth to forgive sins (he says to the paralytic), Up you get! Take your mat and go home. So up he got, took his mat and before their very eyes went off. All were stunned. Everyone glorified God saying, We haven't seen anything like this before!

Levi the tax collector vv13-17

Again Jesus went out beside the sea. The whole crowd was flocking to him, so he started to teach them. And as he walked on he came across Levi, Alpheus' son, sitting at the revenue office. Jesus says to him, Come on—follow me. So he got up and did just that. Later he was having dinner at Levi's house along with his disciples. There were also many tax collectors and sinners—many of whom were following him. When the Pharisees' lawyers saw that he was having dinner with tax collectors and sinners, they kept saying to his disciples, Why's he eating with tax collectors and sinners? On hearing this Jesus says to them, Who needs a doctor—the healthy or the sick? I haven't come to cure the healthy, but the sick. So also I haven't come to call the righteous but sinners.

To fast or to feast? vv18-22

Now John's disciples and the Pharisees were fasting. So some people come to Jesus and ask, Why do John's disciples fast but yours don't? Wedding guests, says Jesus, can't fast while the bridegroom's with them, can they? So long as the bridegroom's with them they can't fast! The day will come when the bridegroom's taken away from them. That's when they'll fast. No one would dream of putting an unshrunk patch onto an old garment. If he did the new piece would pull away from the old, making the hole bigger. Nobody puts new wine into old wine skins, for fear the wine will burst the skins and the wine will be ruined. New wine goes into new wine skins.

Lord of the sabbath vv23-28

One sabbath Jesus and his disciples happened to be walking through cornfields and his disciples began plucking the heads of corn. The Pharisees were saying to him, Look, what do they think they're doing, it's not allowed on the sabbath! He replies, Haven't you heard what David did when he and his friends were hungry and needed food? They went into the house of God (during the tenure of the high priest, Abiathar), and he ate and shared with his companions the consecrated bread reserved exclusively for the priests. The sabbath was made for man, not man for the sabbath. So the Son of Man is Lord even of the sabbath.

Chapter Three

Healing on the sabbath vv1-6

On another occasion he went into the synagogue and a man with a deformed hand happened to be there. It was the sabbath, so they kept their eyes on him to see if he would heal the man, so that they might accuse him. Jesus says to the man with the withered hand, Come, stand here where you can be seen. Then Jesus says to them, Is it lawful to do good or harm on the sabbath—to save a life or kill? But they said nothing. He looked around at them all in anger, grieved at the hardness of their hearts. Jesus says to the man, Stretch out your hand. So he did and was cured. Promptly the Pharisees went out and plotted with Herod's party how they might kill him.

Following Jesus vv7-12

But Jesus and his disciples withdrew to the sea. A huge crowd from Galilee followed—and from Judea, Jerusalem, Idumea, and from across the Jordan—as well as from Tyre and Sidon. Large numbers thronged to see him when they heard what he was doing. So he told his disciples to get a boat ready to stop the crowd from crushing him. He healed so many sick that those ridden with diseases pressed against him, trying to touch him. And unclean spirits, whenever they saw him would fall down in front of him screaming, You're the Son of God! But he gave them strict instructions not to say who he was.

The twelve apostles chosen vv13-19

So he goes up a mountain and calls to him those he wanted, and they came to him. He chose twelve (called apostles) to be with him so he could send them out to preach the good news and continue to have authority to expel demons. These were the twelve he chose: Simon, whom he nicknamed Peter; and James and his brother John, Zebedee's sons whom he called Sons of Thunder; and Andrew and Philip and Bartholomew and Matthew and Thomas and

James, the son of Alphaeus, and Thaddaeus and Simon the Canaanite—and Judas Iscariot who betrayed him.

Satan against Satan vv20-30

So he comes to the house where he was lodging and once again a crowd gather around, so much so that he could not even find time to eat. When his family heard what was going on they came to take him away; for they were saying, He's out of his mind. And lawyers from Jerusalem came down and were saying, He's possessed by Beelzebub and only casts out demons through the prince of demons. Jesus called them and began to speak to them in parables, How can Satan cast out Satan? If a kingdom's divided against itself that kingdom cannot stand. And if Satan rebels against himself and is divided, he won't be able to survive, but will be destroyed. No one can go into a strong man's house to plunder it without first tying up the strong man, only then will he be able to plunder it. Listen carefully; every sin can be forgiven including blasphemy. But for those who blaspheme the Holy Spirit forgiveness is out of the question—because they're guilty of an everlasting sin (because they kept saying, He has an unclean spirit).

His family arrive vv31-35

Then his mother and brothers arrive and standing outside they send for him, calling him. A crowd was sitting around him and they say to him, Your mother and brothers and sisters are outside looking for you. But looking around at those who sat about him he says, Look—here is my mother and my brothers. Anyone who does God's will is my brother and sister and mother!

Chapter Four

Planting seed vv1-9

He began to teach again by the sea. Such a large crowd gathers that he has to get into a boat to sit off shore. So he sat there teaching the crowd who were on the land. He was teaching them using lots of parables, including this one: Listen carefully, a farmer went out to sow. As he did so some seed fell on the path and the birds came and ate it. Other seed fell on rocky ground where there was not much soil and immediately it sprouted because the earth was shallow. But when the sun rose it wilted, and because it had no roots it withered. Yet other seed fell into thorns and the thorns sprang up and choked the seed and it produced no grain. But some fell on fertile soil and produced a crop thirty, sixty, and a hundred times more than had been planted. You all have ears—so listen up!

What are parables? vv10-12

Later, when he was alone, others there along with the twelve started to quiz him about the parables. So he was saying to them, You've been granted insight into God's Kingdom; but to outsiders everything's in parables so that ***by seeing they might see yet not see, hearing they might hear but not grasp, in case they should repent and be pardoned.***

The parable of the seed explained vv13-20

So he says to them, Don't you understand this parable? How then will you make sense of all the parables? The sower plants the word. These are the ones that fall along the path where the word is sown. And as soon as they hear it Satan comes along and snatches away the word sown in them. The rocky ground represents those who receive the message with open arms. But they don't have deep roots and so only last for a while. When hard times or persecution come because of the word they have no staying power and quickly drift away. As for those seeds scattered among thorns, they hear the message, but worldly cares, the deceit of wealth, and lust for other things, seduce them and choke the word so that it's fruitless.

Light under a basket vv21-25

He went on to say, Surely a lamp isn't meant to be put under a basket or under a bed, is it? Obviously not—it's put on a lampstand! For nothing's hidden that won't be revealed. If you've ears—then listen! Pay attention to what you hear! The more you do so the more you'll understand—and more on top of that. So the one who has will be given more. But whoever's nothing, even what he has will be taken from him.

The sprouting seed vv26-34

Jesus continued, The kingdom of God's just like a man casting seed on the earth. He sleeps and wakes, night and day, and all the time the seed is sprouting and growing, but he's no idea how. The earth does this itself, the blade first, then the head of grain, and finally the full head of grain in the blade. When the grain's ripe, it's harvest time—so the sickle's put in! He went on to say, What's the kingdom of God like? What parable shall we use to describe it? It's like a mustard seed; when it's sown it's the smallest seed in all the earth. Yet when sown it grows and grows, larger than any shrub, and sprouts branches big enough for the birds of the air to nest in its shade. With many similar parables he explained the word to them, insofar as they could handle it. He spoke to them only in parables; but to his disciples in private he explained everything.

A storm calmed vv35-41

When it was evening he says to them, Let's cross to the other side. So leaving the crowd behind they take him with them in the boat, just as he was. Other boats came with him. A furious gale sprang up, and waves began to beat against the boat so that the boat was almost swamped. But Jesus was in the stern of the boat, fast asleep on a cushion. So they wake him and say to him, Teacher, Don't you care that we're about to drown? Up he got and rebuked the wind and said to the sea, Silence! Be still! The wind stopped immediately and there was a great calm. He said to them, Why are you afraid? Do you still have no faith? And they were terrified and kept asking each other, Who's this? Even the wind and the sea obey him!

Chapter Five

A possessed man is healed vv1-20

So they arrived at the other side of the sea, in the land of the Gerasenes. Just as Jesus was getting out of the boat, suddenly a demon-possessed man met him from the tombs. He lived there among the tombs, and not even a chain could hold him, because he had often been chained but had ripped them apart, and broken the shackles to pieces. Nobody was strong enough to overpower him. All day and night among the tombs and in the mountains he was screaming and cutting himself with stones. When he saw Jesus in the distance he ran up and fell on his knees before him. He let out a mighty cry saying, What do you want with me, Jesus, you Son of the Most High God? For pity's sake don't torment me! For Jesus was saying, Come out of the man, unclean spirit! What is your name? he began to ask him. Legion, he replies, because we're many. Then he begs him not to banish them from the area. There was a large herd of pigs feeding on the hillside. The demons pleaded with him, Send us into the pigs so we may live inside them. So Jesus gave them permission. The unclean spirits entered into the pigs and the herd, two thousand strong, rushed down the steep incline into the sea and were drowned. The herdsmen fled and spread the news in town and country. People came to see what had happened. So they come to Jesus and see the possessed man, sitting down, fully clothed, in his right mind (the very man who had been possessed by the legion) and they were terrified. Those who saw what had happened to the pigs and to the possessed man told everyone about it. And they began to implore Jesus to leave their region. As he got into the boat the man who had been possessed begs to come with him. But Jesus said, No. Instead, he says, Go home to your own people and tell them everything that the Lord has done for you—and showed you mercy. So off he went to the Decapolis and began to tell everybody what Jesus had done for him, and all were dumbfounded.

The sick cured, the dead raised vv21-43

When Jesus returned to the other side in the boat, an enormous crowd was gathered around him. He was beside the sea. Jairus, one of the synagogue leaders, comes and when he saw Jesus he falls down at his feet and pleads with him, My little daughter's at the point of death, please come and lay hands on her so that she might be healed and live. So Jesus went with him, and a large crowd was following and pressing up against him. Now there was a woman who had a haemorrhage for twelve years. She endured a great deal of suffering at the hands of numerous doctors. She spent all she had, but got no better, in fact she got worse. When she got wind that Jesus was around she slipped through the crowd from behind and touched his clothes. She kept saying to herself, If only I touch his clothes I will be healed. Immediately the bleeding stopped and she knew that she had been cured. Jesus sensed instantly that energy had left him. So he turned around in the crowd and said repeatedly, Who touched my clothes? The disciples kept saying, Look the crowd is jostling you and you ask, Who touched me? But still he kept looking around in the crowd to see who had done it. In fear and trembling the woman came and fell down before him, because she realised what had been done to her, so she owned up. He said to her, Daughter, your faith has made you well! Go in peace and be healed of your illness. As he was saying this people come from the home of the synagogue ruler saying, Your daughter is dead. No need to trouble the teacher further. Jesus overhead what they were saying and says to the synagogue ruler, Don't be afraid, trust me. Jesus would not let anybody else go with him apart from Peter and James and his brother John. So they enter the synagogue ruler's house and Jesus sees the commotion and weeping and loud wailing. And when he entered he says, Why all the pandemonium – and mourning? The child's not dead, only sleeping. They laughed at him. So he takes the child's father and mother, and those who were with him, to where the child was. Taking hold of the child's hand he says to her, *Talitha koum*, meaning, Little girl, get up. And straightaway the girl, aged twelve, gets up and starts walking around. They were utterly amazed. He gave them strict orders to say nothing about this to anyone. Then he told them to give her something to eat.

Chapter Six

Rejection at Nazareth vv1-6

He left there and returns to his hometown. His disciples follow him. On the Sabbath he started to teach in the synagogue. Many who heard him were astonished, Where did he get all this? they asked, who gave him this wisdom? By his own hands he has performed such miracles! He's a carpenter isn't he—Mary's son, the brother of James and Joses and Judas and Simon? And aren't his sisters here with us? And so they took offence. Jesus began to tell them, A prophet's honoured everywhere except in his own country and among his relatives and family. So he was unable to perform even one mighty deed there, apart from laying his hands on a few sick people and curing them. He was amazed by their lack of faith.

The twelve sent out vv7-13

So he went teaching from village to village. Jesus calls the twelve to him and began to send them out in pairs. He gave them power over unclean spirits, and instructed them to take nothing for the journey, except a walking stick—but no bag, bread or purse. They could wear sandals, but not bring two coats. Whenever you enter a house, he was saying, stay there until you leave town. And if anyone doesn't welcome you or listen to what you say, shake off the dust on your feet when you leave, as a sign of their rejection. So they went and proclaimed that people should repent. And they began casting out many demons, and anointing with oil many who were sick—and they were healed.

John the Baptist murdered vv14-29

King Herod heard about what was happening because by now Jesus was well known. This must be John the Baptist come back from the dead, people were saying. This is why he's the power to do such miracles. Some, however, were saying, He's Elijah, others, He's a prophet like one of the old prophets. When Herod heard this he began to say, John, the man I beheaded, has been raised from the dead. For Herod himself had ordered his arrest. He had him shackled and imprisoned, all because of Herodias, his brother Philip's wife, who he had married. John kept reminding Herod, It's illegal to marry your brother's wife. So Herodias had it in for John and wanted to kill him, but was unable to because Herod feared John. For he knew that he was a just and holy man, so he continued to keep him under his protection. He was puzzled by what John had to say, but was still happy to listen to him. But an opportunity arose on Herod's birthday when he hosted a banquet and invited high-ranking individuals, officers and elites from Galilee. So Herodias' daughter came in and danced and delighted Herod and his guests. The king said to the girl, Ask me whatever you wish and I'll give it to you—even half my kingdom. She went out and spoke to her mother and said, What shall I ask for? She replied, The head of John the Baptist. She quickly ran back to the king and said, I want you to give me the head of John the Baptist on a serving plate. The king immediately regretted what he had said but did not feel he could break his promise in front of all his guests. So without delay he sent an executioner and gave him orders to bring back John's head. So he went off and beheaded him in the prison. Then he brought his head on a serving plate and gave it to the girl who gave it to her mother. When his disciples heard what had happened they took his body and placed it in a tomb.

Food in the desert vv30-44

So the apostles come back to Jesus and told him all they had done and taught. He says to them, Come away yourselves to a remote place and rest a while. For there were so many comings and goings that they could not even grab a bite to eat. So they secretly set off in a boat to a remote area. Many witnessed their departure and recognised who they were. So they all ran from the towns and arrived before them. When he got there Jesus saw a great crowd and his heart went out to them, because they were like sheep without a shepherd. And he started to teach them many things. It was now quite late and his disciples came to him and began to say, This is the back of beyond and it's now getting very late; better send them away to the surrounding farms and villages to buy some food for themselves. You give them something to eat, he said. They reply, Do you want us to go and buy two hundred denarii worth of bread and give it to them to eat? How many loaves do you have? he asks—go and see. They had a look and tell him, Five, and two fish as well. Jesus instructed them to sit down in groups of a hundred and groups of fifty on the green grass. He then took the fives loaves and two fish, looked up to heaven, blessed the bread, then broke it and began to give it to his disciples to give to the people. He also shared the fish among them all. Everyone ate. Everyone was satisfied. And they collected the leftovers—twelve baskets full including the fish. Five thousand men had their fill!

A walk on the water vv45-52

Straightaway Jesus made his disciples get into the boat and go ahead to the opposite side, to Bethsaida, while he sends the crowd away. After he sent them off he went up into the mountain to pray. Evening came. The boat was in the middle of the sea, but he was alone on the shore. Now when he saw them straining on the oars, for the wind was against them, he comes towards them walking on the sea making as if to pass them by. It was just before dawn. When they saw him walking on the sea they thought it was a ghost and screamed, because everyone saw him and was petrified. Immediately he spoke to them, and says, Take courage! It's me! Don't be afraid! He came to them in the boat and the wind ceased. They were astonished beyond belief, because they did not understand about the loaves—they were dim-witted.

The sick made well vv53-56

So they crossed over to the other side and came to Gennesaret, where they disembarked. When they got out of the boat they were recognised at once and word got around, so the whole region hurried and brought the sick on mats to where they heard he was. Wherever he went, be it villages, cities or the countryside, they laid out the sick in the market places and begged him that they might just touch the fringe of his clothing: whoever touched him was cured.

Chapter Seven

Clean and unclean food vv1-23

So when the Pharisees and some lawyers come from Jerusalem to see him, they saw some of his disciples eating without washing their hands. Pharisees, and indeed all Jews, do not eat unless they first (in keeping with the tradition of their forefathers) scrub their hands. In the same way unless they purify themselves on returning from the market they do not eat—it is the same with their other customs such as washing cups, pots and bronze utensils. So the Pharisees ask him, Why don't your disciples follow the tradition of the elders, but eat with unwashed hands? Jesus said, Isaiah got it right about you hypocrites when he foretold: ***This people honour me with their lips, but their heart is far from me. Their worship of me is in vain. They mistake human precepts for divine commands.*** He went on to say, How convenient for you to abandon the law of God in order to uphold your tradition! It was Moses who said, ***Honour your father and your mother,*** and, ***Whoever speaks evil of his father and mother, let him be put to death.*** But when you claim that if a person says to his father and mother, Whatever support you would've had from me, I've set aside as a gift for God—you no longer allow him to do anything for his parents! This tradition you hand down undermines God's word—just like many other things that you do. Once again he summoned the crowd and began to address them, Listen carefully and understand what I'm telling you; it's not what goes into a person that makes him unclean, but what comes out! So when he went indoors, away from the crowd, his disciples asked about the parable. Are you clueless too? he replies. Don't you know that everything that goes into a person from outside can't make him unclean because it doesn't enter his heart but his stomach, and then is flushed into the sewer. (For this reason Jesus declared all food clean). He continued, It's what comes out of a person that makes them unclean. Because from within, from a person's heart, comes evil thoughts, sexual immorality, theft, murder, adultery, greed, bad thoughts, deceit, indecency, the evil eye, blasphemy, pride, and foolishness. All this evil comes out of the heart and makes a person unclean.

A woman's faith brings healing vv24-30

So he got up and went to the regions around Tyre. He went indoors, not wishing people to know where he was, but he could not be hidden. Suddenly a woman whose daughter had an unclean spirit arrived and fell at his feet. She was a Greek by birth, a Syro-Phoenician. She begged him that the demon might be driven out of her daughter. He began to say to her, First feed the children, because it's not right to take bread meant for children and throw it to the dogs. But Lord, she says, even the dogs under the table eat the children's crumbs! Jesus replied, Well said! Go—you'll find the demon has left your daughter. When she returned home she found her child lying on the bed—the demon had gone.

A deaf and dumb man healed vv31-37

So he left the district of Tyre and came to the Decapolis region, by way of Sidon, to the Sea of Galilee. They bring a deaf and dumb man to him. They beg Jesus to lay his hands on him. Jesus took him away from the crowd and in private put his fingers into the man's ears and touched his tongue with saliva. He looked up to heaven, sighed and says to him, *Epphata*, which means, Open up! His ears were opened, his tongue was loosened and he began to speak perfectly. He told them not to say anything, but the more he told them the more they spread the news. They were astounded. Everything he has done, they were saying, has been well done—he even makes the deaf hear and the dumb speak!

Chapter Eight

Four thousand fed vv1-10

Once more there was a huge crowd and they had nothing to eat. He called his disciples and says, My heart goes out to the crowd, because they have been with me for three days and have nothing to eat. If I send them home hungry, they'll faint; some of them have come a long distance. His disciples asked, Where can we possibly get enough bread to feed them out here in the desert? He asked, How many loaves do you have? Seven, they said. So he orders the crowd to sit on the ground. He took the seven loaves and gave thanks and broke them and started to give them to his disciples so that they might share them among the crowd. There were also a few fish. When he gave thanks for them he said, Give out these as well. So they ate and were satisfied. And they filled seven baskets with the leftovers. The crowd were four thousand strong. Then he sent them away. Next he set off with his disciples in the boat and came to the region of Dalmanutha.

The Pharisees rebuffed vv11-13

Then the Pharisees came to Jesus and started arguing with him, seeking a sign from heaven, to test him. Exasperated he says, Why does this generation look for a sign? Let me make it clear, no sign will be given to this generation. So he left them, got into the boat, and crossed to the other side.

Warnings about the Pharisees vv14-21

But they forgot to bring bread; and they only had a single loaf with them in the boat. Jesus began to warn them, Look out for the yeast of the Pharisees and the yeast of Herod. They began to debate among themselves the fact that they had no bread. Knowing this he says, Why are you discussing the fact that you've no bread? Are you still blind and ignorant? Are your hearts dull? You've eyes, but don't see, and ears but don't hear. Don't you remember? When I broke the five loaves for the five thousand how many baskets full of leftovers did you pick up? Twelve, they say. And when I broke seven loaves for the four thousand how many baskets of leftovers did you collect? They answer, seven. And he was saying to them, You still don't understand do you?

A blind man sees vv22-26

So they come to Bethsaida and they bring to him a blind man so he might touch him. He took hold of the man's hand and brought him outside the village and when he had spat on his eyes he laid his hands on him and asked, Do you see anything? Looking up he kept repeating, I see men—but I see them as trees walking about. So again Jesus put his hands on the man's eyes, this time he looked intently and saw everything clearly. Jesus ordered him to go straight home saying, Don't enter the village.

Who is Jesus? vv27-30

Jesus and his disciples came into the villages around Caesarea Philippi. On the way there he was asking his disciples, Who do people say that I am? John the Baptist, they answered, others say Elijah, yet others say one of the prophets. So he was asking them, But who do you say I am? Peter says, You're the Messiah! Jesus ordered them not to breathe a word to anyone.

Patient endurance for the gospel vv31-38

So he started to teach them that the Son of Man must suffer much and be rejected by the elders, chief priests and lawyers, and be killed, and three days later rise again. He was saying all this frankly. So Peter took him aside and began to rebuke him. But Jesus turned around, looked at his disciples, and rebuked Peter, and says, Get behind me Satan! You're thinking man's way not God's. And he called the crowd with his disciples and said to them, Whoever wants to follow me, let him deny himself, take up his cross and follow me. Whoever sets out to save his life will lose it; but whoever loses his life for my sake and the sake of the gospel will save it. For how will it benefit a man to gain the whole world yet lose his life? What can a man give up in exchange for his life? For whoever's ashamed of me and of my words in this adulterous, sinful generation, the Son of Man will be ashamed of him when he comes in the glory of the Father and his holy angels.

Chapter Nine

Jesus transfigured vv1-13

And he was saying to them, Truly, I tell you there are some standing here who will not taste death until they see that the kingdom of God has already come in power. Six days later Jesus takes Peter, James and John, privately, up into a high mountain, alone. And his appearance was utterly changed before their eyes. His clothing became blinding, dazzling white—like no launderer on earth could bleach them. And Elijah with Moses appeared to them. They were speaking with Jesus. Teacher, says Peter to Jesus, it's good that we're here, let's make three shelters—one for you, one for Moses and one for Elijah (for he had no idea what to say because they were terrified). Suddenly a cloud started to overshadow them and out of the cloud came a voice, This is my beloved Son—listen to him! And immediately as they looked around they saw no one except

Jesus. On their way down from the mountain he instructed them to tell no one what they saw, at least not until the Son of Man should rise from the dead. And they kept this matter to themselves, speculating as to what it meant to rise from the dead. And so they were asking him, Why do the lawyers say that Elijah must come first? So he said to them, When first Elijah comes he will set about restoring everything. Yet how is it written about the Son of Man, that he should suffer a great deal and be rejected? But what I say to you is this, Elijah has already come, and they did to him as they pleased, just as it's written about him.

A deaf and dumb demoniac healed vv14-29

So when they came to the disciples they saw a large crowd surrounding them and lawyers arguing with them. As soon as the crowd saw Jesus they were astounded. They run to him, greeting him. What are you discussing with them? he asked. Somebody from the crowd said, Teacher, I brought my son to you, because a spirit has robbed him of speech. When the spirit seizes hold of him it slams him to the ground and he foams at the mouth, grinds his teeth and becomes rigid. I asked your disciples to expel it but they couldn't. O faithless generation, sighed

Jesus, how long must I be with you? How long must I put up with you? Bring him to me. So they did. And when the spirit saw Jesus he immediately threw the boy into a convulsion, and falling on the ground he began to roll around foaming at the mouth. Jesus asked the father, How long has he been like this? Since childhood, he answered. It would often throw him into the fire or into water trying to kill him; but if you can help, have pity on us! Jesus said to him, What do you mean—if you can? Everything is possible to the one who believes? Suddenly the child's father began to cry out, I believe—help my unbelief! Once Jesus saw the crowd starting to come together he rebuked the unclean spirit, Out of him! Never enter him again! he said. The spirit cried out and after he had convulsed the boy, he came out. The boy was lifeless. Many thought he was dead, but Jesus took his hand and lifted him to his feet. When he went indoors his disciples asked him privately, Why couldn't we cast him out? He replied, Only prayer can cast out this sort of spirit.

Death, humility, tolerance, and determination vv30-50

After leaving that region they began to make their way through Galilee. He wanted to keep this confidential because he was teaching his disciples, The Son of Man is to be delivered into the hands of men. They will kill him. But three days later he will rise. They had no idea what he meant and were too afraid to ask. They came to Capernaum. When they went indoors he asked them, What were you discussing on the way here? They said nothing, because on the journey they had discussed which of them was the greatest. So he sat down and called the twelve and says to them, If anyone wants to be first, he must be last of all and servant of all. He took a child, and placed it among them, and taking it in his arms he says, Whoever welcomes one of these children in my name, welcomes me; and whoever welcomes me doesn't welcome me, but the one who sent me. John butted in, Teacher, we saw someone expelling demons in your name and tried to stop him. Jesus replied, Don't stop him! No one can do a mighty act in my name and then denigrate me. Whoever's not against us is on our side. The truth is, anyone who gives you a cup of water in my name (because you belong to the Messiah), will by no means lose their reward. But whoever causes one of these little ones who have faith in me to sin, it would be better that a huge millstone be tied around his neck, and for him to be thrown into the sea. If your hand makes you sin—cut it off! It's better for you to go through life crippled than with two hands to end up in hell. If your foot makes you sin—cut it off! It's better to go through life lame than with two feet to be flung into hell. And if your eye makes you sin—tear it out! It's better to enter the kingdom of God with one eye than with two eyes to be thrown into hell, where their worm never dies and the fire is unquenchable. For everyone will be salted with fire. Salt is good but if it loses its saltiness how will you make it salty again? Have salt in yourselves—and be at peace with one another.

Chapter Ten

On divorce vv1-12

Then Jesus left that area and comes to the region of Judea, and beyond the river Jordan. And crowds gather around him and, as was his custom, he began to teach them. Now Pharisees came to him and were asking him, as a test, Is it lawful for a man to divorce his wife? Jesus answered, What did Moses command you? They replied, Moses permitted a man to write a divorce certificate and put her away. But Jesus said to them, He wrote this commandment because of your stubbornness. But from the beginning he made them male and female. Therefore a man will leave his father and his mother and become joined to his wife—and the two will become one flesh. So they're not two but one flesh. Therefore what God has bound together let no one separate.

Back at the house the disciples again began to query this with him. So he says to them, Whoever divorces his wife and marries someone else commits adultery against her. And if she should divorce her husband and marry someone else, she too commits adultery.

Little children blessed vv13-16

They were bringing little children to him so he could touch them. But the disciples told them off. When Jesus saw this he was angry and said to them, Let the children come to me—don't try to stop them. The kingdom of God belongs to people just like them. Let me be frank, whoever doesn't receive the kingdom of God like a child won't enter it. And after he had put his arms around them he blesses them, placing his hands upon them.

A rich man meets Jesus vv17-31

As Jesus was starting his journey a man ran up to him and fell on his knees and began to ask, Good teacher, what must I do to inherit eternal life? Jesus said to him, Why do you call me good? Only God is good. You know the commandments, ***Don't murder, don't commit adultery, don't steal, don't tell lies in court, don't cheat—respect your father and mother.*** He said to him, Teacher, I've kept all these since I was a young man. Jesus looked at him and felt for him. There's one thing missing, he said, Go and sell whatever you have and give the proceeds to the poor, then you'll have treasure in heaven—then come, follow me! This saddened the man and he went away downhearted because he was so rich. Jesus then looked around at his disciples and says, How hard it will be for the rich to enter the kingdom of God. The disciples were astonished at this. Jesus again says, Children, how hard it is to enter the kingdom of God. It's easier for a camel to go through the eye of a needle than for a rich person to enter the kingdom of God. They were even more amazed and kept muttering among themselves, Then who can be saved? Jesus looked intently at them and says, For humans this is impossible, but not for God—for everything's possible with God. Peter then started to say to him, Look, we've left everything and followed you! Jesus answered, Let me make it clear. There's nobody who's left home, brothers, sisters, mother, father, children, or fields because of me, or the gospel, who will not receive a hundred times more on top of homes, brothers, sisters, mothers, children—along with persecutions, and in the age to come, eternal life. But many who are first will be last and the last first.

Jesus predicts his death and resurrection vv32-34

They were on their way to Jerusalem and Jesus was leading the way. They were amazed, and those who followed him became frightened. He took the twelve aside and began to tell them what was going to happen to him. Listen, we're going up to Jerusalem and the Son of Man will be handed over to the chief priests and to the scribes and they'll condemn him to death and will turn him over to the gentiles. They'll mock him, spit on him, whip and kill him. But after three days he will rise.

James and John ask a favour vv35-45

James and John, Zebedee's sons, come to Jesus and say to him, Teacher, we want you to do us a favour. Do what exactly? Jesus asked them. They said to him, Allow one of us to sit on your right and the other on your left in your glory. Jesus replied, You've no idea what you're asking. Can you drink the cup I'll drink, or face the baptism that awaits me? Of course, they replied. Jesus then said, You'll certainly drink the same cup as me, and be baptized with the same baptism. But it's not down to me who will sit on my right or my left—that's already been decided. Now when the other ten heard this they were furious with James and John. So Jesus called them and says, You know that those who are supposed to rule over the gentiles lord it over them, and that their elites exercise authority over them. This won't be the case with you. Instead whoever wants to be great among you must be a servant, and whoever wants to be first will be everybody's slave, because the Son of Man did not come to be served but to serve, and to give his life as a ransom for many.

Blind Bartimaeus receives his sight vv46-52

So they arrive in Jericho. And as he was leaving together with his disciples and a huge crowd, a blind beggar, Bartimaeus, the son of Timaeus, was sitting by the roadside. When he heard that it was Jesus of Nazareth passing by he started to cry out, Jesus, Son of David, take pity on me! Many began to tell him off, in order to shut him up. But he cried out all the more, Son of David, please take pity on me! Jesus stopped in his tracks. Call him, he said. So that's what they did. Be Brave, up you get, they said, he's calling you. So he flung off his cloak and came to Jesus who said to him, What do you want me to do for you? The blind man replied, I want my sight. On your way then, said Jesus, your faith has cured you. Immediately he got back his sight and began to follow Jesus on his journey.

Chapter Eleven

Entering Jerusalem vv1-11

As they approach Jerusalem near Bethpage and Bethany, at the Mount of Olives, Jesus sends two of his disciples and tells them, Head for the village in front of you. As soon as you enter it you'll find a young donkey tied up, on which no one's ever sat. Untie it and bring it here. If anyone should ask you, What are you doing? Just say, The Master needs it—he'll send it straight back. So off they went and found the young donkey tied at a door, outside in the street. They untie it, but some bystanders began to say to them, What do you think you're doing untying the donkey? They told them what Jesus had said. So they let them go. And they bring the donkey to Jesus, throw their cloaks on it, then Jesus sat on it. Many spread out their garments on the road, and others strewed branches they had cut down from the fields. Both those in front and those behind kept shouting ***Hosanna! Blessed is the one who comes in the name of the Lord!*** Blessed is the coming kingdom of David, our father! Hosanna in the highest! So he went into Jerusalem and after he had gone into the temple and had a good look at everything, he headed for Bethany with the twelve because it was getting late.

A fig tree cursed vv12-14

The following day, after they left Bethany, Jesus became hungry. And noticing in the distance a fig tree with leaves, he went to see if he could find anything on it. But when he got there all he found were leaves, because it was not the season for figs. So he said to the tree, May nobody ever eat fruit from you again! And his disciples heard this.

The Temple cleansed vv15-19

So they arrive at the temple. He goes in and starts to drive out those trading there. He was overturning the tables of the moneychangers and the seats of those selling pigeons. He would not allow anyone to bring anything though the temple. He was teaching and saying to them, Isn't it written, ***My House shall be a house of prayer for all nations?*** But you've turned it in to a bandits' hideout. Now the chief priests and legal experts were seeking a way to kill him, because they were frightened of him because all the crowd were amazed at his teaching. When evening came Jesus and his disciples left the city.

The fig tree withered vv20-26

And as they were passing by in the morning they saw the fig tree withered to its roots. And when Peter remembered he says to him, Look, teacher, the fig tree that you cursed has withered! Have faith in God, Jesus says to him. I tell you the truth, if anyone says to this mountain, Be taken up and cast into the sea, and doesn't doubt in his heart, but believes that what he says will happen—so it will be for him. This is why I tell you: whatever you pray and ask for, believe that you've already received it and it will be yours. And when you stand praying, if you hold a grudge against anyone, forgive them, so that your Father in heaven may forgive you your sins.

Jesus' authority questioned vv27-33

So again they come to Jerusalem, and while he was walking in the temple the chief priests and legal experts approach him. They started to ask him, By what authority are you doing these things? Or who gave you the right to do these things? Jesus answered, I'll ask you one question, give me your answer and I'll tell you by what authority I'm doing these things: John's baptism—from God or man, which? They were reasoning among themselves saying, If we say from heaven he'll say, Then why didn't we believe him? But dare we say, from men? (For they were frightened of the mob because everyone thought John was a real prophet.) So they answer Jesus, We don't know. In that case, says Jesus, neither will I tell you by what authority I'm doing these things.

Chapter Twelve

A parable about a vineyard vv1-12

Then Jesus started to teach them using parables. A man planted a vineyard, fenced it off and dug a pit for the winepress and erected a tower, and leased it to tenant farmers, then went away on a journey. After a while he sent a servant to collect some of the grapes. But they seized him, beat him and sent him away empty-handed. Then he sent another servant, and they hit this one on the head and treated him shamefully. So he sent yet another, but they murdered him—and many others: beating some and killing others. All he had left was his one and only son. He was the last one sent. Surely they'll respect my son, says the father. But some of the tenant famers said to themselves, This is the heir, come on, let's kill him and the inheritance will be ours! So they took him and killed him, and dumped him outside the vineyard. So what'll the vineyard owner do now? He'll surely destroy those tenant famers and give the vineyard to others. Haven't you read this scripture: ***The stone rejected by the builders has become the corner stone; this was the Lord's work and we stand amazed?*** So they were seeking to arrest him, but were frightened of the crowd because they knew that the parable was meant for them. So they left him and went away.

Should taxes be paid to Caesar? vv13-17

And they send to him some of the Pharisees and the Herodians to ensnare him with his own words. So when they came to him they say to him, Teacher, we know you're honest and aren't swayed by others, because you pay no attention to outward appearances, but truly teach God's way. Is it lawful to pay tax to Caesar—or not? Should we pay or should we not? But he saw through their hypocrisy and said to them, Why are you testing me? Fetch me a coin. So they brought one. Whose is this image and inscription? Caesar's, they answered. Then give to Caesar what belongs to him and to God what belongs to God. And they were amazed at him.

A trick question answered vv18-27

Now Sadducees, who believe that there is no resurrection, come to him saying, Moses wrote for our guidance that if a man should die and leave a wife childless, his brother should take his wife and raise up offspring for his brother. Now there were seven brothers. The first married her and died, and the second married her and died, leaving no offspring—and the third likewise. So all seven died and left no offspring. Finally the woman died. So whose wife shall she be in the resurrection, because all seven had married her? Jesus began to say to them, Doesn't this show how mistaken you are? You know neither the scriptures nor the power of God. For when the dead are raised they will neither marry nor be given in marriage, but are like the angels in heaven. As for the dead who are raised, haven't you read in the book of Moses, about the bush, how God spoke to him saying, ***I'm the God of Abraham, and the God of Isaac and the God of Jacob?*** He's not the God of the dead but of the living! You're way off the mark.

The great commandment vv28-34

One of the lawyers came and heard them debating. And when he saw how well he tackled their questions, he asked him, What's the most important commandment of all? Jesus answered, This is the most important: ***Hear, O Israel, the Lord our God is one, and you shall love the Lord your God with all your heart, and with all your soul, and with all your mind, and with all your strength.*** The second is this: ***You shall love your neighbour as yourself.*** No other commandment is greater than these. The lawyer said to him, Well said, teacher, that's very true. God is indeed one and there's nobody else but him. And to love him with all your heart, mind and strength, and your neighbour as yourself is more important than all whole burnt offerings and sacrifices. When Jesus saw that he answered thoughtfully, he said to him, You're not far from God's kingdom. After this no one dared question him.

Who is David's son? vv35-37

After this, while he was teaching in the temple, Jesus began to say, How come the lawyers say that Christ is David's son? David himself, guided by the Holy Spirit, said, ***The Lord said to my Lord, sit on my right-hand until I place your enemies under your feet.*** David himself calls him Lord, so how is he his son? And the large crowd was thrilled with what he was saying.

Beware of lawyers vv38-40

He went on to teach saying, Watch out for lawyers who are fond of going about in long robes and of receiving greetings in the markets, and having pre-eminent seats in the synagogues and places of honour at banquets. They devour widows' houses and pretend to pray at length. They'll be judged more harshly.

A widow's gift vv41-44

And as he sat opposite the collection box he was watching the crowd putting money into it. Many rich people were putting in a lot. Then one poor widow came along and threw in two copper coins, equal to a penny. So he called his disciples and said to them, Without a doubt, I tell you, this poor widow has thrown in more than all the others who put offerings into the collection box. Because all the others gave out of their abundant wealth, but she in her poverty gave away her entire livelihood.

Chapter Thirteen

The temple destroyed, the end of the age, the gospel preached vv1-13

As he comes out of the temple one of his disciples says to him, Teacher, look what amazing stones these are—what awesome buildings! Do you see these great buildings? said Jesus, not one of these stones will be left upon another that will not be thrown down. And as he was sitting on the Mount of Olives, opposite the temple, Peter, James, John and Andrew asked him in private, Tell us, when will all these things come about? And what will be the sign that all these things are about to be fulfilled? Jesus began to say to them, Make sure that no one leads you astray. Many will come in my name saying, I'm the One! And they'll deceive many. And when you hear of wars and rumours of wars, don't be alarmed. This must happen, but the end isn't yet. For nation will be raised against nation, kingdom against kingdom. There will be earthquakes in many places, there will be famines—these are but the start of future troubles. But look out for yourselves! They'll hand you over to the councils, and you'll be beaten up in the synagogues and be stood in front of governors and kings for my sake, to bear witness to them. And first the gospel must be proclaimed to all nations. And whenever they put you on trial don't think what to say in advance, but say whatever is given to you. For it's not you who speak but the Holy Spirit. And brother will deliver brother to death and the father his child. Children will rise up against parents and kill them. And all will hate you because of me. But whoever endures to the end will be delivered.

The woes to come vv14-23

And whenever you see the detestable idol standing where it shouldn't be (let the reader understand), then let those in Judea flee to the mountains. Let whoever's on the rooftop not come down and go into his house to take anything. And let him who's in the field not turn back to take his coat. But alas for those pregnant, and those who are breastfeeding at that time. Pray it doesn't happen in winter.

Because then there will be tribulation not seen since the beginning of God's creation, and such as will never happen again. And if the Lord hadn't cut short the days, no one would be saved. But the days will be shortened for the sake of the elect, which he chose. So if anyone says to you, Look, here's the Messiah! Or, Look, he's there! Don't believe a word of it. For false Messiahs and false prophets will be raised up and will perform signs and wonders to deceive, if possible, the elect. So be vigilant, I've warned you about all this in advance.

Cosmic catastrophe vv24-31

But in those days, after that calamity, the sun will be darkened and the moon will not give its light. The stars will start falling from heaven. And the heavenly powers will be shaken. And then they will see ***the Son of Man coming on the clouds*** with great power and glory. And then he will send his angels and gather his chosen ones from the four winds and from the furthest ends of the earth. Learn this lesson from the fig tree: whenever its branch is tender and bears leaves, you know summer is near. It's the same with you: whenever you see these things happen, you can be sure the harvest is near. I tell you the truth: this generation will not pass away until all this takes place. Heaven and earth will pass away, but my words—never!

Watch and pray vv32-37

But as for that day or hour, nobody knows—neither the angels in heaven, nor the Son, but the Father alone. So be ready—because you don't know when this will occur. Watch and pray! It's like a man who leaves his house to go on a journey. He leaves his servants in charge, each with his own task and orders the doorkeeper to keep watch. So keep watch—because you never know when the master of the house is coming back—evening, midnight, dawn or early morning—in case he should come suddenly, without warning, and find you sleeping. What I say to you I say to everybody—be on your guard!

Chapter Fourteen

The plot to kill Jesus vv1-2

Now the Passover and the feast of Unleavened Bread was only two days away. The chief priests and the legal experts were seeking how to arrest him covertly and kill him. But not during the feast, they said, or the people will riot.

Anointing at Bethany vv3-9

When he was at Bethany relaxing at the house of Simon the leper, a woman came with an alabaster jar of perfume filled with pure nard. Opening the jar she poured its contents on his head. Some of the onlookers were angry and grumbled among themselves, What a waste! This ointment could easily have been sold for three hundred denarii and the money given to the poor. So they gave her a good telling off. Leave her alone, said Jesus, why are you picking on her? She has done something beautiful for me. You always have the poor with you, and you'll have every opportunity of doing good for them—but you won't always have me. She did what she could. She anointed my body before burial. I tell you this much, wherever the gospel is proclaimed throughout the whole world, what she did will be told in memory of her.

Judas the traitor vv10-11

Judas Iscariot, one of the twelve, went to the chief priests to betray him. They listened to what he had to say and were delighted and promised him a reward. From then on he was on the lookout for the opportunity to hand him over.

The Lord's Supper vv12-21

It was on the first day of Unleavened Bread, when the Passover lamb was sacrificed, his disciples say to him, Where do you want us to go to prepare the Passover feast for you to eat? He sends two of his disciples and says, Go into the city and you'll meet a man carrying a jar of water. Follow him wherever he goes and say to the householder that the master says, Where's the room to eat the Passover meal with my disciples? He'll show you a large upstairs room, fully furnished and prepared. Get it ready for us. So the disciples went and came into the city and found everything just as he had said. So they got ready for the Passover. Come evening he arrives with the twelve. They were all sitting down and eating when Jesus says, Listen carefully to me. One of you will betray me—someone who's actually eating with me. They were mortified. They kept asking him, Surely it's not me is it? It's one of the twelve, he replied, he's dipping in the dish with me. The Son of Man will depart just as scripture says of him, but as for the one who betrays the Son of Man—bad news: better he'd never been born!

Bread and wine vv22-26

And when they were eating he took bread, blessed and broke it and gave it to them saying, Take, this is my body. He then took the cup, gave thanks and gave it to them. They all drank it. Behold this is my blood of the covenant which is poured out for many. I tell you truly, I'll not drink of the fruit of the vine again until the day I drink it afresh in the kingdom of God. So they sang a hymn and went to the Mount of Olives.

Foretelling what will happen vv27-31

And Jesus says to them, You'll all desert me, just as it's written, ***I'll strike the shepherd and the sheep will be scattered.*** But take courage, I will go ahead of you to Galilee. So Peter was saying, If all the others are scandalised I won't be. The truth is, replies Jesus, today—this very night in fact—before the rooster crows twice, you'll deny me three times. But Peter kept insisting, If I have to I'll die with you. I will never, ever deny you. All the others were saying the same thing.

Praying in a garden vv32-42

So they come to a spot known as Gethsemane. Sit here while I pray, he says to his disciples. And he takes with him Peter, James and John, and terror and deep distress swept over him. And he says to them, My heart is so heavy it could kill me—stay here and watch. He went on a little further, and throwing himself on the ground he began to pray that if possible he might be spared. Abba Father, he kept repeating, everything 's possible for you. Take this cup from me! But not what I want, but what you want. So he comes and finds them asleep, and says to Simon Peter, You're fast asleep are you? Can't you keep awake for a single hour? Watch and pray so you don't fall into temptation. The spirit is willing but the flesh is weak. So he went away again and prayed just as before. And again when he returned he found them asleep, for their eyes were very heavy. And they did not know what to say to him. He comes to them a third time and says, Sleep and rest if you must! The hour has come! The Son of Man is betrayed and handed over to sinners. Come on, get up, let's go! The traitor—he's almost here.

Arrest in the garden vv43-52

Immediately, as he was still speaking, Judas, one of the twelve, comes up to him with a crowd carrying swords and clubs (they had been sent by the high priest, the lawyers and the elders). Now his betrayer had signalled to them saying, Whoever I kiss, he's the one—take him away under close guard. Straightaway Judas went up to Jesus, stood in front of him and says, Rabbi, and then greeted him with a kiss. They then seized him. But a bystander drew his sword and slashed off the ear of the chief priest's servant. Have you come to arrest me with swords and clubs like a criminal? asked Jesus. I was with you every day in the temple teaching, yet you never laid a finger on me. This was to fulfil the scriptures. So all his disciples deserted him and fled. A young man was following, wearing only a linen cloth. They tried to arrest him. But he ran off naked leaving the linen cloth behind.

Jesus tried by the Sanhedrin vv53-65

So they led Jesus to the high priest. And all the chief priests and lawyers come together. Peter followed him but kept his distance, all the way to the high priest's courtyard. He was sitting with the guards, warming himself by the fire. The chief priests and the entire Sanhedrin were searching for evidence against Jesus so that they might put him to death. But they found nothing. Many were giving false evidence, but it was not consistent. Some stood up and testified falsely, We heard him say, I'll destroy this man made temple and in three days build another not made by human hands. But even on this issue their evidence was inconsistent. The high priest got up before them and asked Jesus, Have you nothing to say in your defence? What are these men accusing you of? But he kept silent and said nothing. Again the high priest questioned him, Are you the Christ, the Son of the Blessed One? Yes I am, said Jesus, and, ***You will see the Son of Man sitting on the right hand of Power,*** and ***coming with the clouds of heaven.*** At that the high priest tore his clothes and said, Why do we need any more witnesses? You've heard the blasphemy! What's your verdict? They all condemned him as deserving death. Some of them started to spit on him. They blindfolded him and began to beat him with their fists and said, Prophesy! The guards also punched him.

Peter's denial vv66-72

Now when Peter was below in the courtyard one of the high priest's girl servants approaches. When she saw Peter warming himself she looks straight at him and says, You were with Jesus that Nazarene fellow! But he denied it, I've no idea what you're talking about! He went out into the porch and a rooster crowed. When the servant girl saw him she again started to say to the onlookers, He's one of them. Again he denied it saying, I haven't a clue what you're on about. A short time later the onlookers again kept saying to Peter, You must be one of them, because you're Galilean. He then started to curse himself and swear an oath, Listen, I don't know this man you're all talking about! Immediately a rooster crowed for the second time. Then Peter remembered what Jesus had said to him, Before the rooster crows twice you'll deny me three times. And he broke down in tears.

Chapter Fifteen

Jesus before Pilate vv1-5

Now it was dawn when the chief priests together with the elders and the lawyers held a meeting with the entire Sanhedrin. First they bound Jesus then led him away and handed him over to Pilate. So you're the King of the Jews are you? Pilate asked. So you say, Jesus replies. Now the chief priests were accusing him of all sorts of things. So Pilate began to ask him once more, Have you nothing to say? See how many charges they're bringing against you. Jesus said nothing, much to Pilate's astonishment.

Jesus or Barabbas? vv6-15

At the festival it was his custom to release one prisoner chosen by the people. One of these was Barabbas, who with other rebels had committed murder in the uprising. The crowd went up to Pilate and began to ask that he do as was customary. Shall I release the King of the Jews? says Pilate. (Because he knew full well that it was out of envy that the chief priests had arrested Jesus.) So the chief priests stirred up the crowd even more, so that he might release Barabbas for them. But Pilate repeatedly asked, What then should I do with the so-called King of the Jews? Again they screamed, Crucify him! But Pilate kept asking: what crime has he committed? They screamed all the louder, Crucify him! So Pilate, to placate the crowd, released Barabbas and had Jesus flogged and handed him over to be crucified.

Mocking Jesus vv16-20

The soldiers led him inside the fortress, known as the Praetorium, and they call together the whole company of soldiers and they dress him in purple and twist a crown of thorns and put it on him. And they kept on greeting him with the words, Hail, King of the Jews! They continued to beat him on his head with a rod and were spitting on him. Falling on their knees they began to worship him. And after mocking him they took off his purple robe and dressed him with his own clothes. Then they led him out to be crucified.

The crucifixion of Jesus Christ vv21-32

And they force a certain Simon, from Cyrene (Alexander and Rufus's father), who was passing by, on his way up from the country, to carry his cross. And they bring him to a place called Golgotha, meaning the place of a skull. And they were offering him myrrh flavoured with wine, but he would not touch it. So they crucify him. Then dividing his clothes they cast lots to see which each would take. They crucified him at nine o clock in the morning. An inscription spelled out the charges against him: THE KING OF THE JEWS. And they crucify two criminals with him, one on his right and the other on his left. Passers by began to mock him shaking their heads and saying, Ha! You who said you would destroy the temple and rebuild it in three days—come on then, come down from the cross and save yourself! The chief priests also began to scoff among themselves, He saved others but he can't save himself! Let the Messiah, the King of Israel, come down from the cross right now, so that we might see and believe. Those who were crucified with him joined in the ridicule.

The death of Jesus Christ vv33-41

The whole land was shrouded in darkness from midday until three in the afternoon. At three o'clock Jesus cried out with a loud voice: ***Eloi, Eloi, lema sabachtani.*** This means: ***My God, my God, why have you abandoned me?*** When some of the bystanders heard it they kept on saying, Look, he's calling Elijah! Someone then ran and soaked a sponge in sour wine, put it on a stick and gave it to him to drink, saying, Wait, let's see if Elijah comes to take him down. But Jesus let out a piercing cry and breathed his last. The temple curtain was torn asunder from top to bottom. When the centurion standing there in front of him saw how he died he said, This man really was God's son! Some women were watching what was happening from a distance, Mary Magdalene, and Mary the mother of James the younger and of Joses, and Salome, as well as others. These were among his followers and supporters in Galilee. Many other women who also accompanied him to Jerusalem were there too.

The Burial of Jesus Christ vv42-47

Since it was the evening of the day of Preparation, that is the day before the Sabbath, Joseph of

Arimathaea, a highly regarded member of the council, who was himself awaiting the kingdom of God, plucked up courage to ask Pilate for Jesus' corpse. But Pilate wondered if he were already dead. When the centurion confirmed this, he gave the body to Joseph who then bought linen cloth. After he had taken him down from the cross Joseph wrapped him in the linen and placed the body in a tomb cut out of rock. He then rolled a stone across the entrance of the tomb. Mary Magdalene and Mary, the mother of Joses, were watching carefully where he had been laid.

Chapter Sixteen

The resurrection of Jesus Christ vv1-8

After the Sabbath Mary Magdalene and Mary, James' mother and Salome, bought spices to anoint him. So very early on Sunday morning, just after dawn, they come to the tomb. They were asking each other, Who'll roll back the stone for us? But when they looked up they saw that the stone, a very large one, had already been rolled back. They went into the tomb and saw there a young man dressed in a white robe sitting on the right side. They were shocked to the core. But he said to them, Don't be alarmed. You're looking for Jesus of Nazareth who was crucified—he's risen! He's not here—look, this is where they laid him. Go! Tell his disciples—and Peter—that he's going ahead of you to Galilee, that's where you'll see him, just as he told you. So they rushed out of the tomb in fear and trembling. They said nothing to anyone because they were terrified.

The shorter ending

So they gave a brief account of what they had been told to Peter and those with him. After this Jesus himself, through them, sent out from east to west the sacred and imperishable message of eternal salvation.

The longer ending

It was to Mary Magdalene, from whom he had expelled seven demons, that Jesus first appeared after he had risen on the Sunday. She went and told those who had been with him as they grieved and wept. But when they heard that he was alive and had been seen by her they did not believe it. Later he appeared to two of them as they were heading for the country. He looked different. They headed back and told the others, but they did not believe them. Later on he appeared to the twelve as they were having a meal and rebuked them for their unbelief and stubbornness because they did not believe those who had seen him after he had been raised up. He said to them, Go into all the world and preach the gospel to everybody. Everyone who believes and is baptized will be saved; but whoever doesn't believe will be condemned. And these signs will accompany believers: they will be able to cast out demons in my name, speak new languages, and handle snakes. No deadly drink will harm them and they will lay hands on the sick and they will be healed. So when the Lord Jesus had said all this he was taken up into heaven and sat at God's right hand. So they went out and preached everywhere, the Lord working with them and confirming the message with accompanying signs.

Amen.

Luke

Introduction

Luke, a missionary colleague of Saint Paul, is credited with writing the gospel that bears his name. As well as being a physician, an Eastern Orthodox tradition holds that he was also an artist—the first iconographer, or more precisely "writer" of icons (icons are articles of religious faith, not merely paintings in the conventional sense). Four ancient icons of the Virgin Mary and the Christ child have been attributed to (or were believed to have been copied from) Luke: *Our Lady of Vladimir, Our Lady of Czestochowa,* the *Salus Populi Romani,* and *Our Lady of Perpetual Help*. The veracity of these claims (not least that Mary and her new born son actually posed for one of these paintings) need not concern us here. However, there is a sense in which Luke's two volume literary work, Luke-Acts, might be viewed as an artistic masterpiece of sorts, revealing a keen eye for detail, matched by rich spiritual insights and a solid theological and historical grasp of Christian faith and origins. It has been customary to think of Luke as a Gentile convert, but equally he may have been Jewish, or perhaps even a Hellenistic-Jew (i.e.

coming from a Jewish family that were either domiciled abroad or possibly resident within or recently returned to Judea, and thus culturally influenced by Greek language and education, as well as by the tenets of Second Temple Judaism, as it is known). While we cannot be overly certain about Luke's background, it is clear that he had immense skill and aptitude in showing how the activity of Jesus cohered with the fulfilment of God's promises to Israel. I will develop this point presently. But first, when did Luke write his gospel? What is its relationship to Matthew and Mark (with whom he shared a "synoptic" overview of Christ's life)? And what are its major themes? As with all the gospels, there are difficulties with dating when Luke was written. On the whole scholars tend to push the writing of the gospels to the latter decades of the first century, usually somewhere between 70-100AD (i.e. after destruction of the temple, a generation after Jesus's death and resurrection). But there are no good reasons for assigning Luke's writings to a post-70 date, other than the prejudicial view that neither Jesus nor the Evangelists could have foreseen the sack of Jerusalem (which is predicted in all four gospels). Yet when Jesus preached doom over Jerusalem he was doing no more than prophets like Isaiah and Jeremiah did when they forecast judgment on God's people. Judgment was simply the outworking of divine justice in a society that had forsaken its covenant with God. In this respect the prophets did not require a crystal ball to see how things would pan out for Israel or Judah. A defiant people, steeped in idolatry and materialism, and intent on pursuing dangerous political goals and alliances with untrustworthy neighbours, such as Egypt or Assyria, could only expect a bad outcome. For the prophets, judgement was built into the moral fabric of creation. For Jesus and his followers, it was plain that God's people were on course to repeat history; only in this instance it would come on the heels of rejecting and killing their Messiah. Given this, we might assume that Jesus would indeed have envisioned something like the destruction of the temple in Jerusalem, exactly as the prophets had warned Judah of certain exile to Babylon for spurning Yahweh and his laws. A date for the writing of Luke's gospel therefore need not be pushed back to the closing decades of the first century, based on the premise that Jesus could not have predicted war with Rome. However, if the Jewish historian, Josephus (c.37-100AD), is to be believed, tensions between Jews and Romans escalated over the course of the first century AD. A canny politician, astute military governor, or a religious leader might have sensed the possibilities of future conflict in Palestine, as did the Jewish

High Priest, Caiaphas, as early as 33AD (cf. John 11:49-50). As far as the dating of Luke is concerned, his second volume, Acts, ends with Paul awaiting sentence in Rome for disturbing the peace in Jerusalem. This would give us a date c.62AD as a likely date by which Luke had completed his double volume (or at least this is as far as he had got in penning Acts before other events caused him to break off writing). It is otherwise difficult to explain why Luke would have ended his narrative where he did, without mentioning Paul's martyrdom, which was surely as significant as Stephen's (Acts 7) and James's (Acts 12), and which would have neatly bookended his narrative. More plausible is the scenario in which Paul was released following this, his first imprisonment in Rome, after which he spent time in Spain before a second stint in jail leading to his execution c.64/67AD, under Nero. Either way, we need not subscribe to the view of commentators who go so far as to date Luke's writings to the late first or even the early second century. A date prior to the destruction of the temple in 70AD is entirely feasible. As regards Luke's relationship with the other synoptic writers, it is incontrovertible that he shaped his gospel in a literary mould common to Matthew and Mark, while also inserting special material of his own (often referred to as "L," which included, for example, the nativity stories, the parables of the Good Samaritan and Prodigal Son, and details about Pontius Pilate's execution of Galilean worshippers in Jerusalem, the death of eighteen people on whom a tower collapsed in Siloam, as well as details about Christ's Parousia, which explain its apparent delay). In broad terms Matthew, Mark and Luke fit into the genre of Graeco-Roman literature known as "biography." That is, they include literary features typically found in lives of historically significant people such as emperors, philosophers, military leaders or politicians. This usually comes with a focus on their birth and/or background, upbringing, deeds or exploits, sayings or speeches—details, in other words, of whatever distinguished or set them apart from other people, including an account of their death. This admirably coheres with Luke's stated aim in the prologue of the gospel and Acts. Dedicating his two volume work to Theophilus (a convert to Christ, and high ranking member of the Roman elite or aristocracy), Luke says that his objective is to provide an accurate, trustworthy account of Jesus's life based on eye-witness accounts—including written material (possibly Matthew and Mark and other sources), as well as gleanings from his own research, which likely drew on face-to-face interviews with people who knew Jesus personally, especially the apostles and family members such as Mary, his mother, and his brother (or cousin) James, who went on to lead the early church in Jerusalem according to Luke. Most scholars would also want to register how Luke's preamble to his gospel shares features with Graeco-Roman historiography, such as we find in the writings of Herodotus, Thucydides, Polybius, Philostratus and Josephus—especially regarding their claim to present an "orderly" or "chronological" account of their subject matter. Utilising this literary genre Luke explores the "Jesus event" as a moment in Jewish and world history, which is also climactic both cosmically and transcendently. Lukan scholars refer to this as "salvation history." That is, the message that God's deliverance from sin and death embraces the whole of creation. Luke charts this story from Christ's birth to his ascension, then in the Acts of the Apostles to the point where the gospel of God's kingdom is being proclaimed at the heart of the Roman empire itself, if only from a prison cell. Hence, we see in Luke's gospel a concern about the *historical* reality of God's kingdom and its impact upon the political and social world of the day. In chapters 1-3 he mentions no less than eleven individuals known to "secular" historians outside the bible: Herod the Great, Caesar Augustus, Quirinius, governor of Syria, Tiberius Caesar, Pontius Pilate, Herod Antipas, Herod Philip, Lysanias, ruler of Abilene, the high priests, Annas and Caiaphas, and John the Baptist. As already mentioned, Luke dedicates his work to a high ranking Roman official that he wishes to convince of the reliability of his gospel by reference to flesh and blood people, eye witness accounts, and real events. Key for Luke is answering the question posed by Jesus to his disciples: *Who do the crowds say that I am* (Luke 9:18)? To address this question Luke draws on the Church's collective memory of Jesus's preaching, teaching, healing, exorcism, death and resurrection. Luke saw in this the climax and fulfilment of scripture: of the promises to Abraham, the hope of salvation for Jews and Gentiles alike through Christ, and the eschatological outpouring of the Holy Spirit (promised both by Isaiah and Joel). While it has been customary to highlight the theme of "fulfilment" as being central to Matthew, Luke shows great depth and insight of his own regarding this topic. His infancy narratives (chapters 1-2) evoke an ambience redolent of the early chapters of 1 Samuel. Hannah, like Elizabeth (the mother of John the Baptist), is barren. She prays for a child. When God grants her baby Samuel, she praises God in words that Mary will later echo in the *Magnificat*. Like the boy Samuel, the boy Jesus is also to be found in the temple, going about his Father's business. As Samuel grew up with God's blessing, so too

Luke tells us that Jesus grew up in favour with God, displaying wisdom and a maturity for which the young Samuel was his typological precursor. Here Luke superimposes the stories of Samuel and Jesus over each other in order to evince a rich, interwoven tapestry, which entwines Jesus's destiny in the unfolding purposes of God for his people. This is a subtle way of conveying spiritual truth because Luke does not explicitly tell us what he is doing—he makes no reference to the Book of Samuel, unlike Matthew, who, in his infancy narrative, cites five passages (or "proof texts") from the Old Testament, to show that Mary's virgin conception, Christ's birth in Bethlehem, the massacre of the infants, and the flight to Egypt, were foretold long ago. Luke we assume, expects—or would wish for—Theophilus to pick up on these veiled references to the Book of Samuel, but whether or not he did would very much depend on what level of knowledge or understanding Theophilus would have had of the Old Testament. This would particularly be the case if we consider Luke's account of Mary's visit to Elizabeth. On the surface it is a narrative about two pregnant women sharing about the miracle that had occurred in their lives. However, something more is going on which Luke does not make explicit. The story about Mary's visit to Elizabeth parallels scriptures about the Ark of the Covenant. The Ark contained the Ten Commandments (written on stone), manna (from Israel's time in the wilderness), and the rod of Aaron (the shepherd's staff, symbol of authority and instrument of power, healing and miracles). The lid of the Ark was in turn known as the Mercy Seat (the site where God's glory and presence overshadowed the tabernacle). In 2 Samuel 6 we read of David's decision to move the Ark to Jerusalem. Dancing and celebrating, he stops off at a house on a hill along the route. Here he expresses surprise that the Ark should ever have been given to him in the first place; therefore he brings it to somebody else's lodging where it remained for three months. The resonances with the meeting of Mary and Elizabeth are multiple: Mary arose and went into the hill country of Judea; we read of the baby in Elizabeth's womb leaping for joy because of the divine presence in Mary's womb; like David, Elizabeth ponders why, through Mary's visit, the Lord should grace her with his presence; Mary stayed with Elizabeth for three months, before returning home. The message Luke is seeking to convey here is that Mary is the new Ark of the Covenant—the new abode of the divine presence, the incarnate Word of God, the one destined to wield authority over creation. Whereas Matthew confirms God's incarnate presence by citing an Old Testament prophecy regarding "Emmanuel, God with us," Luke achieves the same end, not through a proof text, but by almost buried, hidden allusions, that only a treasure hunter would find. This is not to say that Luke never quoted scripture (he did—cf. Luke 4:1-30 et al), but it is to say that there were instances where he demanded more of his readers than a surface, or superficial understanding of the gospel. Unlike Matthew, Luke is unprepared in his infancy narrative to spell out everything, or preclude the need for readers to tease out the spiritual or theological nuances or implications of Christ's birth for themselves. This is what we might expect of a writer of gifted intelligence, who also believed, from what we can glean from his writings, that the Holy Spirit was willing and able to open people's eyes to the truth, if they had open, penitent hearts.

But this is always in conjunction with a Christocentric understanding of the Bible. In the closing chapter of his gospel (ch.24) he drives home the necessity of knowing, grasping God's Word, if one is to know and understand Christ and the salvation he offers Jew and Gentile alike. On the road to Emmaus the risen Saviour meets two disciples despondent about the recent events at Passover. They cannot understand or explain Jesus's death, given that he was God's anointed Messiah. Nor can they make sense of reports about the empty tomb and his appearance to other believers. In their thinking there are no categories in which these tragic and mysterious circumstances can be sanitised. Their religious upbringing has led them to an impenetrable brick wall of sorrow, frustration and ignorance. Luke rehearses how the risen Jesus dealt with their spiritual plight. First, he poses a question: was it not necessary that the Messiah should suffer then enter into glory? But they cannot answer this question for reasons already mentioned. To their surprise Jesus directs their thoughts to the scriptures, and shows how Moses and the prophets predicted Christ's suffering, death and resurrection. After this they were enabled to recognise him when Jesus broke bread with them over supper. When they returned to Jerusalem they told the disciples that their hearts had burned within them as Jesus unlocked the scriptures. Once Jesus appears to the rest of the disciples he puts them through their paces in similar fashion. Neither through miracle, sign or wonder, nor even through his actual physical presence in their midst, but rather through biblical exposition alone Jesus makes it possible for his disciples to believe that he had risen from the dead. For Jesus alive in their presence was not enough on its own to foster and nurture faith. Only when he had showed them how everything written about him in Moses, the prophets and the Psalms, had first to be fulfilled, did they begin to comprehend the significance of the trauma both he and they had just undergone. But Luke does not leave it at that. A major theme in Luke and Acts is the Holy Spirit. Left to themselves they still had the capacity to misinterpret scripture and be led astray. Only the indwelling Holy Spirit, who had animated every word and deed of Jesus (Luke 4:1,14), could ensure that they would be morally, spiritually and intellectually equipped to tear down Satan's strongholds and bring good news to the nations. Hence the centrepiece of Luke's theology of fulfilment focuses on Pentecost (Acts 2), when God the Holy Spirit turned the mystery of Christ crucified and raised, into tongues of fire that would burn in millions of people's hearts across twenty centuries.

Chapter One

Opening greetings vv1—4

Since many have taken it in hand to compile a narrative about the deeds that have been fulfilled in our midst (just as the original eyewitnesses and ministers of the word passed them on to us), I too thought it appropriate, after following everything closely from the very beginning, to write a structured account for you, Theophilus, so that Your Excellency may know the reliability of the doctrine that you have received.

The Baptist's birth foretold vv5—25

During the reign of Herod, king of Judea, there was a priest called Zechariah, of the priestly order of Abijah. His wife, Elizabeth, was of the daughters of Aaron. Both were in good stead before God, blamelessly following all the commandments and ordinances of the Lord. But they had no children because Elizabeth was barren and they were getting on in years. Now while he was serving as priest before God, when his rota was on duty, it fell to his lot, in accordance with the priestly custom, to enter the Lord's sanctuary and burn incense. And all the people were outside praying at the hour of incense. And an angel of the Lord appeared to him, standing on the right side of the altar of incense. Zechariah was troubled, gripped with fear when he saw him. But the angel said to him, Don't be afraid, Zechariah, your prayer has been heard. Your wife, Elizabeth, will bear you a son and you'll call his name John. Joy and gladness will be yours, and many will rejoice at his birth. He'll be great in the sight of the Lord. He'll not drink wine or intoxicating liquor. He'll be filled with the Holy Spirit from his mother's womb. He'll convert many of the children of Israel to the Lord their God, and he'll go before him in the spirit and power of Elijah, to turn the hearts of the fathers to the children, and the disobedient to the wisdom of the just, to make ready for the Lord a prepared people. And Zechariah said to the angel, How can I be sure of this? I'm an old man and my wife's advanced in years. And the angel replied, I'm Gabriel. I stand in the God's presence. I've been sent to speak to you and to tell you this good news; and behold, you'll be mute, unable to speak, until these things happen, because you didn't believe my words, which will be fulfilled in due course. Meanwhile, the people who were waiting for Zechariah began to wonder why he was lingering in the temple. When he emerged, he was unable to speak to them. Then they realised that he'd seen a vision in the temple; for he kept making signs to them, and remained dumb. And after the days of his service were complete, he went home. Later, his wife Elizabeth became pregnant, and hid herself for five months, saying, This is what the Lord's done for me, when he looked upon me, and saw fit to rid me of the shame I've had to endure among the people.

The birth of Jesus Christ foretold vv26–38

In the sixth month the angel Gabriel was sent by God to Nazareth, a city in Galilee, to a virgin engaged to a man named Joseph, a descendant of the house of David. The virgin's name was Mary. The angel came in and said to her, Greetings, O favoured woman—the Lord's with you! And she was greatly disturbed, and tried to make sense of this greeting. And the angel said to her, Don't be afraid, Mary, for you've found favour with God. You'll conceive in your womb and give birth to a son, and you'll call him Jesus. He's going to be great, and will be called the Son of the Most High. And the Lord God will give him his father David's throne. He'll reign over Jacob's house forever, and of his kingdom there'll be no end. But Mary said to the angel, How can this be, since I'm a virgin? In reply the angel said to her, The Holy Spirit will come upon you, and the power of the Most High will overshadow you, so the child to be born will be holy—the Son of God. And look, your relative Elizabeth's going to have a son, old as she is, and she's six months pregnant—she who's supposed to be barren! For with God there's no such thing as impossible. Mary then said, Behold, I'm the Lord's servant—so be it—just as you say. Then the angel left her.

Mary's visit to Elizabeth vv39–56

So in those days Mary hastily set out, and went to a Judean town in the hill country, where she went into Zechariah's house and greeted Elizabeth. Now when Elizabeth heard Mary's greeting, the baby jumped in her womb. And Elizabeth was filled with the Holy Spirit, and exclaimed in a raised voice, You're blessed among women! And blessed is the fruit of your womb! What have I done to deserve this—that the mother of my Lord should come to me? For, behold, as the sound of your greeting reached my ears, the baby in my womb jumped in delight. And blessed is she who believed that the Lord would fulfil what he'd spoken to her. Then Mary said:

My soul extols the Lord!

And my spirit rejoices in God my Saviour

For he's regarded the lowly state of his servant

And from now on all generations will called me blessed

For the Mighty One's done great things for me, and his name is holy

His mercy is upon those who fear him from age to age

He's shown the might of his arm

He's scattered the proud in their fantasies

He's cast down the powerful from their thrones and raised up the poor

He's filled the hungry with good things

And sent the rich away empty

He's cared for Israel his servant, mindful of his mercy

As he said to our fathers

To Abraham and his offspring forever

Mary stayed with her about three months before returning home.

The birth of John the Baptist vv57—80

When her time was fulfilled, Elizabeth gave birth to a son. When her neighbours and family heard what great mercy the Lord had shown her, they began to celebrate with her. Eight days after the birth they came to circumcise the child, and were going to call him Zechariah, after his father, but his mother answered, No! He's to be called John. They said to her, But no one in your family has this name. Then they began to make signs to his father, to see what he wanted him to be called. He asked for a writing tablet and wrote, saying, His name *is* John. And they were all astonished. At once his mouth and tongue were opened, and he started to speak, blessing God. Fear came upon all their neighbours, and these things became the talk of the entire hill country of Judea. Everyone who heard them kept them in their hearts, and asked, What then will become of this child? For the hand of the Lord was with him. Then his father, Zechariah, was filled with the Holy Spirit, and prophesied, saying,

Blessed be the Lord, the God of Israel

For he's favourably regarded and accomplished redemption for his people

And he's raised up for us a horn of salvation

In the house of David his servant

As he spoke through the mouth of his holy prophets of long ago

To save us from our enemies, and the grip of all who hate us

To show mercy to our fathers, to remember his holy covenant

The oath he swore to our father, Abraham

That we being rescued from the hands of our enemies

Might fearlessly serve him

In holiness and righteousness

Before him all our days

And you, child, will be called the prophet of the Most High

For you'll go before the Lord to prepare his ways

To make salvation known to his people

Through the forgiveness of their sins

Through the tender mercy of our God

The rising sun will dawn upon us

To give light to those sitting in darkness

And the shadow of death

To guide our feet into the way of peace

And the child grew up and was strong in spirit. He lived in the desert until the day he was made known to Israel.

Chapter Two

The birth of Jesus Christ vv1–7

It came to pass in those days that a proclamation was issued by Caesar Augustus that the entire world should be registered. This was the first registration, and took place when Quirinius was governor of Syria. Everyone went to their hometown to be registered. Joseph, too, went up from the town of Nazareth in Galilee, to David's city, Bethlehem by name, because he was of David's house and family. He went to be registered with his wife-to-be, Mary, who was pregnant. While they were there, the time came for her to give birth to her child. And she delivered a son, her firstborn. She wrapped him in strips of cloth and laid him in a feeding trough, because the lodging was full.

Angels bring good news to shepherds vv8–40

Now in the same area, shepherds were out in the fields guarding their flocks by night. And an angel of the Lord stood before them, and God's glory shone about them, and they were terrified. But the angel said to them, Don't be afraid, I bring you good news of great joy for all the people. Today a Saviour has been born in David's city; he's the Lord, the Messiah. And this will be the sign for you; you'll find the baby wrapped in strips of cloth, lying in a feeding trough. Then all of a sudden a heavenly cohort was with the angel, praising God, and saying, *Glory to God in highest heaven, and peace on earth among people of good will.* When the angels went from them into heaven, the shepherds were saying to each other, Let's go to Bethlehem; let's see this word that has been fulfilled, which the Lord has made known to us. So they went in haste and found Mary and Joseph, and the baby lying in a feeding trough. And when they saw this, they reported what the angel had made known to them about this child. Everyone who heard what the shepherds had to say, were amazed. And Mary kept all these words, cherishing them in her heart. And the shepherds returned, glorifying and praising God, because they had heard and seen everything, just as it had been told them. Eight days later it was time to circumcise the child; and he was called Jesus, as named by the angel before he was conceived in the womb. When the days of purification were fulfilled, they brought him up to Jerusalem to present him to the Lord—as it is written in the Law of the Lord, ***Every male who opens the womb shall be called holy to the Lord***—and to offer a sacrifice, as prescribed in the Law of the Lord—***A pair of turtle doves or two young pigeons.*** Now at the time, in Jerusalem, there lived a man called Simeon. He was upright and devout, awaiting the comfort of Israel, and the Holy Spirit was upon him. And it had been revealed to him by the Holy Spirit that he would not die, until he had seen the Lord's Messiah. And in the Spirit he came into the temple. When the parents brought in their child, Jesus, to perform for him the obligatory customs, as prescribed by the law, he took him up in his arms and blessed him, and said,

Now you're releasing your servant, Lord
In peace, according to your word
For my eyes have seen your salvation
Which you prepared in the sight of all peoples
A light to bring revelation to the Gentiles
And glory for your people, Israel.

And his father and mother are astonished at what is spoken about him. Then Simeon blessed them, and said to Mary, his mother, Behold, this child is marked out for the fall and rising of many in Israel—and for a sign that will be resisted (and a sword will pierce through your own soul too) so that the thoughts of many will be laid bare. There was also a prophetess, Anna, a daughter of Phanuel, of the tribe of Asher. She was advanced in years, having lived with her husband for seven years from when she was a virgin. She had been a widow for eighty-four years. She never left the temple, but night and day, through fasting and supplication, she worshipped. And she appeared at that very hour and began giving thanks to God, and was speaking about the child to all those awaiting the redemption of Jerusalem. And when they had done all that was required of them, as laid down in the Law, they returned to Galilee, to their own town of Nazareth. And the child grew up and became strong, and was full of wisdom; and God's grace was upon him.

The young Jesus confounds scholars vv41–52

Now his parents went to Jerusalem for the Passover feast every year. And when he was twelve years old, they went up, as was customary, to the festival. After the feast was over, the parents began the journey home; but the boy Jesus stayed behind, without his parents' knowledge. Thinking he was in the group, they went a day's journey, and then began to look for him among their relatives and acquaintances. When they did not find him they headed back to Jerusalem to look for him. And so, after three days, they found him in the temple, sitting in the midst of the teachers, listening to them and questioning them. And everyone who heard him was astonished at his understanding and answers. When his parents saw him they were astounded; and his mother said to him, Child, why have you treated us like this? See, your father and I have been searching for you, sick with worry. He said to them, Why were you looking for me? Didn't you know I must be in my Father's house? But they did not understand what he was saying to them. And he came down with them to Nazareth and was obedient to them. And his mother treasured all these things in her heart. And Jesus increased in wisdom and age, and found favour with God and man.

Chapter Three

The Baptist's proclamation vv1–20

In the fifteenth year of Tiberius Caesar's reign, when Pontius Pilate was governing in Judea, and Herod was tetrarch of Galilee, and his brother Philip, tetrarch of the Ituraea and Trachonitis region, and Lysanias, tetrarch of Abilene, during the high priesthood of Annas and Caiaphas, there came a word from God to John, Zechariah's son, in the desert. So he went into the district all around the Jordan, preaching a baptism of repentance for the forgiveness of sins. As it is written in the book of the words of Isaiah, the prophet, ***The voice of one shouting in the desert, Prepare the way of the Lord, make his paths straight. Every ravine will be filled, and every mountain and hill will be made low; the crooked will be made straight, and rough places become smooth. And all flesh will see God's salvation.*** So he began to say to the crowds who came out to be baptised by him, Brood of vipers, who's warned you to flee from the coming wrath? Produce fruits worthy of repentance! Don't start saying to yourselves, We've Abraham as our father. I tell you, God can raise up children for Abraham from these very stones. For the axe is already laid to the root of the trees; therefore any tree that doesn't produce good fruit is cut down and thrown into a fire. So the crowds asked him, saying, What'll we do? Whoever has two tunics, he began to say to them, must share with the one who has none. And whoever has food must do the same. Tax collectors also came to him to be baptised, and said to him, Teacher, what'll we do? Collect no more than the going rate, he said to them. Soldiers also asked him, And what'll we do? He told them, No extortion or blackmail, be content with your pay. Now all the people were full of expectation and were questioning in their hearts regarding John; could he possibly be the Messiah? John answered all of them saying, I indeed baptise you with water; but someone more powerful than I is coming—I'm not worthy even to undo his sandal strap. He'll baptise you with the Holy Spirit and fire. His winnowing fan is in his hand, to clear up his threshing floor and to store the wheat in his barn; but the chaff he'll burn with unquenchable fire. In this way, with numerous exhortations, he continued preaching to the people. But John reproached Herod the tetrarch over the matter of Herodias, his brother's wife—and for all his other misdeeds. And he added to this by locking up John in prison.

The baptism of Jesus the Messiah vv21–22

So when all the people had been baptised, and Jesus also had been baptised, and was praying, the heavens opened, and the Holy Spirit came down upon him in physical form, as a dove. Then a voice came from heaven, You're my well loved son, I take great delight in you.

The family tree of Jesus the Messiah vv23–38

Jesus, when he began his ministry, was about thirty years of age, being the son (as was supposed) of Joseph, the son of Heli, the son of Matthat, the son of Levi, the son of Melchi, the son of Jannai, the son of Joseph, the son of Mattathias, the son of Amos, the son of Nahum, the son of Esli, the son of Naggai, the son of Maath, the son of Mattathias, the son of Semein, the son of Josech, the son of Joda, the son of Joanan, the son of Rhesa, the son of Zerubbabel, the son of Shealtiel, the son of Neri, the son of Melchi, the son of Addi, the son of Cosam, the son of Elmadam, the son of Er, the son of Joshua, the son of Eliezer, the son of Jorim, the son of Matthat, the son of Levi, the son of Simeon, the son of Judah, the son of Joseph, the son of Jonam, the son of Eliakim, the son of Melea, the son of Menna, the son of Mattatha, the son of Nathan, the son of David, the son of Jesse, the son of Obed, the son of Boaz, the son of Sala, the son of Nahshon, the son of Amminadab, the son of Admin, the son of Arni, the son of Hezron, the son of Perez, the son of Judah, the son of Jacob, the son of Isaac, the son of Abraham, the son of Terah, the son of Nahor, the son of Serug, the son of Reu, the son of Peleg, the son of Eber, the son of Shelah, the son of Cainan, the son of Arphaxad, the son of Shem, the son of Noah, the son of Lamech, the son of Methuselah, the son of Enoch, the son of Jared, the son of Mahalaleel, the son of Cainan, the son of Enos, the son of Seth, the son of Adam, the son of God.

Chapter Four

The Messiah tempted vv1—13

Jesus, full of the Holy Spirit, returned from the Jordan and was led in the Spirit to the desert where, for forty days and nights, he was tempted by the devil. During that time he ate nothing, and by the end was famished. The devil said to him, If you're the Son of God, order these stones to become bread. But Jesus answered him, It's written, ***Man can't survive on bread alone.*** And bringing him up, he showed him, in a flash, all the kingdoms of the world. Then the devil said to him, To you I'll give all this power with its glory; for it's been given to me, and it's mine to give to whoever I please. If you worship me, it's all yours. Jesus answered him, It's written, ***Worship the Lord your God and only serve him.*** Then he took him to Jerusalem and placed him on top of the temple, and said to him, If you're the Son of God, hurl yourself down from here, because it's written, ***He'll give his angels orders concerning you, to keep you safe.*** And, ***Their hands will bear you up in case you strike your foot against a stone.*** Jesus replied, It's said, ***Don't test the Lord your God.*** So when the devil had exhausted every kind of temptation, he left him until an opportune time.

The Messiah starts his ministry vv14–30

And Jesus returned to Galilee in the power of the Spirit. News about him spread throughout the surrounding countryside. And he was teaching in their synagogues, being praised by all. And he came to Nazareth, his hometown, and as usual he went to the synagogue on the sabbath day. And a scroll of the prophet Isaiah was handed to him; he unrolled it, and found where it was written, ***The Spirit of the Lord is on me, for he has anointed me to preach good news to the poor, to preach release for prisoners and to restore sight to the blind, and to set free the oppressed, to proclaim the year of the Lord's favour.*** Jesus rolled up the scroll, gave it back to the steward and sat down. Every eye in the synagogue was glued on him. And he began to say to them, Today, in your ears, this scripture is fulfilled. And everyone began to criticise him, astonished at the gracious words that poured out of his mouth. Isn't this Joseph's son? they asked. And he said to them, No doubt you'll quote to me this proverb, Doctor, heal yourself! What we heard you did at Capernaum, do here also in your hometown. But truly, I tell you, no prophet's welcome in his hometown. There were many widows in Israel, I assure you, in Elijah's time, when the heavens were shut up for three and a half years, and there was a great famine in the land; yet Elijah wasn't sent to any of them, except to a widow at Zarephath in Sidon. And there were many lepers in Israel in Elisha the prophet's time, and not one of them was cleansed, except Naaman the Syrian. When those in the synagogue heard this they were beside themselves with rage, and they got up and drove him out of the town. They brought him to the brow of the hill on which their town was built, so that they could throw him off, but passing through the crowd, he went on his way.

Teaching and healing in Capernaum vv31–37

So we went down to Capernaum, a city in Galilee, and began teaching them on the Sabbath. They were amazed at his teaching, because he spoke with authority. Now in the synagogue there was a man with the spirit of an unclean demon, and he cried out with a loud voice, Away! What have you to do with us, Jesus of Nazareth? Have you come to destroy us? I know who you are—God's holy one! But Jesus rebuked him, Be quiet—come out of him! So the demon flung him down in their midst and came out of him, without causing him any harm. And amazement gripped them all and they were saying to each other, What's this word? For with authority and power he commands the unclean spirits, and they come out? And stories about him began to circulate throughout the surrounding region.

Many healed vv38—41

When he had got up and left the synagogue he went into Simon's house. Now Simon's mother-in law had a high fever, and they asked him about her. So he stood over her and rebuked the fever and it left her. Straightaway she got up and began to serve them. As the sun was setting, everyone who had anyone sick with various diseases brought them to him; and he laid hands on each of them and cured them. Demons too came out of many, screaming, saying, You're the Son of God! But he rebuked them and would not let them speak, because they knew he was the Messiah.

Preaching in synagogues vv42–44

At daybreak, he left and went to a desert place. And the people kept looking for him, and came to him, and would have prevented him leaving them. But he said to them, I must proclaim the good news of the kingdom of God to other towns as well; this is why I was sent. So he began preaching in the synagogues of Judea.

Chapter Five

First disciples called vv1—11

While the crowd was pressing against him to hear the word of God, he was stood beside lake Gennesaret. He spotted two boats by the lake; but the fishermen had left them and were washing their nets. He got into one of the boats, owned by Simon, and asked him to put out a little from the land. And he sat down and started teaching the crowds from the boat. After he had finished speaking, he said to Simon, Put out to the deep and let down your nets for a catch. Simon replied, Master, we've been working all night but caught nothing; but if you say so, I'll let down the nets. So they did this, and caught a huge number of fish, such that their nets began to tear. They waved to their colleagues in the other boat to come and help them. They came and filled both boats, but they started to sink. When Simon Peter saw this, he fell to his knees before Jesus, saying, Leave me—I'm a sinful man, Lord! For he and all those with him were amazed at the catch of fish they had hauled in—this included James and John, the sons of Zebedee, Simon's partners. But Jesus said to Simon, Don't be afraid; from now on you'll be catching people. And once they had brought the boats to shore, they left everything and followed him.

Cleansing a leper vv12–16

While he was in one of the towns a man covered by leprosy fell on his face when he saw Jesus, and begged him, saying, Lord, you can make me clean if you want to. Jesus stretched out his hand and touched him, saying, I want to—be clean! Instantly the leprosy left him. And he warned him to say nothing to anyone. Go and show yourself to the priest and make an offering for your cleansing, as Moses prescribed—this will be proof for them. But now there was even more talk about him than ever; and great crowds were coming together to hear him and to be cured of their illnesses. But he would retire to deserted places and pray.

A paralytic healed vv17–26

Once, when he was teaching, there sat there Pharisees and legal experts who had come from every village in Galilee, Judea and Jerusalem; and the healing power of the Lord was with him. And look, men were bringing a paralysed man on a stretcher, and they were trying to bring him and lay him before Jesus. But finding no way to do so, because of the crowd, they went up onto the roof and let him down with his stretcher through the tiles, right in front of Jesus. Seeing their faith, he said, Man, your sins have been forgiven you! And the legal experts and the Pharisees began to debate, saying, Who's this speaking blasphemies? Who can forgive sins, except God alone? But Jesus knew what they were thinking, and answered them, Why do you vex yourselves over this? What's easier to say, Your sins are forgiven? Or, Get up and walk? But so that you may know that the Son of Man has authority to forgive sins, he said to the paralysed man, I tell you, up you get—pick up your stretcher and go home! And straightaway he got up in front of them, picked up what he was lying on, and went home, glorifying God. Fear gripped them all and they were saying, We've seen startling things today.

A tax collector called vv27—32

Afterwards, he went on his way and saw Levi, a tax collector, sitting in the tax office. And he said, Follow me. So leaving everything, he got up and follows him. Then Levi gave a sumptuous feast in Jesus' honour. There were many tax collectors and other sorts also eating with them. And the Pharisees and their legal experts were grumbling at his disciples, saying, Why do you eat and drink with tax collectors and sinners? In reply Jesus said, The healthy don't need a doctor, only the sick. I haven't come to call the upright to repent, but sinners.

To fast or feast? vv33—38

And they said to him, John's disciples fast often and recite prayers, as do the disciples of the Pharisees, but yours eat and drink. Jesus said to them, You can't make the wedding guests fast while the bridegroom's still with them, can you? The days will come when the bridegroom's taken from them, that'll be the time to fast. And he began to tell them a parable. Nobody tears a patch from a new garment and puts it on an old one. If so, the new one will be rent, and the patch from the new one won't match the old. So also, nobody puts new wine into old wine skins; if he does the new wine will burst the skins and it'll be spilled, and the skins ruined. But new wine must be put into fresh wine skins. And nobody wants new wine after drinking the old, for he says, The mature's good.

Chapter Six

Jesus, Lord of the Sabbath vv1–5

One sabbath he happened to be walking though some cornfields. His disciples began to pluck some corn heads, rubbing them in their hands and eating them. But some Pharisees said, Why are you doing what's unlawful on the sabbath? Haven't you read, Jesus replied to them, what David did when he was hungry, himself and those with him? How he entered God's house and took and ate the Bread of the Presence (which was illegal, except in the case of the priests), and gave it to his companions. Then he said to them, The Son of Man is Lord even over the sabbath.

A man with a withered hand vv6–11

On another sabbath he went into the synagogue and began to teach. And a man whose right hand was shrivelled up was also there. Now the legal experts and the Pharisees were keeping an eye on him, to see whether he would heal on the sabbath, and so give them an excuse to accuse him. But he was aware what they were thinking, and said to the man with the withered hand, Get up, and stand here in the middle. So he got up and stood there. Then Jesus said to them, Let me ask you this question, Is it permitted to do good or harm on the sabbath, to destroy life or save it? And he looked around intently at everybody, and said to him, Stretch out your hand. So he did, and his hand was restored. Overcome with rage, they were discussing with each other what they might do to Jesus.

The twelve chosen vv12—19

In those days he went to the mountain to pray; and he was praying to God all night long. Next day he called his disciples, and out of them chose twelve whom he named apostles: Simon, whom he nicknamed Peter, Andrew his brother, and James and John, and Philip and

Bartholomew, and Matthew, and Thomas, and James the son of Alphaeus, and Simon who was called the Zealot, and Judas the son of James, and Judas Iscariot, who turned traitor. He came down with them and stood on level ground. With him were a large crowd of his disciples, and a huge number from all Judea, Jerusalem, and the coastal area of Tyre and Sidon. They came to listen to him and to be cured of their illnesses. Those afflicted with unclean spirits were cured, and the crowd was trying to touch him because he exuded power, and healed them all.

Blessings and curses vv20–49

And he directed his gaze at his disciples, and began to say, Happy are the poor, for the kingdom of God is yours. Happy are those who hunger now, for you'll be satisfied. Happy are those who weep now, for you'll laugh. Happy are you whenever people hate, exclude, and revile you, and cast out your name as evil on account of the Son of Man. Rejoice in that day and leap for joy! For your reward in heaven will be great. For this is how their fathers used to treat the prophets. But woe to you who are rich, for you already have your comfort. Woe to you who are filled now, for you'll go hungry. Woe to you who are laughing now, you'll be grieving and weeping. Woe to you when people speak well of you, for your fathers used to do the same to false prophets. But I say to you who listen, Love your enemies, do good to those who hate you, bless those who curse you and pray for those who mistreat you. If someone slaps you on the cheek, offer the other; and to the one who takes your cloak, don't stop him stealing your tunic as well. Give to all who ask you, and if someone takes your belongings, don't demand them back. Do to others what you'd want them to do to you. What's the good of loving those who love you? Even sinners love those who love them. And what's the point of doing good to those who do good to you? Even sinners do the same. If you lend to those who'll pay you back what credit is that to you? Even sinners lend to sinners, to receive the same again. Rather, love your enemies, do good and lend while expecting nothing in return—and you'll be greatly rewarded, and be sons of the Most High—for he too is kind to the ungrateful and the wicked. Don't judge, and you won't be judged; don't condemn, and you won't be condemned; forgive, and you'll be forgiven; give, and it'll be given to you—an abundance, pressed down, shaken together, overflowing, will be poured into the folds of your garment. For what you measure out to others will be measured out to you. And he told them a parable, Can a blind man lead a blind man? Won't they both fall into a ditch? A pupil is not superior to his teacher, but when he's fully qualified he'll be like his teacher. Why do you spot the fleck in your brother's eye, but fail to notice the plank in your own? How can you say to your brother, Brother, permit me, I will take out the fleck in your eye, when you don't notice the plank in your own? Hypocrite! First remove the plank in your own eye, and then you'll see clearly to remove the fleck from your brother's eye. A good tree doesn't produce rotten fruit, nor again does a bad tree produce good fruit. Each tree is known by its fruit. Figs are not harvested from thorn bushes, or grapes from a bramble bush. The good person, out of the heart's good treasure, brings forth good, whereas the wicked brings forth wickedness; because the mouth speaks out of the heart's abundance. Why do you call me Lord, Lord, and don't do what I tell you? Everyone who comes to me, and hears and does what I say, is like this: he's like a man building a house. He dug deep and laid the foundation on a rock. When the flood came the river battered against the house and couldn't shake it, because it was soundly built. But the one who hears but doesn't act, is like a man who builds a house on ground without a foundation. When the river burst against it, it collapsed in an instant— and the ruin of that house was immense!

Chapter Seven

A centurion's servant healed vv1–10

After he said all this to the people he entered Capernaum. And a certain centurion had a greatly valued servant who was ill, at the point of death. When he heard about Jesus, he sent Jewish elders to him to ask him to come and cure his servant. And coming to Jesus they began to beseech him earnestly, saying, He's deserving that you should do this for him, because he loves our nation and it was he who built for us our synagogue. So Jesus started to accompany them, but when he was some distance from the house, the centurion sent some friends to him to say to him, Lord, I'm not worthy that you should come to my house—that's why I didn't presume to approach you in person. But speak a word, and let my servant be healed. For I also am under orders, and have soldiers under my authority. If I say to one of them, Go, he goes, or, Come, and he comes; and to my servant, Do this, and he does it. When Jesus heard this he was astonished and turned to the crowd that was following him, and said, I tell you, Not even in Israel have I found such faith. When those who had been sent returned to the house, they found the servant well.

A widow's son restored to life vv11–17

Thereafter he went into a town called Nain, and his disciples and a large crowd were following him. As he drew near to the town gate, look—a dead man was being carried out. He was the only son of his mother, a widow. Quite a crowd from the town accompanied her. When he saw her, the Lord, moved with pity, said, Stop weeping. Then he went up and touched the coffin. The bearers stood still and he said, Young man, I tell you, get up! And the dead man sat up and began speaking, and he restored him to his mother. Fear gripped them all, and they glorified God, saying, A mighty prophet has been raised up among us, and God has come to his people. And news of him spread throughout Judea and the surrounding countryside.

Now John's disciples reported back to him all that had happened. So John, summoning two disciples, sent them to the Lord, saying, Are you the one who is to come or should we look for someone else? When they came to Jesus, the men said, John the Baptist has sent us to you to ask, Are you the one who is to come or should we look for someone else? That very hour Jesus healed many people of diseases, plagues and evil spirits, and restored sight to many blind people. In reply he said to them, Go tell John what you've seen and heard: ***The blind regaining sight,*** the lame walking, lepers cleansed***, the deaf hearing, the dead raised,*** the poor having good news proclaimed to them. Happy the one who isn't offended by me! After John's messengers had gone back he began to speak to the crowds about John. What did you go to the desert to see? A reed shaking in the wind? What did you go out to see? A man dressed in luxurious clothing? Look, those who wear expensive garments and live a life of luxury belong in royal palaces. So what did you go out to see? A prophet? Yes, I tell you—more than a prophet. This is the one about whom it's written, ***Behold, I'm sending my messenger before you, who will prepare your way in advance.*** I tell you, no one born of a woman is greater than

John. And yet the one who's the least in the kingdom of God is greater than he is. When all the people (including the tax collectors) heard this, they acknowledged God to be in the right, having themselves been baptised with John's baptism. However, the Pharisees and lawyers rejected God's plan for them, since they were not baptised by him. To what shall I compare this generation? What are they like? They're like little children sitting in the marketplace, calling to each other, We played the flute for you, but you didn't dance; we wailed for you, but you didn't cry. For John the Baptist has come neither eating bread nor drinking wine, and you say, He's got a demon. But the Son of Man's come, eating and drinking, and you say, Look at him! A glutton and a drunk! A friend of tax collectors and sinners! Even so, all her children justify wisdom.

Anointed by a sinner vv36—50

One of the Pharisees invited Jesus to dinner, and so he went to the Pharisee's house and took his seat. And look, a woman known in the town to be a sinner heard that he was dining in the Pharisee's house. So she brought an alabaster flask of perfume and went and stood behind him, weeping at his feet. Her tears wet his feet, and she wiped them with the hair of her head. She kept kissing his feet, and anointed them with the perfume. When his host, the Pharisee, observed this he thought to himself, If this fellow were a prophet he'd know what sort of woman is touching him—she's a sinner. But Jesus said to him, Simon, I want to tell you something. Go ahead, teacher, he replied. A certain moneylender had two debtors; one owed five hundred denarii, and the other fifty. When neither could pay, he cancelled both debts. Now which should love him the more? Simon answered, The one whose larger debt he cancelled, I presume. Correct, Jesus said to him. Then turning to the woman, he said to Simon, See this woman? I came to your house and you didn't give me water for my feet; but she's wet my feet with her tears and wiped them with her hair. You didn't give me a welcome kiss, but she's been kissing my feet from the moment she came in. You didn't anoint my head with oil, but she wiped my feet with perfume. For this, I assure you, her sins, though many, are forgiven her—for she loved much. But whoever's forgiven little, loves little. And he said to the woman, Your sins are forgiven. Then the other guests began to say among themselves, Who's this who forgives sins? And he said to the woman, Your faith has saved you—go in peace.

Chapter Eight

Women followers of Jesus vv1-3

Soon afterwards he was progressing through cities and villages, preaching and heralding the kingdom of God, and the twelve were with him, together with some women who had been cured of evil spirits and illnesses: Mary, called Magdalene, from whom seven demons had been driven out, and Joanna, the wife of Chuz, Herod's chamberlain, Susanna, and many others, who catered for them out of their own pockets.

The parable of the sower vv4–8

As a large crowd was gathering, and people joined from one town after another, he addressed them by means of a parable. A sower went out to sow his seed. And some of the seed he sowed fell on the footpath and was trampled underfoot, and the birds of the air gobbled it up. Some fell on rock, and as it sprouted it dried up for lack of moisture. And some fell among thorns, and as they grew together the thorns choked them. But some fell on fertile soil, and when it produced a crop it yielded a hundredfold. Whoever's got ears to hear—listen!

The purpose of the parables vv9–15

And his disciples were asking him, What's this parable about? He said, You've been given to know the mysteries of the kingdom of God; but for the rest, there's parables, so that, ***Seeing they may not see; and hearing they may not understand***. This is the parable—the seed's the word of God. Those by the wayside are the ones who've heard. Then comes the devil and snatches the word from their heart, to stop them believing and being saved. The ones on the rock are those who, when they hear, receive the word with joy, but have no root—they believe for a while, but in time of testing they fall away. And those that fell among thorns are the ones who listen but go off and are choked by anxieties, riches and worldly pleasures, and so bear no fruit. But as for that in the fertile soil, they're the ones who listen to the word of God and hold fast to it with a good and virtuous heart, and yield fruit with patience.

Covering a lamp vv16–18

After lighting a lamp no one covers it with a jar, or hides it under a couch, but puts it on a stand so that those who come in can see the light. For there's nothing hidden that won't be revealed, nor secret that won't be made known and brought to light. So mind how you listen; for the one who has will be given more; but the one who's nothing will lose even what he thinks he has.

Jesus and his family vv19–21

Then his mother and brothers turned up, but they could not get to him on account of the crowd. So he was informed, Your mother and brothers are standing outside wanting to see you. But he answered them, My mother and my brothers are the ones who hear the word of God and do it.

Calming a storm vv22–25

Once he got into a boat with his disciples, and said to them, Let's cross over to the other side of the lake. So they set off. And as they were sailing he fell sleep. And a storm of wind swept down the lake and they were being swamped, and in peril. They came and woke him up saying, Master, Master, we're drowning! He roused himself, rebuked the wind and surge of water, and it ceased—all was calm. Then he said to them, Where's your faith? In dread and awe they say to each other, Who's this? He even commands the wind and the sea, and they obey him!

A demoniac healed vv26–39

So they sailed to the region of the Gerasenes, opposite Galilee. As he stepped ashore, a man from the city who was possessed by demons met him. For a long time he had worn no clothes nor lived in a house, but in the tombs. When he saw Jesus, he screamed and prostrated himself before him, and at the top of his voice shouted, What do you want with me, Jesus, Son of the Most High God? I implore you, Don't torment me! For he had commanded the unclean spirit to leave the man—for it had often convulsed him. He was kept locked up with chains and shackles; but he would break the bonds, and be driven by the demon into desert haunts. Jesus then asked him, What's your name? Legion, he replied, because many demons had entered him. And they kept beseeching him not to order them back into the abyss. Feeding on the nearby hill was a large herd of pigs; so they begged him to be allowed to go into those. And he gave them permission. Then the demons left the man and entered the pigs, which bolted down the steep incline into the lake and drowned. The herdsman who saw it fled, and spread the news in town and country. So people came to see what had happened, and when they got to Jesus, they found the man from whom the demons had quit, sitting at the feet of Jesus, fully clothed and in his right mind. And they were afraid. Then the eyewitnesses related how the man possessed of a demon had been restored. All those in the surrounding area of the Gerasenes asked him to leave them; because they were struck with great fear. So Jesus got into the boat and made his way back. But the man from whom the demons had been expelled kept begging to be with him, but he sent him away, saying, Go back home, and tell how much God has done for you. So he returned, and proclaimed throughout the town how much Jesus had done for him.

A sick woman and a dead girl vv40–56

When Jesus returned the crowd welcomed him, because they were all anticipating him. And look, a man named Jairus, a synagogue ruler, came and fell at Jesus' feet beseeching him to come to his house, because his only daughter, twelve years of age, was dying. As he was going, the crowd thronged him. And there was a woman who suffered from haemorrhages for twelve years; and although she spent all her money on doctors, no one could cure her. She came up behind him and touched the hem of his cloak, and instantly her haemorrhage stopped. Who touched me? asked Jesus. When everyone denied it, Peter said, Master, the crowds are mobbing, pressing against you. Someone touched me, said Jesus, because power's gone out of me. When the woman realised that she had not gone unnoticed, she came trembling and prostrating herself before him, and in the presence of all she confessed why she had touched him, and how she had been immediately made well. He then said to her, Daughter, it's your faith that's saved you—Go in peace. As he was speaking, someone from the ruler of the synagogue's house came, saying, Your daughter's died; no need to trouble the teacher further. But Jesus, hearing this, said, Don't be afraid; believe and she'll be saved.

And when he came to the house, he allowed nobody to go in with him except, Peter, John and James, and the child's parents. Everyone was weeping and mourning for her. But he said, Don't weep; she's not dead, just sleeping. And they were laughing at him, convinced she was dead. But taking her by the hand, he said, Child, get up! And her breath returned, and she got up at once. He ordered that she be given something to eat. Her parents were amazed; but he ordered them not to tell anyone what had happened.

Chapter Nine

Jesus sends out the twelve disciples vv1-6

And he called the twelve together and gave them power over all demons and to cure illnesses. And he sent them out to proclaim the kingdom of God and to heal. And he said to them, Don't take anything for your journey—no walking stick, or bag, no bread or money, and don't have two tunics. And when you visit a house, lodge there, and then depart. And wherever they don't welcome you, as you leave that town, shake off the dust from your feet as a witness against them. So off they went, and as they made their way through the villages they were preaching the gospel and healing everywhere.

Jesus troubles Herod vv7–9

Now when Herod the tetrarch got wind of all that was going on, he was at a loss, because it was said by some that John had risen from the dead, but by others that Elijah the prophet had appeared, and by still others that one of the ancient prophets had been raised. Herod said, I certainly beheaded John—so who's this I keep hearing about doing all these things? And he was eager to meet him.

Five thousand fed vv10–17

When the apostles got back they told him everything they had done. And he took them and set off privately to a town called Bethsaida. But when the crowds learnt this, they went after him. And he welcomed them, and began to speak to them about the kingdom of God, and he healed those in want of a cure. As the day was drawing to its close, the twelve came and spoke to him. Send the crowd away, so they can go into the surrounding villages and countryside, to find a place to stay and get food. For here we're in a desert scape. You feed them yourselves, he said to them. We've only five loaves and two fish, they replied—unless we're to go and buy food for all these people; for they numbered about five thousand men. And he said to his disciples, Get them to sit down in groups of about fifty each. So they did this, and they all sat down. And he took the five loaves and two fish, looked up to heaven, and blessed them. He then broke the loaves and started to hand them out to his disciples to set before the crowd. And they all ate their fill, and there were twelve baskets of leftovers.

Peter's confession vv18–22

And it happened once that while he was praying alone, the disciples were with him. And he asked them, saying, Who do the crowds say that I am? They replied, John the Baptist—but others Elijah—still others that one of the ancient prophets has arisen. But who do you say that I am? he asked. Peter answered, God's Messiah. But he gave them strict instructions not to tell anyone, saying, The Son of Man must suffer much and be rejected by the elders, chief priests and lawyers, and be killed and on the third day be raised.

The cost of following Jesus vv23–27

And he began to tell them all, If anyone wants to join me let him forget himself, take up his cross each day, and follow me. For whoever seeks to save his life will destroy it; but whoever abandons his life for my sake will preserve it. For what's the profit if someone gains the whole world, but destroys or ruins himself? If anyone's ashamed of me and of my message—it's him the Son of Man will be ashamed of when he comes in his glory, and the glory of the Father and of the holy angels. But I tell you truly, there are some standing here who won't by any means taste death before they see the kingdom of God.

The Messiah transfigured vv28–36

Eight or so days after these sayings, he took Peter, James and John with him, and went up into the mountain to pray. While he was praying the appearance of his face became different and his clothing white as lightening. And behold, two men were talking with him—Moses and Elijah—who appeared in glory. They were speaking of his exodus that he was about to fulfil in Jerusalem. Peter and those with him were overcome with sleep, and when they woke up they saw his glory, and the two men standing with him. As they were leaving him, Peter said to Jesus, Master, it's good for us to be here—let's put up three tents, one each—for you, Moses and Elijah—not thinking what he was saying. And as he was saying this, a cloud appeared and overshadowed Jesus, Moses, and Elijah. And the disciples were afraid as those three entered into the cloud. And a voice came out of the cloud, saying, This is my Son, my chosen one—pay heed to him! After the voice had spoken, Jesus was found alone. And they kept quiet and told no one at that time about anything they had seen.

Exorcism and a prophecy vv37–45

The following day, when they came down from the mountain, a great crowd met him. It was then that a man from the crowd shouted out, Teacher, I beg you, look at my son—my only child—see—a spirit's seizing, convulsing him—he's screaming now—frothing—and it's bruising him—and won't leave him without a struggle. I begged your disciples to cast it out, but they couldn't. Jesus answered, Faithless and perverse generation! For how long am I to be with you and tolerate you? Bring your son here. While he was coming, the demon tore and convulsed him. But Jesus berated the unclean spirit, healed the boy and restored him to his father. And all were astounded at the majesty of God. While they were marvelling at everything he was doing, Jesus said to his disciples, Make sure these words sink into your ears. The Son of Man's going to be handed over into the custody of men. But they did not understand what he said, and its meaning was concealed from them, lest they figure it out. And they were afraid to ask him what it meant.

A dispute about rank vv46–48

A debate arose among themselves about which of them was the greatest? But Jesus, realising what they were thinking took a little child and put him beside him, and said to them, Whoever receives this little child in my name receives me, and whoever receives me receives him who sent me. For whoever's least among you all—he is great.

Who is for or against Jesus? vv49–50

John intervened and said, Master, we saw someone expelling demons in your name, and we tried to stop him, because he's not one of us. Don't stop him, Jesus said to him, because anyone who's not against you is for you.

Jesus unwelcome in Samaria vv51–56

When the days were about to be fulfilled for him to be taken up, he set his face to go to Jerusalem. And he sent messengers before his face, who went and arrived at a Samaritan village, to prepare for him. But they did not welcome him there, because he was intent on going to Jerusalem. And when James and John, his disciples, saw this they said, Lord, do you want us to summon fire down from heaven to consume them? But he turned and rebuked them, and they went on to another village.

The cost of discipleship vv57–62

As they travelled along the road, someone said to him, I'll follow you wherever you go. Jesus said to him, Foxes have holes, and the birds of the air have nests; but the Son of Man's nowhere to lay his head. To somebody else, he said, Follow me. But he replied, Lord, let me go and bury my father first. Jesus said to him, Let the dead bury their own dead—but you, go and proclaim the kingdom of God. Yet another said, I'll follow you, Lord, but first let me go and bid farewell to those at home. But Jesus said to him, No one who puts his hand to the plough, and keeps looking back, is fit for the kingdom of God.

Chapter Ten

Seventy sent vv1–12

After these things the Lord appointed seventy others and sent them ahead of him in pairs to every town and place where he himself was going to visit. And he was saying to them, The harvest's abundant, but the labourers few. So entreat the Lord of the harvest that he might send labourers into his harvest. Go forth! See! I'm sending you as lambs in the midst of wolves. Don't take a wallet, backpack or sandals—and don't say, Hello, to anyone on the way. Whenever you enter a house first say, Peace to this house! And if there's a son of peace there, your peace will rest upon it—but if not, it'll return to you. Stay in the same house, eating and drinking what they give you, for the labourer deserves his keep. Don't go from one house to the other. Whenever you enter a town and they welcome you, eat whatever they give you.

Cure that town's sick and say to them, God's kingdom's come near to you. But whenever you enter a town that doesn't welcome you, go out into its streets and say, Against you we shake off even the dust of your town that clings to our feet. But know this—God's kingdom has drawn near. I declare to you, on that day it'll be more tolerable for Sodom than for that town.

Woe to surrounding towns vv13-16

Woe to you Chorazin! Woe to you Bethsaida! For if the mighty works performed in your midst had happened in Tyre and Sidon, they would've repented long ago, and sat in sackcloth and ashes. But it'll be more tolerable for Tyre and Sidon than for you. As for you Capernaum, you think you'll be exalted to heaven do you? You'll be brought down to Hades! Whoever listens to you listens to me, and whoever rejects you rejects me, and whoever rejects me rejects the one who sent me.

The return of the missionaries vv17–20

The seventy returned joyfully, saying, Lord, in your name even the demons submit to us! And he said to them, I watched Satan fall like lightning from heaven. See, I've given you authority to tread on serpents and scorpions, and over all the power of the enemy—and nothing at all will harm you. However don't rejoice in this, that the spirits submit to you, but rejoice that your names are written in heaven.

Rejoicing in the Father's will vv21–24

In that same hour he exulted in the Holy Spirit, and said, I thank you, Father, Lord of heaven and earth, because you've hidden these things from the wise and learned and revealed them to little children. Yes, Father, for this was fitting in your sight. Everything's handed over to me by my Father; and no one knows who the Son is except the Father, or who the Father is except the Son, and to anyone to whom the Son chooses to reveal him. He turned to the disciples and said, privately, Happy are the eyes that see what you see. For I tell you, there are many prophets and kings who wanted to see what you see, but didn't see, or to hear what you hear, but didn't hear.

And look, a lawyer stood up to test him, saying, What do I have to do to inherit eternal life? He answered him, What's written in the Law? How do you read it?

He answered, ***You must love the Lord your God with all your heart, soul and might, and love your neighbour as yourself.*** And he said to him, Correct! Do this and you'll live. But wanting to justify himself he said to Jesus, And who's my neighbour? Jesus responded, A certain man was going down from Jerusalem to Jericho and fell in with robbers, who stripped, battered him and fled, leaving him half dead. By chance a priest was travelling the same road. Now when he saw the man, he passed by on the other side. Similarly, a Levite arriving at the scene saw him and also passed by on the other side. But along came a Samaritan, who was on a journey, and when he saw the man he was moved with pity and approached him, bandaged his wounds, pouring oil and wine over them. He mounted him on his own animal and led him to an inn and looked after him. Next day he took two denarii and gave them to the innkeeper, saying, Take care of him, and I'll reimburse you for any additional expenditure when I return. Now which of these three do you think turned out to be a neighbour to the man who fell among the robbers? The one who was kind to him, he replied. You go and do the same, said Jesus.

Mary and Martha vv38–42

So as they went on their journey, Jesus came to a village where a woman named Martha welcomed him. She had a sister, Mary, who sat at the Lord's feet listening to what he had to say. But all the serving distracted Martha. So she went up to him and said, Lord, don't you care that my sister's left me to serve on my own? Tell her to help me. But in answer the Lord said, Martha, Martha, you're fretting and worrying over lots of things—but one thing matters: Mary's chosen the better part, and she won't be deprived of it.

Chapter Eleven

Jesus teaches how to pray vv1–4

Once Jesus was praying in a certain place. When he had finished, one of his disciples said to him, Lord, teach us to pray as John taught his disciples. And he said to them, Whenever you pray, say, Father, may your name be revered. May your kingdom come. Give us each day our daily bread. Forgive us our sins, for we also forgive those indebted to us. And don't let us yield to temptation.

Praying shamelessly vv5–13

And he said to them, Which of you'll have friend and he'll go to him at midnight and say to him, Friend, lend me three loaves; for a friend of mine who's traveling has turned up and I've nothing to give him. Now suppose he replies, Don't bother me; the door's locked and my children are in bed with me. I can't get up now and give you anything! I tell you, even if he won't get up and give him anything because he's his friend, he'll eventually rouse himself and give him whatever he needs because he's so shameless. So I'm telling you, Ask, and it'll be given to you; search, and you'll find; knock, and it'll be opened to you. For everyone who asks receives, those who search find, and to those who knock it'll be opened. And is there any father among you who, if his son asks for a fish, will give him a snake instead? Or, if he asks for an egg, will give him a scorpion? If you, though bad, know how to give good gifts to your children, how much more will the heavenly Father give the Holy Spirit to those who ask him.

Casting out demons by Beelzebul? vv14–23

Now Jesus was expelling a mute demon; and when the demon had left, the mute man began to speak, and the crowds were dumbfounded. But some said, He's expelling demons through Beelzebul, the prince of demons; but others, in order to test him, kept demanding from him a sign from heaven. But he read their minds and said to them, Every kingdom divided against itself will face ruin; and a house at war with another house falls. So, if Satan is at war with himself, how will his kingdom prevail—for you say that by Beelzebul I cast out demons? But if it's through the Lord of the flies that I expel demons, by whom do your sons expel them? Therefore they themselves will be your judges. But if it's by the finger of God that I cast out demons, then the kingdom of God has come upon you. When a strong man, fully armed, stands guard over his own house, his belongings are secure. But when someone stronger attacks and overpowers him, he carries away all the weapons on which he relied and divides up the booty. Whoever's not with me is against me, and whoever doesn't gather with me, scatters.

The return of an evil spirit vv24–26

Whenever the unclean spirit leaves someone, it passes through waterless areas looking for rest, and when it does not find any it says, I'll go back to my home that I left. And on its return it finds the house swept and in order. It then goes and brings seven other spirits more evil than itself, and they go in and live there, and the final condition of that person is worse than it was before.

The truly blessed vv27–28

As he was saying this, a woman in the crowd raised her voice and said to him, Happy's the womb that bore you, and the breasts at which you fed. But he said, No, happy are those who hear the word of God and keep it!

A generation condemned vv29–32

As the crowds were growing he began to say, This generation's an evil generation—It seeks a sign, but none will be given to it, except Jonah's sign. For as Jonah became a sign for the inhabitants of Nineveh, so will the Son of Man be to this generation. The queen of the South will rise up together with the men of this generation and condemn them. She came from the ends of the earth to listen to the wisdom of Solomon, but behold, someone greater than Solomon is here! The inhabitants of Nineveh will rise up together with this generation at the judgment and condemn it, because they repented after Jonah's preaching, and behold, someone greater than Jonah is here!

The inner light vv33–36

Nobody lights a lamp then puts it in a secret place, but on a lamp stand, so that those who come in may see the light. Your eye's the lamp of your body. If your eye's healthy, your entire body's filled with light; but if it's unhealthy, your whole body's full of darkness. So take care that the light in you isn't darkness. If then your body's infused with light—with no dark regions—it'll be as completely bright as when a lamp shines its rays on you.

Pharisees and lawyers rebuked vv37–54

While he was speaking, a Pharisee invited him to dine with him, so he went and reclined at table. The Pharisee was shocked to see that he did not wash before dinner. But the Lord said to him, You Pharisees wash the outside of the cup and the dish, but inside you're full of greed and evil. Fools! Didn't the one who made the outside also make the inside? Instead, give alms from the heart and, look, everything will be clean for you. Woe to you Pharisees! For you tithe mint, rue and every garden herb, but neglect justice and the love of God. You should have done these things without neglecting the others. Woe to you Pharisees! For you love the front seat in the synagogues and being saluted in the market places. Woe to you! For you're like unmarked graves, over which people walk without realising. Then one of the lawyers breaks in, Teacher, you also insult us with these words. Woe also to you lawyers! he said. For you heap unbearable burdens on people, and don't lift so much as a finger to help. Woe to you! For you built the tombs of the prophets your fathers murdered. So you're complicit in, and approve your fathers' doings, because they killed them, and you erect their tombs. Because of this, the wisdom of God also said, I'll send them prophets and messengers, and some they'll kill and persecute. So the blood of all the prophets, shed since the beginning of the world, will be held against this generation—from the blood of Abel to that of Zechariah, who perished between the altar and the sanctuary. Yes, I tell you, it'll be required of this generation. Woe to you, lawyers! You've taken the key of knowledge but didn't enter yourselves, and you hindered those who were entering. As he left there, the scribes and Pharisees began to press him hard, and to quiz him about many things—lying in wait to catch him out—in case he might say something.

Chapter Twelve

The leaven of the Pharisees vv1–7

Meanwhile, a crowd of thousands had gathered together, so that they were trampling on each other. He began to say first to his disciples, Beware the leaven of the Pharisees—hypocrisy. There's nothing hidden that won't be revealed, or concealed that won't be made known. So what you've said in the dark will be heard in the light, and what you've whispered in private will be proclaimed from the rooftops. My friends, I tell you, don't fear those who kill the body—that's all they can do. I'll show you whom to fear; fear him who, after he's killed, has power to throw into hell. Yes, I tell you, that's the one to fear! Aren't five sparrows sold for tuppence? Yet not one of them's forgotten before God. But even the hairs on your head are all numbered. Don't worry; you're worth far more than many sparrows.

Acknowledging Jesus, the Messiah vv8–12

And I tell you, everyone who acknowledges me before men, the Son of Man also will acknowledge him before God's angels. And anyone who disowns me before men will be disowned before God's angels. And everyone who speaks a word against the Son of Man will be forgiven; but anyone one who blasphemes against the Holy Spirit won't be forgiven. When they indict you in the synagogues and before the rulers and authorities, don't be anxious about how to defend yourself or what to say, for the Holy Spirit will, at that very moment, instruct you what to say.

Useless riches vv13–21

Then someone in the crowd said to him, Teacher, tell my brother to divide the inheritance with me. But he said to him, Man, who put me over you as judge or arbiter? And he said to them, Watch out—guard against all greed. Life isn't about having an abundance of possessions. Then he told them a parable. There was once rich man whose farm produced plentiful crops, and he thought to himself, What'll I do? I don't have enough space to store my crops. So this is what I'll do. I'll pull down my barns and build bigger ones, and store all my grain and goods there. And I'll then say to myself, You've enough goods stored for many years—relax, eat, drink, be merry. But God said to him, Fool! This very night your life will be required of you. So who'll own everything you've set aside? Thus it'll be for everyone who stores up treasure for himself, but isn't rich toward God.

No need to worry vv22–34

And he said to his disciples, Therefore, I tell you, don't worry about your life—what to eat, or about your body, what to wear. There's more to life than food, and there's more to the body than clothing. Look at the ravens! They don't sow or reap, they've no storeroom or barn, and yet God feeds them. How much more valuable are you than the birds? Which one of you by worrying can add a single cubit to his life? If you can't do so small a thing as this, why worry about the rest? Ponder the lilies—how they grow, they neither spin nor weave, and yet I tell you, even Solomon in all his pomp wasn't attired like one of these. But if God so clothes the grass—here today and tossed into the furnace tomorrow—how much more will he clothe you—faithless people! And quit your preoccupation with food and drink—stop fretting. For every nation on earth's preoccupied with these things, and your Father knows that you need them. Instead, look for God's kingdom, and all these things will be given to you. Don't worry, little flock, for your Father's pleased to give the kingdom to you. Sell your belongings and give to the needy. Make for yourselves purses that won't wear out, a treasure in heaven that won't fail, where neither thief can get near it or moth destroy. For where your treasure is, that's also where your heart will be.

Be Ready vv35–48

Gird up your loins, and keep your lamps burning. Be like those who wait for their master to return from the wedding feast, so they may open the door for him at once, as soon as he arrives and knocks. Happy are the servants whom the master finds awake when he returns. Truly, I tell you, he'll put on an apron, sit them down, and will come and serve them. Should he come about midnight, or at dawn, and find them awake, they'll be blessed. But be sure of this, if the master of the house were to know when the burglar was coming, he wouldn't have left his house to be broken into. So you must be ready, because the Son of Man's coming when you least expect him. Peter said, Lord, is this parable for us or for everyone? The Lord replied, So who's the faithful and prudent manager whom the master will appoint over his household, to give them their corn allowance when due? Happy's the servant whom the master finds so doing when he arrives. Seriously, I tell you, he'll appoint that person to be in charge of all his affairs. But if that servant says to himself, My master's arrival is delayed, and starts to mistreat his young male and female servants, and to eat, drink and get drunk. The master of that servant will arrive unexpectedly, and at an unknown hour, and will dismember him and bury his remains with the faithless. But that servant, who knew his master's wishes, yet didn't prepare for them or carry them out, will get a severe beating. But the one who didn't know, yet did what deserved a beating, will receive a light beating. To the one who's been given much, much will be required; and from the one who's been entrusted with much, even more will be expected.

Division not peace vv49–53

I've come to cast fire upon the earth—how I wish that it were already ablaze! I've a baptism to be baptised with, and how distressed I am until it's accomplished. Do you think I've come to bring peace on earth? No, I tell you—discord! From now on five members of a household will be divided, three against two and two against three. There'll be division; father against son and ***son*** against ***father***, mother against daughter and ***daughter against mother,*** mother-in-law against daughter-in-law and ***daughter-in-law against mother-in-law.***

The signs of the times vv54–56

And then he said to the crowds, Whenever you see a cloud forming in the west you say, It's going to rain; and that's what happens. And whenever you see a southerly wind blowing you say, There'll be scorching heat; and that's what happens. Hypocrites! You know how to read the face of earth and sky, but you don't know how to interpret the present moment.

Compromise better than litigation vv57–59

And why don't you judge for yourselves what's right? As you and your opponent are going to the judge, try to settle with him before you get there, in case he drags you before the judge, and the judge hands you over to the bailiff, and the bailiff put you in prison. And I tell you; you'll not get out until you've paid the last penny.

Chapter Thirteen

Repent or die vv1–5

Many who were present there at that very moment told him about the Galileans whose blood Pilate had mingled with their sacrifices. Do you think, he said to them, these Galileans were worse sinners than all the other Galileans because they suffered in this way? No, I tell you; but unless you repent, you'll perish just like them. Or take the eighteen on whom the tower of Siloam fell and killed—do you think they were worse offenders than all the inhabitants of Jerusalem? No, I tell you; but unless you repent you'll all likewise face destruction.

The barren fig tree vv6–9

Then he began to tell them this parable. A man had a fig tree planted in his vineyard. He came to it looking for fruit, but found none. So he said to the vine-tender, Look, I've been coming for three years expecting fruit on this fig tree—but nothing! Cut it down. Why should it use up the soil? But he replies, Sir, leave it for another year, until I loosen the soil around it, and put on manure. Then if it bear fruit next year, well and good; but if not, then you can cut it down.

A woman cured on the sabbath vv10–17

And he was teaching on the sabbath in one of the synagogues. Suddenly there was a woman there crippled by a spirit for eighteen years. She was bent double and could not straighten herself. When Jesus saw her he called out, and said to her, Madam, you're free from your disability—and he laid hands on her. Instantly she straightened up and began to glorify God. But the synagogue leader, furious that Jesus had cured her on the sabbath, started to say to the congregation, There's six days for work—come and be cured on one of those, not on the sabbath. But in reply the Lord said,

Hypocrites! Doesn't each one of you on the sabbath untie his ox, or his donkey, from the manger and lead it to water? And shouldn't this woman, a daughter of Abraham, bound for all of eighteen years by Satan, be released from this bondage on the sabbath day? And as he said this, his opponents were ashamed, and the entire congregation were rejoicing at all the glorious things that were being done by him.

The mustard seed parable vv18–21

He was saying therefore, What's the kingdom of God like? And to what shall I compare it? It's like a mustard seed which someone planted; it grew into a tree and the birds nested in its branches. And again he said, To what shall I compare the kingdom of God? It's like leaven that a woman took and hid in three measures of flour, until it was all leavened.

The narrow door vv22–30

He was journeying through towns and villages, teaching and travelling towards Jerusalem. Someone said to him, Lord, will only a few be saved? He said to them, Fight to enter through the narrow door. For I tell you, many will try to get in, but few will succeed—especially when the householder gets up and shuts the door. You'll then begin to stand outside the door, and to knock on the door, saying, Sir, open for us. Then he'll answer, I don't know where you're from. Then you'll begin to say, But we used to eat and drink with you, and you taught us in our streets. But he'll say, I don't know where you're from—***away from me all you evil doers***. There'll be weeping and grinding of teeth when you'll see Abraham, Isaac and Jacob, and all the prophets in the kingdom of God, but you yourselves thrown out. People will come from east and west, north and south, and recline at table in the kingdom of God. But watch out! Those who are last will be first, and those who are first will be last.

Herod's plan vv31–35

In that very hour some Pharisees came and were saying to him, Get away—leave here—Herod wants to kill you! He said to them, Go tell that fox, Look, I'm casting out demons and curing people today and tomorrow, and I'll finish up on the third day. However, I must journey today, tomorrow and the day after, because it's not fitting that a prophet should perish away from Jerusalem. O Jerusalem, Jerusalem, that murders the prophets and stones those sent to it. How often did I want to gather your children together, as a hen gathers her brood under her wings, but you wouldn't. Your house is abandoned—look! And I tell you, you won't see me until you say, ***Blessed is the one coming in the name of the Lord.***

Chapter Fourteen

To heal on the sabbath or not vv1–6

One sabbath he went to have dinner with a ruler of the Pharisees, and they were eyeing him carefully. And who was there but a man with dropsy. Jesus asked the lawyers and Pharisees, saying, Is it lawful to cure people on the sabbath or not? They remained silent. So he took hold of the man, healed him, and discharged him. And he said to them, Suppose your child or ox fell into a well on the sabbath, wouldn't you pull it out straightaway? But they could not answer this.

Dining etiquette vv7–11

And noting how the guests were choosing places of honour, he started to tell them a parable.

When someone invites you to a wedding banquet, don't sit down in the best seat, in case someone more distinguished than you has been invited by him, and the one who invited both of you will come and say to you, Give him this place. Then you will begin with shame to take the lowest place. Instead, whenever you're invited, go and sit in the lowest place, so that when your host comes he might say, Friend, move up higher. In this way you'll be honoured among your fellow guests. For whoever exalts himself will be humbled, and whoever humbles himself will be exalted.

Invitations to a feast vv12–24

And he also began to say to his host, Whenever you give a dinner or feast, don't invite your friends or your siblings or your relatives or affluent neighbours—they'll only invite you back, and you'd be repaid. But when you throw a dinner party, invite the poor, the crippled, the lame and the blind. Then you'll be happy—because they won't have anything to give you in return—but you'll be repaid at the resurrection of the just. When a fellow guest heard this, he said to him, Happy are those who'll eat bread in the kingdom of God. So he said to him, There was once a man who gave a great banquet and invited many guests. When it was time for the banquet, he sent his servant to tell those invited, Come—everything's ready! But each of them began to make excuses. The first one said to him, I've bought a field and must go and see it; kindly excuse me. Another said, I've bought five oxen and am going to examine them; kindly excuse me. And another said, I've just got married and can't come. So the servant returned and reported all this to his master. In anger the master of the house said to his servant, Go out quickly to the streets and lanes of the town and bring the poor, the crippled, the blind and the lame, in here. And the servant said, Sir, what you ordered has been done and there's still room. And the master said to the servant, Go out then to the highways and hedgerows and insist that people come in so that my house may be filled. For I tell you, none of those men originally invited will taste my banquet.

The cost of discipleship vv25–33

Great crowds were accompanying him, so he turned and said to them, If anyone comes to me and doesn't hate his father and mother, his wife and children, his brothers, and sisters, and yes, even his own life, can't be my disciple. Whoever doesn't carry his own cross and follow me can't be my disciple. For which one of you would plan to build a tower without first sitting down and working out the cost, to see if he's enough to complete it, otherwise he might lay its foundation but won't have the resources to finish it? Then all who see it will begin to mock him, saying, This man started to build, but couldn't finish it. Or what king, setting out to do battle with another king, wouldn't first sit down and weigh up whether with ten thousand troops he could engage in battle with an opposing twenty thousand? And if not, while the other is still at a distance, wouldn't send emissaries to sue for peace? Therefore, any of you who won't renounce all he has, cannot be my disciple.

Tasteless salt vv34–35

Salt is good; but if it loses its taste how can its saltiness be restored? It's of no use either for the earth or the dung heap. It's thrown away. You've got ears— listen up!

Chapter Fifteen

A lost sheep vv1–7

Now all the tax collectors and sinners were drawing close to him to hear him. But the Pharisees and legal experts kept grumbling about him, This fellow welcomes sinners and eats with them. So he told them this parable. Suppose one of you had a hundred sheep and lost one of them, wouldn't he leave the ninety-nine in the desert and go after the lost sheep until he should find it? And after finding it he places it joyfully onto his shoulders, went home, calls together his friends and neighbours, saying to them, Rejoice with me, because I've rescued my lost sheep! I tell you so, there'll be greater happiness in heaven over one sinner who repents than over ninety-nine upright persons who don't need to repent.

The lost coin vv8–10

Suppose a woman with ten silver coins were to lose one; wouldn't she light a lamp, and sweep the house, and search meticulously until she should find it? And after she finds it, she calls together her friends and neighbours, saying, Celebrate with me, because I've found the coin I lost! So I tell you, there's joy among the company of God's angels over one sinner who repents.

The lost son and the broken family vv11–32

And he said, A man had two sons. And the younger of them said to his father, Father, give me the share of my inheritance; so he divided his property between them. A few days later, after he'd liquidated his assets, the younger son left for a far away country, where he wasted his money on reckless living. After he'd spent everything a severe famine occurred in that country, and he began to experience hardship. So he became a hired hand to one of the citizens of that region, who sent him into his fields to feed pigs. He would've been glad to feed himself with the husks the pigs ate; but nobody gave him any. When he came to himself he said, How many of my father's hired hands have more than enough bread to eat, but I'm perishing of hunger here? I'll rouse myself, go to my father and say to him, I've sinned against heaven and before you. I'm no longer worthy to be called your son—class me as one of your servants. So up he got, and went to his father. And while he was still a long way off, his father spotted him. Filled with emotion he ran, fell upon his neck, and kissed him. And the son said to him, Father, I've sinned against heaven and before you; I'm no longer worthy to be called your son. But his father said to his servants, Hurry up, bring out the best robe and clothe him; put a ring on his finger and sandals on his feet. Bring out the fatted calf and slaughter it—let's feast and be happy! For this, my son died and is alive again; he was lost and now is found. So they began to celebrate. Now his elder brother was in a field. As he got near to the house, he heard the music and dancing. And he called one of the servants to him, and asked, what's all this about? He said to him, Your brother's arrived and your father's killed the fatted calf, because he's received him back safely. But he became angry and refused to go in. His father came out and kept pleading with him. But he answered his father, Look, all these years I slave for you without disobeying a single command of yours; yet you've never given me so much as a goat to celebrate with my friends. But when this son of yours turned up, who's devoured your living with prostitutes, you kill the fatted calf for him. And he said to him, Son, you're always with me, and all I have is yours. It was fitting that we celebrate and be happy, for this your brother was dead and has come back to life, he was lost and has been found.

Chapter Sixteen

The dishonest manager vv1–13

And he began to tell his disciples, There was once a rich man who had an administrator, and allegations were made about him that he was squandering his property. So he called him and said to him, What's this I hear about you? Audit your management accounts, for you can no longer be administrator. And the administrator said to himself, What'll I do, since the master is taking the administration away from me? I'm not strong enough to dig, and too ashamed to beg. I know what I'll do, so that when I lose my job as administrator people will welcome me into their homes. So he summoned his master's debtors one by one. He began to say to the first, How much do you owe my master? One hundred measures of oil. So he said to him, Take your record and sit down quickly and write fifty. Then he said to another, And you, how much do you owe? He replied, A hundred measures of wheat. And he says to him, Take your account and write eighty. And the master applauded that unrighteous manager because he'd acted with cunning. For the children of this age are more cunning in dealing with their own generation than are the children of light. And I tell you, make friends for yourselves of unrighteous wealth, so that whenever it fails you they will welcome you into the eternal dwellings. One faithful in the least thing is also faithful in much; and one who's unrighteous in the least thing is also unrighteous in much. So, if you've been unfaithful with respect to unjust gain, who's going to trust you with true riches? And if you've been unfaithful with what belongs to another, who'll give you what is your own? No servant can serve two masters, for he'll hate one and love the other, or he'll be devoted to the one and despise the other. You can't serve God and mammon.

The Law and the kingdom of God vv14–17

And Pharisees, being lovers of money, were listening to all this and sneering at him. And he said to them, You're the very ones who put on a show of righteousness before men; but God knows your hearts. For what's esteemed by men is an abomination in God's sight. The law and the prophets were until John, from then on the good news of God's kingdom is being preached and everyone is desperate to enter it. But it's easier for heaven and earth to pass away than for one stroke of a letter of the law to be left out.

Divorce and adultery v18

Everyone who divorces his wife and marries another commits adultery; and anyone who marries a divorced woman commits adultery.

Lazarus and the wealthy man vv19–31

There was a wealthy man who was dressed in purple and expensive linen who used to feast lavishly every day. At his gate squatted a poor man called Lazarus, covered in sores. He longed to be fed with what fell from the wealthy man's table—even the dogs passing by began to lick his sores. One day the poor man died and was carried by the angels into Abraham's presence. The wealthy man also died and was buried. And in the Realm of the Dead he raised his eyes, being in unbearable pain, and sees Abraham in the distance and Lazarus at his side. And he called out, Father Abraham, have pity on me! Send Lazarus to dip the tip of his finger in water and cool my tongue, for I'm in agony in this flame. But Abraham said, Child, you enjoyed the good life whilst alive; and Lazarus, for his part, suffered bad things and now he's comforted whilst you're in torment. Furthermore, a great chasm's opened up between us; so that those who want to pass from here to you may not; and nobody can cross from there to us. And he said, Then I beg you, father, send him to my home—for I've five brothers—to warn them, lest they also come to this place of torment. But Abraham said, They've Moses and the prophets, they ought to listen to them. And he said, No, father Abraham, but if someone from the dead goes to them, they'll repent! And he said to them, If they don't listen to Moses and the prophets they won't be convinced if someone should arise from the dead.

Chapter Seventeen

Warning against yielding to temptation vv1–4

And he said to his disciples, Enticements to stumble are bound to come, but woe to the one through whom they come. It'd be better for such a person to have a millstone tied around his neck and be thrown into the sea than that he should cause one of these little ones to stumble. Watch out! If your brother sins, rebuke him; if he repents, forgive him; and if he sins against you seven times a day, and turns to you and says, I repent, you shall forgive him.

Teaching about faith vv5—6

And the apostles said to the Lord, Increase our faith! The Lord replied, If you've faith like a grain of mustard seed, you could say to this mulberry bush, Be uprooted and planted in the sea—and it would obey you.

Teaching about true service vv7–10

Will any of you with a servant who ploughs or tends sheep say to him when he comes in from the field, Please—do take a seat? Won't he say instead, Prepare supper for me—put on your apron—wait on me while I eat and drink—then you eat and drink. He doesn't compliment that servant because he did what was ordered, does he? So it is with you, whenever you've done all your duties, say, We're unworthy servants, we've only done our job.

Cleansing ten lepers vv11–19

He began to pass between Samaria and Galilee as he was journeying towards Jerusalem. And as he was entering a certain village ten lepers—who stood at a distance—met him. They shouted to him, saying, Jesus, Master, pity us! When he saw them, he said to them, Go show yourselves to the priests. And as they went they were cleansed. But one of them, when he saw that he has was cured, went back praising God loudly, and fell on his face at the feet of Jesus, thanking him. And he was a Samaritan. Jesus said, weren't ten cleansed? Where are the nine? Was no one found to return and glorify God except this foreigner? So he said to him, Up you get—be on your way! Your faith has cured you.

How God's kingdom will come vv20—37

When asked by some Pharisees when God's kingdom would come, he answered them, saying, God's kingdom won't come by observation, nor will they say, Look, it's here, or it's there—for God's kingdom's within you. And he said to his disciples, The time will come when you'll long to see one of the days of the Son of Man, but won't see it. And they'll say to you, Look there—or here! Don't follow or pursue. For just as lightning flashes and lights up the earth under heaven from one end to the other, so will the Son of Man be in his day. But first he must suffer much and be rejected by this generation. Just as it was in the days of Noah, so it'll be in the days of the Son of Man: they were busy eating, drinking, marrying, being given in marriage, until the day Noah entered the ark, then the flood came and destroyed them all. So also, as in the days of Lot: they were eating, drinking, buying, selling, planting, building. But on the day Lot left Sodom, fire and sulphur rained down from heaven and destroyed them all. It'll be like this on the day the Son of Man is revealed. On that day, anyone on the rooftop with belongings inside the house, mustn't come down to collect them; anyone out in the fields mustn't go back for them. Remember Lot's wife! Whoever tries to save his life will lose it; and whoever loses his life will keep it. I tell you, on that night there'll be two in one bed; one will be taken and the other abandoned. There'll be two women grinding together at the same mill; one will be taken and the other abandoned. And they say to him, Where, Lord? He replied, Where the corpse is, there the vultures will be gathered.

Chapter Eighteen

Pray without ceasing vv1–8

And he began to tell them a parable about the need to pray always and not give up, saying, There was a judge in a certain town who neither feared God nor cared about people. And in that town there was also a widow who kept coming to him, saying, Vindicate me against my opponent! For a time, he wouldn't; but eventually he said to himself, Although I don't fear God nor care about people, I'll give this widow justice, to stop her wearing me out with her continual coming. And the Lord said, Hear what this unjust judge is saying. Won't God then give justice to his chosen ones who cry out to him day and night? Will he delay long over them? I tell you he'll quickly give them justice. But will the Son of Man find faith on earth when he comes?

Two ways of praying vv9–14

He also told this parable to some who regarded themselves as upright, and treated others with disdain. Two men went up to the temple to pray, one a Pharisee and the other a tax collector. Stood there, the Pharisee prayed thus to himself: God, I thank you that I'm not as others—extortioners, wrongdoers, adulterers—or even like this tax collector. Twice a week I fast; I tithe a tenth of my earnings. But the tax collector, standing far off, did not deign even to lift his eyes to heaven, but kept beating his breast, muttering, God, pity me a sinner! I tell you, this man, not the other, went home justified. Everyone who exalts himself will be humbled, but whoever humbles himself will be exalted.

Blessing children vv15–17

People even used to bring babies to him, so that he might touch them. But when the disciples saw it, they began to tell them off. But Jesus called for them, saying, Let the infants come to me, don't stop them, for it's to such as these that the kingdom of heaven belongs. In truth, I tell you, whoever won't receive the kingdom of God as a little child won't enter it—ever.

Costs and rewards vv18–30

A certain ruler once asked him, saying, Good teacher, what must I do to inherit eternal life? Jesus answered him, Why do you call me good? Nobody's good—except God alone! You know the commandments, ***Don't commit adultery, don't murder, don't steal, don't commit perjury, honour your father and mother.*** And he replied, I've kept all these since I was a youth. When Jesus heard this, he said to him, You lack one thing: sell all you've got and give it to the poor, and you'll have treasure in heaven—then come follow me. On hearing this he became sad, because he was very rich. When Jesus saw him becoming downcast, he said, How hard is it for those with wealth to enter God's kingdom. It's easier for a camel to go through a needle's eye than for a rich man to enter God's kingdom. Those who heard this said, Then who can be saved? And he replied, What's impossible for you is possible for God. Then Peter said, Look, we've left everything to follow you! And he said to them, In truth, I tell you, there's nobody who's left home, wife, brothers, parents or children for the sake of the kingdom of God, who won't receive much more in this life, and eternal life in the age to come.

Jesus foretells his death again vv31–34

Then Jesus took the twelve aside and said to them, Look, we're going up to Jerusalem, and there, everything that's been written about the Son of Man by the prophets will be accomplished. He'll be handed over to the gentiles—mocked, insulted, spat upon. After flogging him, they'll kill him—but he'll rise again on the third day. But they understood none of this, for the saying was hidden from them, and they were unable to grasp what was said.

Healing near Jericho vv35–43

As he drew near Jericho there was a blind man sitting by the roadside begging. When he heard a crowd passing through, he asked, What's going on? Jesus of Nazareth is going by, they told him. Then he shouted out, Jesus, son of David, pity me! Those in front were telling him off, to silence him. But he cried out all the more, Son of David, pity me! Jesus stopped and ordered the man to be brought to him. When he came near him, he said, What do you want me to do for you? Lord, he answered, let me see again. Then see again! said Jesus to him—your faith has saved you! Immediately he regained his sight, and began following Jesus, glorifying God—and all the people, when they saw it, gave glory to God.

Chapter Nineteen

Zacchaeus finds salvation vv1–10

He entered and was passing though Jericho, and there was a man there, named Zacchaeus. He was the head tax collector and was wealthy. He was keen to see who Jesus was, but was unable because of the crowd, for he was short. So running on ahead, he climbed up a sycamore tree to catch sight of him, for he was about to pass that way. When Jesus reached the spot he looked up and said to him, Zacchaeus, quick—come down—for I must stay at your house today. So he got down hastily and was happy to welcome him. All who saw this began to grumble, saying, He's a gone to be a guest of a sinner. Zacchaeus stood there and said to the Lord, Look—I give half my assets, Lord, to the poor. And if I've extorted anything from anyone, I'll give it back four times over. Today, Jesus said to him, salvation's come to this house, because he's a son of Abraham too. For the Son of Man came to seek and save the lost.

Putting God's gifts to good use vv11–27

As they were listening to this, he went on to tell a parable, because he was nearing Jerusalem and people were thinking that God's kingdom was to appear without delay. There was once an aristocrat, he said, who went to a far-off land to receive for himself a kingdom, and then return. So he called ten of his servants, gave them ten pounds, and said to them, Trade until I return. But his citizens began to hate him and sent a delegation to him, saying, We don't want this man to reign over us. When he returned, having received the kingdom, he ordered these servants, to whom he'd given the money, to be called before him so that he might know what trading they'd done. The first came before him saying, Lord, your pound has made ten pounds. Good servant, he said to him, well done. Because you've been trustworthy in a very small matter, take control of ten cities. And the second came, saying, Lord, your pound has made five pounds. And to him he said, You, rule over five cities. Then another came, saying, Lord, here's your pound. I've kept it safe in a handkerchief. I was in fear of you because you're a stern man; you seize what you haven't deposited and reap what you haven't sown. He says to him, Scoundrel! Your own words condemn you! You knew I was a stern man, stealing what I didn't deposit, and reaping what I didn't sow. Why then didn't you put my money in the bank, so that on my return I might have collected it with interest? And he said to those standing by, Take the pound from him, and give it to the one who's ten pounds. But Lord, they said to him, he has ten pounds! I tell you, to everyone who has, more will be given; but from the one who has nothing, even what he has will be seized. And as for those enemies of mine who didn't want me to reign over them—bring them here and slaughter them in front of me.

Jesus enters Jerusalem vv28–40

After he had said this, he continued journeying ahead, up to Jerusalem. When he drew near to Bethphage and Bethany, at the hill called the Mount of Olives, he sent on two of his disciples, saying, Go to the village opposite, and as you enter it you'll find a colt tethered there on which nobody's ever sat. Untie it and bring it. If anyone asks you, Why are you untying it? say this: Because the Lord needs it. Those who were sent went and found it just as he had told them. And as they were untying the colt, its owners said to them, why are you untying the colt? And they said, Because the Lord needs it. So they brought it to Jesus, flung their cloaks on the colt, and sat Jesus on it. And as he rode along, they spread their cloaks on the road. When he was getting near (already at the foot of the Mount of Olives), the whole crowd of disciples began to rejoice and praise God with a loud voice for all the mighty works they had seen, saying, ***Blessed is*** the king ***who comes in the name of the Lord!*** Peace in heaven and glory in the highest! But some Pharisees in the crowd said to him, Teacher, rebuke your disciples. But he answered, I tell you, if these shall be silent, the stones will cry out.

Weeping over Jerusalem vv41–44

And when he came close to the city, he wept at the sight of it, saying, If only you knew—on this very day—yes you—the things that make for peace! But now they're hidden from your sight. For the time's coming upon you when your enemies will erect siege works against you, surround you, and hem you in on every side.

And they'll hurl you—and your children with you—to the ground, and they'll not leave one stone standing upon another: for you didn't know the time of your visitation.

Purging the Temple vv45–48

And he went into the temple and began to drive out those who were trading, saying to them, It's written, ***My house shall be a house of prayer,*** but you've made it ***a den of robbers***. And he was teaching in the temple daily. The chief priests, legal experts and the elders of the people, were looking for a way to kill him, but could not find the means to do so, because all the people were hanging on his words.

Chapter Twenty

The authority of Jesus questioned vv1–8

Once when Jesus was in the temple, teaching and proclaiming the good news to the people, the chief priests and legal experts and the elders were present. They spoke, saying to him, Tell us, by what authority do you do these things, or who gave you this authority? He answered them, I'll also ask you a question. Tell me, was John's baptism from heaven or from men? They debated among themselves, saying, If we say from heaven, he'll say, Why didn't you believe him? If we say from men, all the people will stone us because they're sure that John was a prophet. So they answered that they did not know from where. Then Jesus said to them, So neither will I tell you by what authority I do these things.

Wicked tenants vv9–18

And he began to tell the people this parable. A man planted a vineyard, leased it to tenants and went abroad for a long time. Eventually, he sent a servant so that they'd give him some of the produce of the vineyard. But the tenants beat him and sent him away empty-handed. So he sent another servant; but they beat him as well and treated him disgracefully. He then sent a third; but this one they also wounded and cast him out. So the master of the vineyard said, What'll I do? I'll send my dear son; perhaps they'll respect him. But when the tenants saw him, they began to discuss among themselves, saying, This is the heir. Let's kill him, so the inheritance will be ours. So after they drove him out of the vineyard, they murdered him. What then will the master of the vineyard do? He'll come and destroy those tenants and hand over the vineyard to others. When they heard this, they said, Surely not! But he looked at them intently and said, Then what's the meaning of this scripture, ***The stone rejected by the builders has become the cornerstone?*** Everyone who falls on that stone will be broken to pieces; and it'll crush anyone on whom it falls.

Paying tax to Caesar vv19–26

The legal experts and the chief priests were planning to seize him, there and then, because they knew that he spoke this parable against them, but they were afraid of the people. So they kept him under surveillance and sent out spies who pretended to be sincere, so that they might catch him out in his speech. In this way they could hand him over to the jurisdiction and authority of the governor. So they asked him, Teacher, we know that what you say is right, and you're impartial, and truly teach God's way. Is it lawful to pay tribute to Caesar or not? But he saw through their trickery and said to them, Show me a coin. Whose image and inscription does it have? Caesar's, they said. So he said to them, Then give to Caesar what belongs to Caesar, and to God what belongs to God. And they could not (with the people present) catch him out in anything he said, but were forced into silence, astonished by his reply.

Questions about the resurrection vv27–40

And some Sadducees came, who say there is no resurrection. They asked him a question, saying, Teacher, Moses wrote for us, ***If any one's***

brother dies, leaves a wife, and is childless, his brother should marry the wife and rear children for his brother. Now there were seven brothers, and the first married her and died childless. Then the second married her, and the third, and so on, until all seven had married her—but left no children. Eventually the woman also died. Now at the resurrection, whose wife will the woman be, since all seven had married her? And Jesus said to them, The children of this age marry, and are given in marriage; but those deemed worthy of sharing in that age, and in the resurrection from the dead, won't marry or be given in marriage, for they can no longer die—for they're like angels and sons of God, since they share in the resurrection. Even Moses showed that the dead are raised, in the scripture about the bush, where he calls ***the Lord, the God of Abraham, and the God of Isaac, and the God of Jacob***. For he's not the God of the dead, but of the living. In him they're all alive! At this, some of the legal experts responded, Teacher, well said! And they no longer dared to question him.

Who is David's son? vv41–47

And he said to them, How can they say that the Messiah is David's son? For David himself says in the book of Psalms, ***The Lord says to my Lord, Sit down at my right hand, until I make your enemies your footstool for your feet***. Therefore David calls him Lord, so how can he be his son?

Beware of lawyers vv45—47

In the hearing of all the people he said to his disciples, Beware of the legal experts, who like to parade in long robes, and love to be greeted in the marketplaces, and who take the best seats in the synagogues, and places of honour at feasts, who devour the houses of widows, and say long prayers for show. They'll incur the most severe judgment.

Chapter Twenty-One

Out of her poverty vv1–4

And he looked up and saw the wealthy putting their gifts into the offering box. Then he saw a poor widow putting in two small coins. And he said, Truly, I tell you, this destitute widow has put in more than all the rest. For they've all given gifts out of their surplus, but she in her wretchedness has put in her entire livelihood.

The destruction of the temple foretold vv5–9

And while some of them were talking about the temple, and how it was adorned with beautiful stones and votive offerings, he said, As for these stones you're looking at: the time will come when not a stone will be left upon a stone that won't be torn down. And they asked him, saying, Teacher, when will this happen? And what'll be the sign of these things happening? And he said, Watch out that you're not led astray, for many will come in my name, saying *EGO EIMI—I* AM, and, The time has come! Don't go after them. When you hear of wars and insurrections, don't be alarmed, because these things must first take place, but the end won't follow immediately.

Wars and terrors to come vv10–19

Then he began to say to them, Nation will be raised against nation, and kingdom against kingdom. Everywhere there'll be massive earthquakes, famines, pandemics, terrors and mighty signs from heaven. But before all this, they'll lay hands on you, persecute you and deliver you to synagogues and prisons. And you'll be brought before kings and governors because of my name. This will be your chance to bear witness. Settle in your hearts not to mount a defence in advance. I myself will give you words and wisdom which none of your opponents will be able to withstand or contradict. You'll even be handed over by parents, brothers, relatives and friends, and they'll kill some of you. On account of my name everyone'll hate you.

But not a hair of your head will perish. By your endurance you'll gain your souls.

The fall of Jerusalem foretold vv20–24

And when you see Jerusalem surrounded by armies, you'll know that its desolation is near. Then let those in Judea—flee to the mountains, those inside the city—escape, and let those in the countryside—keep away! For these are days of vengeance, to fulfil all that's written. Woe to pregnant women or those nursing infants in those days! For there'll be great distress in the land and wrath against this people. For they'll fall by the edge of the sword and be carried off captive to all nations, and Jerusalem will be trampled underfoot by pagans—until the times of the Gentiles are fulfilled.

The coming of the Son of Man vv25–28

And there'll be signs in sun, moon and stars, and turmoil on earth among nations, anxiety at the roaring and surging of sea and waves. People will faint with fear and foreboding of what's coming upon the world. For ***the powers of heaven*** will be shaken. And then they'll see

the Son of Man coming in a cloud with power and great glory. Now when these things start to happen, straighten up, raise your heads, for your redemption's near.

The parable of the fig tree vv29–33

And he told them a parable. Look at the fig tree—all the trees in fact. As soon as their leaves appear, you see and know for sure that summer's almost here. So it is when you see these things happening you know that the kingdom of God is near. Truly, I tell you, this generation will certainly not pass away until all these things happen. Heaven and earth will pass away, but my words won't pass away.

Be on your guard vv34–38

Be on guard, so that carousing, drunkenness and worldly cares don't weigh down your hearts—so that day won't surprise you, like a trap. For it'll come upon all who live on the face of the whole world. But stay awake, at all times—praying for the strength to escape all that's going to happen, and to stand before the Son of Man. And each day he was in the temple teaching, but at night he went out and stayed on the hill called Olivet. And in the early morning, all the people would come to him in the temple to hear him.

Chapter Twenty-Two

The plot to kill Jesus vv1–6

Now the feast of Unleavened Bread, known as Passover, was imminent. The chief priests and legal experts were looking to find a way of putting him to death, because they were in fear of the people. Then Satan entered Judas, called Iscariot, one of the twelve. He went out and plotted with the chief priests and officers how he might hand him over to them. They were pleased, and agreed to give him money. He consented, and kept looking for an opportunity (when the crowd was not around) to hand him over to them.

Celebrating the Passover vv7–13

So the day of Unleavened Bread dawned, when the Passover lamb was to be slaughtered.

And he sent Peter and John saying, Go, make preparations for us to eat the Passover. They said to him, Where do you want us to get it ready? He said to them, When you've entered the city a man carrying a jar of water will meet you. Follow him to the house he's going to, and you're to say to the house owner, The teacher asks you, Where's the guest room I'm to eat the Passover with my disciples? He'll show you a large furnished upper room—prepare it there. So off they went and found it exactly as he had told them; and they prepared the Passover.

The first communion vv14–23

At the appointed hour, he sat at table with the apostles. And he said to them, How greatly I've longed to eat this Passover with you before I suffer. For I tell you, never again will I eat it until it's fulfilled in the kingdom of God. Then he took a cup, and after giving thanks, he said, Take this, and share it among yourselves; for I'm telling you, from now on I'll not drink the fruit of the vine until the kingdom of God comes. Then he took the bread, and after giving thanks, broke it, and gave it to them, saying, This is my body, given for you—do this in memory of me.

And after they had eaten, he did the same with the cup, saying, This cup, poured out for you, is the new covenant in my blood. However—look—the hand of the betrayer's with me on the table. For the Son of Man goes as it's been ordained—but woe to that one by whom he's betrayed. Then they began to question one another as to which of them could be about to do this.

Who is the greatest? vv24–30

Then a quarrel broke out among them—which of them should be seen to be the greatest. But he said to them, The kings of the gentiles lord it over them, and those in authority call themselves benefactors—but not in your case. No, the greatest must become like the youngest, and the leader like the servant. For who's greater, the one who dines or the waiter? Isn't it the one who dines? Yet I'm among you as the waiter. You're the ones who've stood by me in my trials. And I assign to you—as my father's assigned to me—a kingdom; so that you may eat and drink at my table in my kingdom, and sit on thrones judging the twelve tribes of Israel.

Peter's denial foretold vv31–34

Simon, Simon, watch out; Satan's demanded all of you—to sift you all like wheat. But I've prayed for you, Simon, that your faith won't buckle. And when you've turned back, strengthen your brothers. But he said to him, Lord, I'm ready to go with you to prison and to death! I tell you, Peter, he replied—the rooster won't cry out today before you deny—three times—that you know me.

Two swords vv35–38

And he said to them, When I sent you out with no purse, bag or sandals, did you lack anything? Not at all, they replied. And he said to them, But now the one who has a purse, let him take it—and a bag too. And whoever's without a sword must sell his coat and buy one. For I tell you, this scripture must be fulfilled in me, namely ***He was classed among outlaws.*** For what's written about me has its fulfilment. And they said to him, Lord, here's two swords. That's enough, he replied.

Jesus prays on the Mount of Olives vv39–46

So he went out, and as was his habit, went to the Mount of Olives; and his disciples followed him. And when they reached the spot he said to them, Pray you don't succumb to temptation. Then he left them about a stone's throw away and knelt and prayed, saying, Father, take this cup from me; yet not my will but yours be done. And an angel from heaven appeared strengthening him. In agony he was praying more earnestly, and his sweat was like great drops of blood falling to the ground. Then he arose from prayer, and when he came to his disciples, he found them sleeping for sorrow. And he said to them, Why are you sleeping? Get up and pray, that you don't succumb to temptation.

Jesus betrayed and arrested vv47–53

While he was still speaking, look, a crowd—and the one called Judas, one of the twelve, came leading them. He came up to Jesus to kiss him. But Jesus said to him, Judas, would you betray the Son of Man with a kiss? And when those around him saw what was going to happen, they said, Lord, shall we strike with a sword?

And one of them struck a bondservant of the High Priest with a sword and cut off his right ear. But Jesus said, Enough of this! And he touched the ear and healed him. Then Jesus said to the chief priests, temple staff and elders, who had come out to him, Have you come out against a robber with swords and clubs? When I was with you day after day in the temple, you never laid hands on me. But this hour is yours and the power of darkness.

Peter denies Jesus vv54–62

They arrested him and led him away, bringing him to the high priest's house; and Peter was following at a distance. And when they had kindled a fire in the middle of the courtyard and sat down together, Peter sat down among them. And a servant girl saw him sitting there at the fire. She looked closely at him and said, This fellow was also with him. But he denied it, saying, Woman, I don't know him. A little later someone else saw him and said, You're also one of them. But Peter said, No man, I'm not! About an hour later someone else insisted, saying, This one was with him for sure, for he's also a Galilean. But Peter said, Man, I don't know what you're talking about. And suddenly, as he was still speaking, the rooster crowed. And the Lord turned and looked at Peter. And Peter remembered the word of the Lord, how he said to him, Before the rooster crows today, you'll deny me three times. And he went outside and wept bitterly.

Jesus mocked and tried vv63–71

And the men holding Jesus in custody began to mock and beat him. They blindfolded him and kept asking him, saying, Prophesy! Who hit you? And they kept uttering many other things, blaspheming him. At daybreak, the elders of the people, both chief priests and legal experts assembled, and they led him to their council, saying, If you're the Messiah, tell us. But he said to them, If I tell you, you won't believe; and if I question you, you won't answer. But from now on ***the Son of Man*** will be ***seated at the right hand*** of God's power. And they all said, Are you the Son of God, then? He answered them, You yourselves say that ***I am***. Then they said, What further evidence do we need? We have heard it ourselves from his own lips.

Chapter Twenty-Three

Jesus before Pilate vv1–5

Then the entire multitude of them got up and brought him before Pilate. They began to accuse him, saying, We've found this man inciting our nation and encouraging them not to pay tribute to Caesar, and claiming that he's the Messiah, a king. Pilate asked him, saying, Are you the king of the Jews? And he replied, So you say. Then Pilate said to the chief priests and the crowds, I find this man not guilty. But they kept insisting, saying, He stirs up the people with his teaching throughout Judea, from Galilee, where he began, even to here.

Jesus before Herod vv6–17

When Pilate heard this he asked whether this man was a Galilean. On learning that he was under Herod's authority, he sent him over to Herod who was also in Jerusalem at that time. When Herod saw Jesus he was pleased, because he had wanted to see him for a long time, for he kept on hearing about him, and hoped to see some sign being done by him. So he questioned him at length, but Jesus said nothing to him in reply. And the chief priests and legal experts stood by, vigorously accusing him. And Herod and his soldiers poured contempt and mockery on him; and putting a sumptuous robe on him, they returned him to Pilate. So on that very day Herod and Pilate became friends; for previously there was enmity between them. Pilate then summoned the chief priests, the rulers and the people, and he said to them, You brought this man to me as someone who has been inciting the people. Look, I've examined him before you, and I've not found him guilty of any of the charges you made against him. Neither did Herod, because he sent him back to us. And it's plain he's done nothing to deserve death. I will therefore punish and release him.

Jesus condemned vv18–25

But they were all crying out, saying, Away with this man! Release Barabbas for us (he was a man imprisoned for insurrection in the city, and for murder). Pilate, wanting to release Jesus, addressed them again. But they kept shouting, Crucify him! Crucify! He asked them a third time, Why? What wrong has he done? I've found him not guilty of a capital crime—so I'll punish and release him. Then with loud shrieks they kept on demanding that he be crucified, and their voices prevailed. So Pilate gave in to their wishes. He released the man they had been asking for (the one who had been thrown into prison for insurrection and murder) and handed Jesus over, according to their wishes.

The crucifixion of Jesus vv26–43

As they led him away, they grabbed a certain Simon, a Cyrenian, who was up from the country, and they laid the cross on him to carry behind Jesus. And a great throng of people was following him, including women who were beating their breasts and wailing for him. But turning to them, Jesus said, Daughters of Jerusalem, don't weep for me, but for yourselves and for your children. For I tell you, the day is coming when it'll be said, Blessed are the barren, and the womb that never gave birth, and the breasts that never gave suck. Then they'll begin *to* ***say to the mountains, Fall on us, and to the hills, Cover us***. For if they do all this when the wood is green, what'll happen when it's dry? Two others—criminals—were led away to be put to death with him. When they reached the place known as the Skull, they crucified him there with the criminals, one on his right and the other on his left. And Jesus said, Father, forgive them; for they don't know what they're doing. ***And dividing his clothing among them, they threw dice.*** And the people stood by and looked on. But the rulers were sneering, saying, He saved others—let him save himself if he's the Messiah, God's Chosen One! The soldiers also mocked him, coming up and offering sour wine, and saying, If you're the King of the Jews, save yourself! There was also an inscription over him: This is the King of the Jews. One of the hanged criminals kept blaspheming him, saying, Aren't you the Messiah? Save yourself and us! But the other rebuked him, saying, Don't you fear God, since you're under the same sentence? It's justice for us, because we're only getting what our deeds merit; but this man's done nothing wrong. And he said, Jesus, remember me when you come into your kingdom. And he said to him, Truly I tell you, you'll be with me in paradise today.

The death of Jesus vv44–49

Now about noon, until three o'clock, there was darkness over the whole land. The sun was eclipsed and the temple curtain torn in two. Then Jesus said with a loud voice, Father, ***I commit my spirit into your hands.*** After saying this, he breathed his last. When the centurion saw what had happened, he praised God, saying, Clearly this man was innocent. And when all the crowds that had gathered for this sight saw what had taken place, they returned home beating their breasts. All his acquaintances, and the women who had followed him from Galilee, stood at a distance watching all this.

Jesus interred vv50–56

And look, there was man called Joseph from the town of Arimathea, a member of the council, a good and upright man, for he did not consent to their plan of action. He was waiting for the kingdom of God. This man went to Pilate and asked for the body of Jesus. And he took it down, wrapped it in linen, and laid it in a tomb carved out of rock where no one had ever been laid. It was the day of Preparation and the sabbath was imminent. The women who had come with him from Galilee followed and noted the tomb and saw how his body was interred. And they returned and prepared spices and ointments, and rested on the sabbath, according to the commandment.

Chapter Twenty-Four

The resurrection of Jesus vv1–12

Now early on Sunday morning they went to the tomb, taking the spices they had prepared. And they found the stone rolled away from the tomb, but when they went in, they did not see the body of the Lord Jesus. While this perplexed them, behold, two men in gleaming robes stood beside them. They were startled and bowed their faces to the ground, but the men said to them, Why do you look for the living among the dead? He isn't here. He's risen! Remember what he told you while he was still in Galilee. The Son of Man must be handed over to sinful men and be crucified, and on the third day rise. Then they recalled his words. So they returned from the tomb and reported all this to the eleven and the others. The women were Mary Magdalene, Joanna and Mary the mother of James, and the other women with them. They kept telling all this to the apostles, but their story seemed to them an idle fantasy, and they would not believe them. But Peter got up and ran to the tomb; he stooped down and sees only the linen wrappings, and he took himself off, astonished by what had happened.

The road to Emmaus vv13–35

And look, on this very same day two of them were going to a village called Emmaus, about seven miles from Jerusalem, and they were talking together about all that that happened. While they were talking and discussing with each other, Jesus himself drew near and began to walk with them. But their eyes were kept from recognising him. And he said to them, What's this you're discussing with each other as you walk along? They stood still, downcast. Then one of them, named Cleopas, said to him, Are you the only one in Jerusalem who doesn't know about all the things that have being gone on there lately? And he said, What things? And they said to him, About Jesus of Nazareth, a prophet mighty in deed and word before God and all the people. How our priests and leaders handed him over to be condemned to death and crucified him. But we—we had hoped that he himself was the one to redeem Israel. Yes, and today—this is the third day since these things happened—and some of the women in our group astonished us. They were at the tomb early. When they didn't find his body they came back saying that they'd seen a vision of angels who told them that Jesus was alive. Some of our group went to the tomb and found it just as the women had said, but didn't see him. And he said to them. What fools you are, and slow to believe in your heart all that the prophets have spoken. Wasn't it necessary for the Messiah to suffer all this before entering into his glory? And starting from Moses and all the prophets he expounded to them what the scriptures said about himself. So they came near to the village where they were going, and he made as if to go further, but they urged him strongly, saying, Stay with us, because it's almost evening and it's getting late. So he went in to stay with them. Now when he had sat down he took bread, blessed and broke it, and gave it to them. And their eyes were opened, and they recognised him; and he vanished from their sight. And they said to each other, Wasn't our heart on fire while he was speaking to us on the road, while he was opening the scriptures to us? And there and then they got up and went back to Jerusalem. They found the eleven, and those gathered together with them, saying, It's true, the Lord has risen and has appeared to Simon! And they themselves began to explain what had happened on the road, and how, by breaking bread, he was made known to them.

The risen Christ appears to his disciples vv36–49

As they were discussing these things, Jesus himself stood among them and says, Peace be upon you. Frightened and startled, they thought they were seeing a ghost. And he said to them, Why are you alarmed? Why do questions arise in your heart? Look at my hands and my feet; see—it's really me. Touch me and see—a ghost doesn't have flesh and bones as you see that I have. And having said this, he showed them his hands and feet. And as they were still disbelieving for joy and wondering, he said to them, Have you anything here to eat? So they gave him a piece of grilled fish and he took it and ate in front of them. And he said to them, These are my words that I spoke when I was still with you, that everything written about me in the Law of Moses and the Prophets and the Psalms must be fulfilled. Then he opened their mind to understand the scriptures, and said to them, Thus it's written: the Messiah must suffer and rise from the dead on the third day, and repentance and forgiveness of sins be proclaimed to all nations, starting from Jerusalem. You're witnesses of these things. And look, I'm sending upon you my Father's promise. But stay in the city until you are clothed with power from on high.

The Ascension of Jesus vv50–53

Then he led them out as far as Bethany, and with uplifted hands he blessed them. While he blessed them he was separated from them and was received into heaven. And they worshipped him and returned to Jerusalem with great joy, and remained continually in the temple praising God.

Amen.

John

Introduction

Since the late second century AD the gospel of John has been regarded as the most spiritual and theologically sophisticated of the four Evangelists. However its mystical overtones, and explicit attribution of divinity to Jesus of Nazareth, have, since the nineteenth century in particular, led to it being neglected or spurned as a credible historical source for the life of Christ. Aside from doubts regarding his deity, the veracity of his miracles and the authenticity of the deep, almost philosophical inflexion of his teaching, there is also the more mundane question of authorship: for the gospel purports to be an eyewitness account of Jesus' public career. But how could an illiterate fisherman who had hung out with Jesus in the late twenties of the first century AD, be still alive at the close of that century, writing a rarefied meditation on the life of his Master, while somehow also finding time to pen an apocalyptic fantasy, known as the Book of Revelation (to say nothing of letters he wrote to churches over which he appears to have had some kind of pastoral oversight)? Whence his education? Whence his familiarity with Greek notions, such as that of the *Logos,* which John translates as "Word," but which can also refer to the "reason" or "rationale" behind the cosmos? And how could he have taken the giant intellectual leap of identifying this same *Logos* with a peasant from Nazareth in Galilee? Furthermore, what is the likelihood of an uneducated fisherman coming up with the idea that God became flesh incarnate—a notion that was as alien to Jewish thought as it was blasphemous? One might also ask if such an individual would have had facility in speaking or writing Greek, as we must assume that John did if he penned the fourth gospel? There is also the question of how John, a Galilean fisherman, was known by the high priest—and sufficiently well known to be granted access into the inner court of the high priest's lodgings, where Jesus himself was being held prisoner prior to his trial (John 18:16). These are formidable questions, to be sure. But they are not insurmountable. Although we do not have all the details about the origins and background to the gospel that we might like, it is still possible to say something about the author and the possible date in which he wrote the gospel that bears his name.

The best place to address these issues is with the earliest physical evidence that we have regarding the gospel itself. Papyrus 52 (in the John Rylands Library, Manchester) contains the earliest fragment of John (i.e. ch18: 31-33). This was found in Egypt, and has been dated on palaeographic evidence to as early 120AD. It takes little imagination to see how this might have been a copy of an earlier copy which originated in neighbouring Palestine. If John had been an older teenager when he first met Jesus, it would not be beyond the bounds of possibility that he might still have been alive in the late first century, as a man in his eighties. However we need not assume this. Nor need we paint ourselves into a corner trying to defend a date for the composition of the fourth gospel. Why have scholars been so insistent that John was written late? Two reasons stand out: the depth of theological reflection about Christ that appears to transcend what we find in the synoptic gospels. There is also the fact that in so many ways John's narrative differs from the other three, not only as regards new material that we don't find in the synoptic gospels (e.g. John's lengthy teaching chapters centred on the Last Supper, chs. 13-17), but also in the way he can take up material common to Matthew, Mark and Luke, and imbue it with a new or deeper significance (e.g. Jesus' teaching about the Trinity, his understanding of being "sent" as implying his "pre-existence," or the locating of the cleansing of the temple near the start of Jesus' ministry). All this, it is assumed, required a longer period of theological gestation before the author of John could share his fresh perspective on Christ's life, death and resurrection. This may be true. But it need not imply that John was written between 90 or 100AD. Many similar insights about the deity of Christ can be found, for example, in the writings of Paul written much earlier in the 40s to mid–60s AD (e.g. Phil 2:5-11; Rom 1:1-4). The liberal Cambridge scholar, Bishop J. A. T. Robinson, argued that the whole of the New Testament might feasibly have been written before the destruction of the temple in 70AD (*Re-dating the New Testament,* 1976), and that John contained some traditions about Jesus that were earlier than the synoptic gospels (*The Priority of John,* 1984). His point, at any rate, is that there is no indisputable evidence that John was written late or that it could not have been produced much earlier than many contemporary scholars suggest. Thus we are not obliged to entertain the idea that an old disciple, anywhere between eighty to a hundred years old, penned the gospel. A disciple of similar age to Jesus would have been seventy when Jerusalem fell to the Romans in 70AD. If, as we might imagine, Jesus' disciples were younger than Jesus, then in 70AD they might have been aged about sixty years—an eminently reasonable age for a healthy individual to assume the task of writing up apostolic memoirs about the Messiah. Moreover, if John, the "beloved disciple," had been an older teenager during Christ's ministry (also conceivable), he would have been younger still—perhaps in his mid-50s by 70AD. This is worth bearing in mind, because the Book of Revelation, traditionally attributed to the author of the fourth gospel, has central to its message the destruction of the temple in Jerusalem, and the creation of a new heavens and a new earth, with God and Christ becoming the immanent, divine presence in the New Jerusalem. Its detailed emphasis on the replacement of the old religious cult in Jerusalem would make sense if John, incarcerated on the island of Patmos for preaching the gospel, had heard about the tragedy that had befallen the Jews and was motivated by the Spirit (as he claims he was) to give a godly perspective on the future course of history and the fate of God's people. Assuming that Revelation was written in the aftermath of the sack of Jerusalem, this might reasonably push back the composition of the fourth gospel to sometime during the 60s AD. We cannot, of course, be certain about this, but I have at least tried to show how such a scenario might be feasible, and how the "beloved disciple" might have composed his gospel within the lifespan of a first century Jew prior to 70AD.

Here we should note that earliest title of the fourth gospel was simply, "According to John." Whoever this individual was, there was clearly no need to identify him any further, no more than there was a need to identify or explain who Matthew, Mark or Luke were. For clearly these people were established figures in the first Christian communities to which they belonged, and did not need to be distinguished from other individuals who might have born the same name. Their names carried sufficient weight and authority on their own, such that people would have known immediately who they were. The apostle John, the son of Zebedee, referred to in the synoptic gospels, is known as the "beloved disciple" throughout the fourth gospel. This individual, according to a passage in the final chapter of John, witnessed first hand Jesus' ministry, death and resurrection, and also, we are informed, wrote a narrative about it in the vein of the other gospels, even though his style and content was markedly different in places, as I've already mentioned. It is on the basis of his claim to be an eyewitness of Jesus' ministry that "we know that his testimony is true" (21:24-25). No other gospel comes as clean about the identity of the author as does John. Matthew contains no self-reference; Mark tells us nothing about himself; Luke, while upfront about being a missionary companion of Paul's, is coy about giving personal details (such as the fact that he was as doctor by profession). What is striking about John is the claim that he was Jesus' closest disciple. If indeed he was, then this put him in a unique position to tell us things about Jesus that might not have been known to, or were perhaps less understood or appreciated by, the other Evangelists. It also opens up the possibility that, contrary to what many biblical critics have claimed over the past two hundred years, that John might have reliable data about Jesus—in particular about his messianic consciousness and self-understanding as God's Son. For these are very much at the theological heart of his gospel. I shall return to this presently.

The conviction that John—the son of Zebedee, or the "beloved disciple"—was the author of the gospel that bears his name was as good as universal in the post-apostolic era. Between the mid-second and mid-third century (roughly between 150-250AD), the belief that John was the author of the fourth gospel was universally upheld by such notables as: Irenaeus, Justin Martyr, Clement of Alexandria, Theophilus, Bishop of Antioch, Tertullian, Origen, as well as by the author of the Muratonian Canon (the earliest known list of writings that made up the New Testament). In fact no other person is identified as the author of John's gospel in the post-apostolic period. In the absence of any better evidence (e.g. that the gospel was written by an unknown John, or perhaps by an individual known as John the Presbyter) it makes sense to work with the notion that the fourth gospel was linked with somebody who was an eyewitness of Jesus' ministry.

What then of the gospel itself? What is it exactly? What are its contents? We may loosely identify it with the genre of Graeco-Roman biography, which I've touched upon more fully in my introduction to Luke. But it is not simply biography. None of the gospels are. In John 20:31 the author states that his aim in writing is to encourage Christians to *"hold fast to your belief that Jesus is the Messiah, the Son of God, and that by believing you may have life in his name."* How does he set about achieving this objective? Matthew begins his gospel with a genealogy that links Jesus with King David. Mark opens his message by rooting the good news about Jesus in the prophetic writings. Luke starts his narrative with the story of the incarnation. John begins on an altogether different scale. He sets the tone for his gospel by stating at the outset that Jesus, the Word, pre-existed, was with God in the beginning, and was himself "God," the creator of all things. By this John attests that Jesus is wrapped up in the meaning of the word "God." Throughout his gospel emphasis is placed on Jesus' relationship as Son of God to his Father. John tells us that Jesus expresses the will and mind of God. God is seen to be speaking, working through Jesus, both in word and deed. To meet Jesus is to encounter God, says John; in the Son's humanity the face of the Father is revealed, his flesh and blood existence among us. According to John, it will no longer be possible to speak of God without reference to Jesus. To be ignorant of Jesus is to be ignorant of God. We can only know God's Fatherhood or pray to him through the Son. Anything that God has to say to us, whether regarding his salvific purposes for mankind, the promise of the Holy Spirit, the meaning of "eternal life," the threat of judgement, are solely revealed in the person of his Son, Jesus of Nazareth, the Messiah. As I stressed in the introductions to Matthew and Mark in particular, the Evangelists knew that Jesus was divine. It is just that John articulates this truth in a startling, arresting fashion that draws out profound, cosmic-shattering implications. So while John takes us on a journey that coheres with the synoptic outline of Christ's ministry of preaching, teaching, healing and miracle working, he leads us deeper into the significance of Jesus' words and deeds, which are more implicit than explicit in the other Evangelists. John calls them "signs." As with a road sign, a sign points beyond itself. Thus a signpost for Dublin or Wembley Stadium signifies a direction to such and such a place, but not the destination itself. In John's gospel Jesus performs seven signs: turning water into wine, healing a royal official's son, curing a paralytic, feeding five thousand, walking on water, restoring sight to a blind man, raising Lazarus from the dead. John wants us to see in these a deeper significance than just physical healing, nature miracles, or the resuscitation of a dead corpse. The seven signs disclose God's saving presence and activity among his people in the person of his well beloved son. But they also flood light on the reader, demanding critical self-examination. For John is not merely a chronicler of healings or miracles, but wants rather to challenge his readers to discern under the Spirit's guidance whether they themselves stand under God's grace or judgment. For one of the most cutting truths in the fourth gospel is that some who imagine they are God's people, or disciples of Jesus, are not in fact, but rather are children of the devil (John 8:44). Thus Jesus did not come into the world to condemn the world, says John, because it was already condemned. Humanity stands under divine judgment for preferring light to darkness and for pursuing evil deeds. The seven signs invite us to square up to the reality of God present and at work in his Son, the only one through whom salvation and deliverance can be found. When Jesus turns water into wine we are given a foretaste of the marriage of heaven and earth. The healing of a royal official's son, a man paralysed for thirty eight years and the restoration of sight to a man born blind, point beyond Jesus' thaumaturgical powers to his capacity to deal with the deeper disease, paralysis and blindness that sin brings into our lives. In the feeding of the five thousand and walking on water he assumes the mantle of Yahweh in feeding Israel in the desert and demonstrating his control over nature and the forces of chaos. Ultimately, in raising Lazarus back to life, Jesus signposts his own death and resurrection, and calls us to trust him in the face of our own mortality and the Day of Judgment. For John, what we believe about Jesus is crucial to our salvation. Hence also his seven "I am" sayings, that draw us into the mystery of Christ, beyond the superficial level of those who misinterpret Jesus by hailing him as a prophet, moral teacher or healer, or for that matter, at the other extreme, a fraud or blasphemer. Instead, John invites us to ponder Christ's claims and how he realised them in people's lives: I am the bread of life, the light of the world, the door of the sheep, the resurrection and the life, the good shepherd, the way, the truth and the life, the true vine. Only through experience could such claims be validated. And this is the point about the fourth gospel. John does not invest in theory or abstraction, like the Gnostics would later. Christ's claims are experiential, or existential. The claim that Jesus is God incarnate is an extravagant one, and can only be meaningful if somehow people truly encounter the divine in his presence. "My Lord and my God!" cries doubting Thomas after he encounters the risen Lord (John 20:28). But this is only possible through the Holy Spirit who will come to indwell, comfort and teach the disciples, when Jesus is finally exalted to glory (John 16:5-16). The seven "I am" sayings relate also to our deeper, inner needs and dispositions. Jesus satiates our hunger for spiritual reality; he is the light in the darkness of our sin and world; the door through which we find nourishment and protection, and shepherd-like guidance throughout our days; he is the way to God, the truth about God, and God's very life within us, through the Holy-sanctifying-setting-apart-Spirit; he is the true vine, no less, by means of which we may draw on his endless, illimitable resources in order to flourish and bear fruit for God. No gospel writer so explores the nature of our union with Christ, as profoundly as does John. (It is a mark of the significance of this motif of "union" in John that the seventeen year old Karl Marx composed an essay in 1835 entitled "The Union of the Faithful with Christ," based on John 15.)

Perhaps the idea that John came from priestly stock should be explored more fully, not just to explain his priestly forename, or his acquaintance with the high priest in Jerusalem, but also to deepen our understanding of his theological concerns about God dwelling on earth in human form (also the climactic theme of the Book of Revelation). For John, Jesus is the new temple and Passover lamb, as well as being the high priest who intercedes to the Father on behalf of his redeemed people (John 17). When Jesus dies, he dies as the Passover lambs are being sacrificed in the temple. His is truly a Passover sacrifice—a sacrifice that will end all blood sacrifices (the Christian Emperor Theodosius finally banned animal sacrifices in the fourth century AD). John also has a lot to say about how Jesus brought to fulfilment the meaning and significance of other key Jewish feasts, including Tabernacles and Hanukkah, known also as "the Festival of Lights" (cf. John 8:12, where Jesus describes himself as "the light of the world"). But it is John's ultimate concern that his readers experience these truths in their own lives, and so be strengthened and encouraged to keep on "believing" that Jesus is who he says he is—"the Messiah, the Son of God." To this extent, then, while being the most theologically demanding of the four, John's gospel is conspicuously the most practical.

Dr Brendan Devitt

Chapter One

The divinity of Jesus Christ vv1-18

The Word was there right from the start. He was with God—indeed the Word was God. Everything was made through him, and nothing was made apart from him. There was life in him and this life was the light of everyone. The light stands shining in the darkness and the darkness could not smother it.

A man named John was sent by God. He came as a witness to testify to the light so that everyone might believe through him. He himself was not the light but only a witness to it. The true light that illuminates everyone was coming into the world. He was in the world, the world was made by him, but the world never knew him. He came to his own people, but they did not receive him. But to those who did accept him, to those who believed, he gave the right to become children of God. These were born not as a result of physical birth, nor of human choice, or a husband's will, but by the will of God. Now the Word became flesh and lived among us and we were enraptured by his glory, the glory of the one and only Son who came from the Father, brimful of grace and truth.

John testifies about him and cried out saying, This is the one I spoke of when I said, The one who comes after me is ahead of me, because he ranks before me. And out of his fullness we have all received endless grace. Although the law was given by Moses, grace and truth came through Jesus Christ. Nobody has ever seen God, but his one and only Son who comes straight from the Father's heart, he has fully revealed him.

John's testimony vv19-34

Now this is John's witness when the Jews sent priests and Levites from Jerusalem to ask him, Who are you? He made clear, and did not dissemble but said plainly, I'm not the Christ. So they said to him, Well are you Elijah? No, he replied. Are you the Prophet then? No, he answered. Then who are you? they asked, so that we may tell those who sent us. Who do you claim to be? He replied in the words of Isaiah the prophet, I'm ***the voice of one shouting in the desert, make straight the way of the Lord.***

Now among those who had been sent out were some Pharisees. They too examined him and said, If you're neither the Christ, nor Elijah, nor the Prophet how come you're baptising? John said, True, I'm baptising with water, but in your midst stands someone you don't know. Although he comes after me I'm unworthy even to untie the strap of his sandals. All this happened in Bethany on the other side of the Jordan where John was performing baptisms.

The next day John sees Jesus walking towards him and says, Look! There's the lamb of God, he's the one who blots out the world's sin! This is the one I spoke about when I said, There comes after me a man who is greater than me because he ranks before me. I myself didn't know him. But I came baptising with water for this reason: that he might be made known to Israel. And John testified saying, I saw the Spirit come down from heaven as if it were a dove, and alight on him. I myself didn't know him but the one who sent me to baptise with water said to me, On whom you see the Spirit descend and remain, he's the one who baptises with the Holy Spirit. I saw it myself, with my own eyes and I testify that this man is the Son of God.

Jesus' first followers vv35–42

Again the following day John was standing with two of his disciples. And looking intently on Jesus as he walked about John said, Look! There's the lamb of God! So when those two disciples heard him saying this they went after Jesus. Jesus turned around and when he saw them following says, What can I do for you? They replied, Rabbi (which means teacher), where do you live? He says to them, Come and see. So they went and saw where he was staying and remained with him that day because it was four o'clock in the afternoon. It was, in fact, Andrew, Simon Peter's brother, who was one of those who had heard John preach and then followed Jesus. Now the very first thing Andrew did was to find his brother, Simon, and say to him, You'll never guess, we've found the Messiah (which means Christ)! Andrew brought him to Jesus. Jesus gave him a long hard look and said, So, you're Simon, John's son are you? You'll now be known as Cephas (which means Peter).

Jesus calls two more, Philip and Nathanael vv43–51

The next day Jesus decided to go to Galilee where he came across Philip. He says to him, Follow me!

Now Philip hailed from Bethsaida, Andrew and Peter's town. Philip then finds Nathanael and says to him, Wait till you hear, we've found the one that Moses and the prophets wrote about in the law—Jesus, Joseph's son from Nazareth! Nathanael replied, Can anything good come out of Nazareth? Philip answers, Come and see! Now Jesus saw Nathanael coming towards him and says, Lo and behold! An Israelite devoid of cunning! Nathanael says to him, How come you know me? Jesus answered, Before Philip called you while you were sitting under the fig tree I spotted you. Nathanael replied, Rabbi, you're the Son of God, indeed you're the King of Israel! Is it because I told you that I saw you under the fig tree that you believe? said Jesus. You're going to see greater things than this. Let me tell you, you'll see heaven wide open and the angels of God ascending and descending on the Son of Man.

Chapter Two

A sign at a wedding vv1–11

Three days later there was a wedding in Cana, Galilee. The mother of Jesus was there, and Jesus and his disciples had also been invited to the wedding. And when the wine had run out Jesus' mother says to him, All the wine has gone. Then Jesus says to her, Lady, why is that my problem? My hour hasn't arrived yet. Jesus' mother says to the waiters, Whatever he tells you be sure to do it. Now there were six stone water jars standing nearby, used for Jewish purification rites, each able to hold twenty or thirty gallons. So Jesus says to the waiters, Fill them with water. So they filled them to the brim. Then he says to them, Draw some and take it to the master of ceremonies; so they did. When the master of ceremonies tasted the water which had become wine, not knowing where it had come from (although the waiters were in the know), he beckons the bridegroom and says, Everyone serves the best wine first and then when everybody's drunk, the inferior wine, but you've kept back the good wine until now! This, the first of Jesus' signs, was done in Cana, Galilee, and in this way he displayed his glory and his disciples believed in him.

Jesus in Capernaum and in Jerusalem where he purges the temple vv12–25

Then after this Jesus went down to Capernaum together with his mother, brothers and disciples, but only stayed there for a few days. As the Jewish Passover was approaching Jesus went up to Jerusalem. In the temple he came across people selling cattle, sheep and pigeons, as well as money-changers sitting at their tables. Jesus made a whip out of cords and drove them all out of the temple, including the sheep and cattle. And he scattered the coins of the money-changers and overturned their tables. And he addressed those selling pigeons, Get these out of here! Stop making my Father's house a bazaar! Now his disciples remembered that it was written, ***Zeal for my Father's house will utterly consume me.*** So the Jews shot back, What sign can you show us to prove you've a right to do all this? Jesus replied, Destroy this temple and in three days I'll raise it up. The

Jews said, This temple has been in the throes of construction for forty-six years and are you seriously claiming that you can rebuild it in three days? (He was in fact speaking of the temple of his body.) So when he had risen from the dead his disciples remembered that he had said this, and they believed the scriptures and the word that Jesus had spoken.

Now while Jesus was in Jerusalem during Passover time, many put their trust in his name because they all saw the signs he was performing. But Jesus did not trust them because he knew only too well what was in their hearts.

Chapter Three

A night visitor vv1–15

It was after dark when a man called Nicodemus, a prominent Jew, came to Jesus and said to him, Rabbi, we of course know that you're a teacher come from God because no one can do the incredible signs that you do unless God is with him. Jesus replied, I tell you the truth, unless a person is reborn he cannot see the kingdom of God. Nicodemus says, How can an old man be reborn? He cannot enter his mother's womb a second time, can he? Unless, said Jesus, you're well and truly born by water and the Spirit you'll be unable to enter the kingdom of God. Whatever's born of the flesh is flesh; whatever's born of the Spirit is Spirit. Don't be amazed that I said you must be reborn. The wind blows where it wants to and you hear its sound, yet know neither where it's coming from nor where it's going. So it is with everyone born of the Spirit. Nicodemus replied, You can't be serious! Jesus said, Are you a respected teacher in Israel yet can't grasp these things? Be assured, we know what we're on about, we testify to what we've seen, but you people don't accept our witness. If I told you about earthly matters and you don't believe, how then would you believe if I were to tell you of heavenly things? No one's ever gone up into heaven but he who came down from heaven, the Son of Man. And just as Moses lifted up the snake in the desert, so must the Son of Man be raised aloft, so that everyone who trusts in him may have eternal life.

God's love for the world vv16–21

It is because God loved the world so very much that he gave his Son, his only Son, that everyone who has faith in him should not die but have eternal life. For God did not send his Son into the world to judge it, but in order that the world might be saved through him. Whoever has faith in him is not judged, but whoever does not have faith in him has already been condemned because he has not had faith in the name of God's one and only Son. Now this is the verdict, that light has come into the world and people loved darkness rather than light because their behaviour was evil. For everyone who practises wickedness detests the light and dares not come to it for fear his deeds might be exposed; whereas everyone who practises truth comes to the light so it may be plainly seen that their good works are rooted in God.

John testifies about Jesus vv22–36

Afterwards, Jesus and his disciples went into Judea and he remained with them there for a time and continued to baptise. As it happened, John was baptising in Aenon, near Salem, because there was plenty of water there. And folk kept coming to be baptised because John had not yet been thrown into prison. Now a dispute arose between some of John's disciples and a Jew about ritual cleansing. And so they came to John and said to him, Teacher, that man who was with you on the other side of the Jordan, the one you testified about, is baptising and everyone's flocking to him. Listen, said John, nobody can receive anything unless it's given to him from heaven. You yourselves can vouch that I said in no uncertain terms that I'm not the Christ, but the one sent ahead of him. It's the bridegroom who has the bride, right? The best man who's waited around in expectation is overjoyed when he hears the bridegroom's voice. In the same way my joy is perfected. His influence must continue to increase and mine diminish.

The one who comes from above is superior to all; whereas the one from the earth belongs to the earth and speaks in an earthly manner. However, the one who comes from heaven surpasses everyone. He bears witness to what he has seen and heard, yet nobody accepts what he has to say. But whoever has taken his message on board can vouch that God is truthful. Because the one that God has sent speaks God's very words. For God does not give the Spirit in a limited way. The Father loves the Son and has entrusted everything to him. Whoever has faith in the Son has eternal life, but whoever disobeys the Son will not experience life, on the contrary, the wrath of God will continue to dog his steps.

Chapter Four

Discourse at a well vv1–42

Now when Jesus got wind that the Pharisees had heard he was recruiting and baptising even more followers than John (although Jesus did not actually baptise but his disciples did), he left Judea and once more headed for Galilee. This meant he had to go through Samaria. So he comes then to a Samaritan town called Sychar (which was near the piece of ground that Jacob gave to his son, Joseph). Jacob's well was there. Exhausted from his journey, Jesus sat down by the well. It was about midday.

Along comes a Samaritan woman to draw water. Jesus says to her, Give me a drink (because the disciples had gone off to the town to buy food). The Samaritan woman says to him, How come you, a Jew for goodness sake, are asking for a drink from me a Samaritan woman? (For Jews have nothing to do with Samaritans.) Jesus said to her, If only you'd known God's gift and who it is who's saying to you, Give me a drink, you would've asked him and he would've given you fresh flowing water. Really, sir? says the woman, but you don't even have a bucket and the well's deep! So where are you going to get this fresh flowing water of yours? Come off it, you aren't greater than our father Jacob are you, who gave us the well and drank from it himself with his sons and his flocks? Everyone, said Jesus, who drinks this water will be thirsty again. But whoever drinks the water I give will thirst no more. The water I give will become an inner fountain of water bubbling up to eternal life.

I tell you what, says Jesus, go and call your husband and come back here. The woman said to him, Actually, I don't have a husband. You're right, says Jesus, you've had five and the man you're living with now isn't your husband. You speak the truth! The woman says to him, So you're a prophet, sir. Our fathers worshipped on this mountain but you Jews say that it's in Jerusalem where worship should really take place. Believe me, woman, says Jesus, the time is coming when you'll worship the Father neither on this mountain nor in Jerusalem. You Samaritans worship in ignorance; we Jews worship with knowledge because salvation comes from the Jews. But, listen, the hour's coming and is already here when true worshippers will worship the Father in spirit and truth—these are the kind of worshippers God wants. God is Spirit, so we must worship him in spirit and truth. The woman says to him, I know that the Messiah, called Christ, is coming and whenever he comes he'll explain everything to us. That's me, says Jesus, the very one who's speaking to you right now.

Just then his disciples came back and were amazed to see him talking to a woman, but no one dared ask, What do you want from her? Or, Why are you talking to her? The woman left her water jar and went off to the town and says to one and all, Come and see a man who's told me everything I've ever done! Surely this can't be the Messiah, can it? The people left the town and began to make their way to Jesus.

Meanwhile the disciples were pressing him saying, Teacher, eat for heaven's sake! But he said, I've food to eat that you don't know about. The disciples began to say among themselves, Nobody's brought him anything to eat, have they? Jesus says, This is my food: to obey God and complete his work. People say, don't they, the harvest's four months away? But just raise your eyes and look at the fields—they're gleaming white and ready for harvest! The reaper's already getting his wages and gathering together a crop for eternal life so that both sower and reaper may rejoice together. The saying, One sows and another reaps, is spot on. But remember, I sent you to reap what you didn't work for; others have laboured and you've reaped their reward.

Therefore, many Samaritans from the town believed in him because of the woman's testimony, He told me everything I've ever done. The Samaritans approached Jesus and implored him to remain with them. So he stayed with them for two days. Many more believed in him because of his message, and were saying to the woman, We no longer believe because of what you said. We've heard with our own ears and know for sure that this man is the Saviour of the world.

An official's son healed vv43–54

Two days later Jesus returned to Galilee (for Jesus himself had stressed that a prophet has no honour in his home town). When, therefore, he arrived in Galilee all the locals welcomed him because they had seen all he had done at the festival in Jerusalem, for they were there as well. Then Jesus came to Cana in Galilee where he had changed water into wine. And there was a certain royal official in Capernaum whose son was ill. When he heard that Jesus had left Judea for Galilee he sought him out and repeatedly begged him to come down and cure his son, for he was at the point of death. Jesus said to him, Unless you all see signs and wonders you refuse to believe! Sir, pleads the official, come down before my little boy dies! Go, says Jesus, your son is alive and kicking. The man believed what Jesus had said to him and hurried home. While he was en route his slaves met him and told him that his child had recovered. So he asked them, When did he get better? Yesterday, at about one o'clock, the fever left him, they replied. It dawned on the father that that was the very hour when Jesus had told him, Your son lives! So both he and his entire household believed in Jesus. This was Jesus' second sign after his arrival in Galilee from Judea.

Chapter Five

A sign at a pool and the reaction vv1–18

Now there was a Jewish festival so Jesus went up to Jerusalem. And there by the Sheep Gate was a pool that has five colonnades (called Bethesda in Hebrew). Among them lay many who were disabled, blind, lame, and paralysed. One of those lying there had been disabled for thirty-eight years. When Jesus saw him and was aware that he had been in that state for so long, he says to him, Do you want to be healed? Sir, replies the sick man, I've no one to put me into the pool whenever the water is disturbed by the angel, and as I'm making my way there someone else gets in before me. Up! says Jesus, take that mattress of yours and start walking! Immediately the man was cured. He picked up his mattress and began to walk. This happened on the Sabbath. So the Jews were asking the man who had been healed, You there, what do you think you're doing? It's against the law to carry your mattress on the Sabbath. The man protested, The one who healed me said, Pick up your mattress and start walking! They questioned him further, Who exactly told you to pick up your mattress and walk? But the man who had been healed was clueless because Jesus had made himself scarce on account of the crowd. Later on Jesus finds the man in the temple and said to him, See! You've been made well! But give up your sins in case something worse happens to you. The man went away and told the Jews that it was Jesus who had made him well. Now, because he was healing on the Sabbath the Jews were hot on Jesus' heels. But Jesus responded, My Father and I are working in tandem. This was the reason they redoubled their efforts to kill him because not only did he break the Sabbath but he kept saying that God was his own Father, thus making himself equal with God.

Jesus went on, I tell you in all truthfulness there is nothing the Son can do on his own; he can only do what he sees the Father doing. Whatever the Father does the Son does as well. For the Father loves the Son and shows him all he's doing; and he will show him greater works than these in order to amaze you. For just as the Father raises the dead and gives life to them, so too the Son gives life to whoever he chooses. For the Father does not judge anybody; rather he has handed over all judgment to the Son, so that all should revere the Son just as they revere the Father. For whoever doesn't revere the Son doesn't revere the Father who sent him.

I tell you in all truthfulness whoever hears my message and has faith in the one who sent me has eternal life and won't be judged, but has passed from death to life. Listen carefully, the hour's coming, I tell you, and now is when the dead will hear the voice of God's Son and those who hear it will come to life. For just as the Father has life in himself so too he's granted the Son to have life in himself. And he's given him authority to execute judgment because he's the Son of Man. Don't be shocked at this, because the hour's coming when all who are in their graves will hear his voice and come out: those who've done good to a resurrection of life; those who've done evil to a resurrection of judgment.

On my own I can do nothing; I judge as I hear and my judgment is just because I don't seek my own will but the will of the one who sent me. If I testify about myself then my testimony isn't true. But there's someone else who testifies about me and I know his testimony is true. You yourselves sent messengers to John and he's testified about the truth. Not that I need man's testimony; the reason I'm saying these things is so that you may be saved. John was a bright burning lamp and you were happy enough to bask in his light for a time. But my testimony's greater than John's because the works which the Father's given me to finish—these very works that I'm now doing—are proof that the Father's sent me. And the Father himself who sent me has testified about me, yet you've never heard or seen him. And because you don't believe in me, his messenger, his word finds no place in your heart. You scrutinise the scriptures because you think they'll lead you to everlasting life, but it's these very scriptures that point to me. Even so you refuse to come to me so that you may have life. I don't accept praise from anyone. But I know you've no love for God in your hearts. I've come in my Father's name and yet you want nothing to do with me. If, however, anyone else should come in his own name you'd gladly accept him. How can you possibly believe when you accept praise from one another while you neglect to seek God's approval?

Don't think that I'll accuse you before the Father; the one who accuses you, on whom you've pinned your hopes, is Moses himself! For if you'd believed Moses then surely you would've believed me, because he wrote about me. But if you don't believe his writings how will you believe my words?

Chapter Six

A sign for the hungry vv1–15

Afterwards Jesus crossed the Sea of Galilee, otherwise known as the Sea of Tiberias. A large crowd continued following him because they saw the signs he was performing on the sick. Jesus climbed the mountain and sat down there with his disciples. It was Jewish Passover time. Jesus looked up and saw a huge crowd streaming towards him. He says to Philip, Where can we buy bread to feed them? Now he said this to test him because he knew what he was going to do. Well, answered Philip, eight months' wages won't buy enough bread for each of them to have even a morsel.

Just then, Andrew, Simon Peter's brother (one of the disciples) says to him, There's a young lad here who has five barley loaves and two small fish, but what's that among so many? Jesus said, Make the people sit down (it was a very grassy area). So the menfolk sat down, about five thousand of them.

Jesus took the bread and after he had given thanks he distributed it among those who were sitting down, and also the fish. When they had had enough Jesus says to his disciples, Make sure you pick up all the leftovers, leave nothing behind. So they gathered them up and filled twelve baskets. When the people saw the sign that Jesus had done they began to say, Truly this is the Prophet who's to come into the world! When Jesus realised that they were planning to seize him forcibly and make him king, he withdrew again to the mountain alone.

A sign on the water vv16–23

At sunset his disciples went down to the sea, got into their boat and began to sail to Capernaum. By now it was dark and Jesus had still not joined them. A gale was starting to whip up the waters. When they had rowed about three or four miles out to sea they clapped eyes on Jesus advancing towards them on foot! They froze in terror but Jesus says to them, Don't panic it's only me! They welcomed him into the boat and before they knew it they had reached their destination.

The next morning the crowd that had been standing on the other side of the shore noticed that there had only been a small boat there and that Jesus had not got into it with his disciples, who had left without him. However, there were small boats from Tiberias that came near to the place where the people had eaten the bread after the Lord had given thanks.

The Bread of Life vv24–53

Now when the crowd saw that neither Jesus nor his disciples were there they got into the small boats and came to Capernaum searching for him. And when they found him on the other side they said, Rabbi, when did you get here? Jesus said, I know you're seeking me not because of the signs you saw but because you ate your fill of the bread. Don't labour for the food that perishes but for the food that lasts forever. The Son of Man will give it to you, because it's on him that God the Father has set his seal of approval. So they said to him, What do we have to do in order to perform God's works? Jesus replied, Don't worry about works, your job's simply to believe in the one sent by God. They said, What sign can you show us so that we may see it and put our trust in you? What miraculous deed can you perform? Our fathers ate manna in the desert, as scripture records, ***He gave***

them manna from heaven to eat. Listen to me carefully, said Jesus, it wasn't Moses who gave you manna from heaven, but it's my Father who continues to give you real bread from above. For the bread which God gives is the one who comes down from heaven, and it's this bread that gives life to the world. Well Master, they said, then keep on giving us this bread! I am the bread of life, said Jesus; whoever comes to me will never go hungry, and whoever has faith in me will never thirst again.

But as I've already made clear, although you've seen me you don't believe in me. Everyone that the Father gives to me will come to me, and whoever comes to me I'll never turn away. For I've come down from heaven not to do my own will but the will of the one who sent me. And this is his will, that I should lose none of those that he's given me, but that I should raise them up on the last day. This is what my Father wants, that everyone who sees the Son and comes to have faith in him should have eternal life, and I'll raise him up on the last day.

When they heard this the Jews began to grumble among themselves because he said, I'm the bread which came down from heaven. Isn't this Jesus, the son of Joseph? they asked; don't we know his father and his mother? How for goodness sake can he say, I've come down from heaven? Stop muttering among yourselves, said Jesus. No one's able to come to me unless the Father who sent me draws him, and I'll raise him up on the last day. It states in the prophets, ***They will all be taught by God.*** All who've heard and learned from the Father come to me. Not that anyone has actually seen the Father except the one who's from God, he alone has seen the Father.

Let me assure you, whoever believes has eternal life. I am indeed the bread of life. Your fathers ate manna in the desert and died. But here's the bread that has come down from heaven; if anyone eats it they won't die. I am the life giving bread that came down from heaven; whoever eats this bread will live forever, and the bread that I'll give for the life of the world is my own flesh.

This was too much for the Jews who began arguing with each other, How can he give us his flesh to eat? Jesus addressed them, Listen, unless you eat the flesh of the Son of Man and drink his blood you're spiritually dead. Anyone who feeds on my flesh and drinks my blood will live forever and I'll raise him up on the last day. Because my flesh is real food and my blood is real drink. Whoever eats my flesh and drinks my blood remains in me and I in them. For just as the Father who lives sent me (and I live because of the Father) so whoever feeds on me will live because of me. This is the bread that came down from heaven, it bears no resemblance to the bread your fathers ate yet still died. Whoever feeds on this bread will live forever.

Jesus said these things when he was teaching in the synagogue at Capernaum. So when many of his followers heard this they said, This teaching's very hard, who can stomach it? But Jesus, aware that his followers were moaning said, Are you shocked? Then what if you were to see the Son of Man ascending to where he was before? It's the Spirit that gives life; the flesh is worthless. Can't you see that it's the life-giving Spirit that I'm speaking about? But there are some of you who simply don't believe (he knew from the outset those who would not believe, and who it was that would betray him). He went on, This is why I've said to you, nobody can come to me unless it's been determined by the Father. Because of this some of his followers turned back and no longer accompanied him.

Therefore Jesus said to the twelve, You don't want to desert me like the others do you? Master! Simon Peter said, to whom would we go? You've got the words of eternal life, and we've come to believe and know that you're the Holy One of God. Jesus replied, Didn't I choose you, the twelve, and yet one of you is a devil? (This was a reference to Judas, the son of Simon Iscariot, one of the twelve, who was about to betray him.)

Chapter Seven

Jesus goes to the Tabernacles festival vv1–13

Later on Jesus was travelling around Galilee, for he did not want to go up to Judea because the Jews were seeking to kill him. Now the Jewish festival of Tabernacles was approaching. His brothers said to him, You should leave here and go up to Judea so that your followers can see the miracles you're doing. Nobody can attract attention if they work in secret. Show yourself to the world! (For not even his brothers had faith in him.) Jesus says to them, It's not my time right now, but you can always seize the opportunity. The world cannot hate you, but it hates me because I expose its wicked ways. Go on, you go up to the festival, I'm not going to this one because it's not the right time for me. So he stayed behind in Galilee.

When, however, his brothers had gone up to the festival he himself went after all, but privately not publicly. Now the Jews were searching for him at the festival and asking, Where is he? Among the crowds there was plenty of gossip about him. Some said, He's a decent fellow, but others said, No, he's leading people astray. However, nobody actually spoke about him openly for fear of the Jews.

Jesus teaches in the temple vv14–24

It was halfway through the feast when Jesus went up to the temple and began to teach. The Jews were astonished; He's had no education, they said, so where did he get all this knowledge? Jesus replied, These aren't my own ideas; they come from the one who sent me. If anyone wants to do God's will he'll know whether my teaching is mine or God's. Whoever speaks on his own authority seeks his own glory; but whoever seeks the honour of the one who sent him is truthful and upright. Wasn't it Moses who gave you the law? And yet none of you keep it! Tell me, why do you want to kill me? The crowd answered, You've a demon! Who's trying to kill you? Jesus said, I performed a single miracle and you're all astonished! Moses gave you circumcision (although of course it doesn't come from Moses but the fathers) and so you circumcise a man on the Sabbath. If a man is circumcised on the Sabbath so that the law of Moses be not broken, why are you angry because I healed a man on the Sabbath? Judge justly, not by outward appearances!

Who is Jesus? vv25–31

Then some of those who lived in Jerusalem began to say, This is the man they're trying to kill, isn't it? He speaks frankly, yet they say nothing to him. Could it be that the authorities know he's the Christ? But we know where this man comes from; whenever the Messiah appears no one will know his origins.

Jesus cried out while teaching in the temple, You know me and you know where I've come from, do you? I've not come on my own authority but he who sent me is true and you don't know him. But I know him because I've come from him, and it's he who sent me. On account of this they were bent on seizing him but nobody laid so much as a finger on him, for his time had not yet come.

Nevertheless, many in the crowd had faith in him, and they were saying among themselves, When the Christ comes surely he won't do more miracles than this man, will he?

The Pharisees attempt to arrest Jesus vv32–53

When the Pharisees heard the crowd arguing about him they linked up with the chief priests and dispatched guards to arrest him. Jesus then said to them, I'm only with you for a short time and then I go to the one who sent me. You'll look in vain for me because where I'm going you cannot come.

The Jews said to each other, Where will he go that we won't be able to find him? Does he have it in mind to go to our people dispersed among the gentiles, and teach the Greeks as well? Whatever did he mean when he said, You'll search for me but not find me, and, Where I am you cannot come?

Now on the last and most important day of the feast, Jesus stood up and cried out, If anyone's thirsty let him come to me and drink. Whoever has faith in me, as scripture says, ***From within him rivers of living water will flow.*** This was a reference to the Spirit that those who had faith in him were to receive, although not immediately for Jesus had yet to be exalted.

When the crowd heard what he said they began to ask, Surely this is the Prophet, isn't it? Others were saying, He's the Christ! Yet others made the point, But the Christ won't come out of Galilee, will he? Doesn't scripture say the

Christ descends from David and comes from Bethlehem, David's hometown?

So there arose a disagreement in the crowd because of Jesus. Some of them were eager to arrest him, but no one dared lay a finger on him.

Eventually the guards reported back to the chief priests and Pharisees who asked them, Why haven't you arrested him? They replied, Nobody ever spoke like him. The Pharisees retorted, Don't tell us he's deceived you as well? Have any of the rulers or the Pharisees put their faith in him? No way! But this crowd are in ignorance of the law and so are cursed. Nicodemus, one of their number who had previously visited Jesus butted in, Just a minute, does our law condemn a man without first hearing what he's to say in his defence? Are you a Galilean too? they asked. Check it out: no prophet hails from Galilee! Then they all went home.

Chapter Eight

Jesus saves an adulteress vv1–11

Jesus then went to the Mount of Olives. At dawn he came again to the temple and all the people kept coming to him and so he sat down and began to teach them. The scribes and the Pharisees brought a woman to him who had been caught committing adultery. They stood her in front of them all and said, Teacher, this slut has been caught red handed! Now in our law Moses ordered us to stone such a creature; so what do you say? (They said this to trap him, so that they might accuse him.)

Jesus, however, bent down and began writing with his finger on the ground. But because they kept needling him he straightened up and said, If any of you are sinless by all means be the first to stone her. He bent down and resumed writing on the ground. When they heard this they began to leave one at a time, beginning with the Elders, until Jesus and the woman were alone. Then Jesus stood up and said, Woman, what's going on? Where is everybody? Did no one condemn you? She replied, No one, sir. Then, said Jesus, I certainly don't condemn you. Now off you go—and no more sinning!

Jesus the light of the world vv12–30

Then Jesus spoke to them again and said, I am the light of the world, whoever follows me will not walk in pitch darkness but will have the light of life. The Pharisees said, Hang on, you're giving evidence about yourself, so it's unreliable. Jesus replied, Even if I'm giving evidence about myself my evidence is reliable, for I know where I came from and where I'm going to, whereas you know neither where I came from nor where I'm going. You judge at face value; I judge no one. But even if I were to judge, my judgment's true because my judgment's aligned with that of my Father who sent me. It states in your own law that the evidence of two men is trustworthy. I give evidence on my own behalf and the Father who sent me corroborates my evidence.

Then they started to ask him, Where's this Father of yours then? Jesus replied, You know neither me nor my Father.

If you knew me you would've known my Father.

He spoke these words in the treasury as he taught in the temple and no one dared arrest him because it was not yet his time. So again he said to them, I'm going away and you'll look for me but you'll perish in your sin. Where I'm going you cannot come. At this the Jews began to ask, He's not going to kill himself, is he? Is that why he says, Where I'm going you cannot come?

And he went on, You're from below, I'm from above; you're of this world, I'm not of this world. This is why I told you that you'll die in your sins, for if you don't believe who I am, you'll die in your sins.

So who are you then? they asked. Jesus replied, What I've been telling you from the outset. I've much to tell you about yourselves and much to judge. But he who sent me is true and I only tell the world what I've heard from him (they had no idea that he was speaking to them of his Father). Therefore, said Jesus, when you've lifted up the Son of Man you'll know that I am who I claim to be and that I only pass on what the Father's taught me. The one who sent me is with me. He hasn't deserted me, because I constantly do what pleases him. As he said all this many believed in him.

Jesus said to those Jews who had put their trust in him, If you continue to stay true to my teaching then you're truly my disciples. And you'll come to know the truth and it'll liberate you. They replied, We're descendants of Abraham and have never been enslaved by anyone, so how can you tell us we'll be liberated? Jesus answered, Listen, everyone who sins is enslaved to sin. A slave doesn't have the right to live in the house permanently, but an heir does. So if the Son liberates you, you'll be well and truly freed! I know you're Abraham's descendants, but you're bent on killing me because my word finds no place in your hearts. I've told you those things that I've seen in the very presence of my Father, but you act out what you've heard from your father. We'll have you know, they said, our father's Abraham. Jesus responded, If you really were Abraham's children you'd be doing what Abraham did. But now you seek to kill me, someone who's told you nothing but the truth that I heard from God. Abraham didn't behave like this! You're merely acting like your father. At least, they said, we weren't born outside marriage! We've one father and one father only, namely God himself.

Then Jesus said to them, If God were your father you'd love me, because I come from

God and was sent by him. I haven't come on my own initiative—he sent me. Why do you fail to understand what I'm saying? Because you're stone deaf! You belong to your father, the devil, and your instinct is to carry out your father's desires. He was nothing but a murderer right from the start and was always a stranger to the truth, because there's no truth in him. Whenever he lies he does so because it's his nature. He's simply a liar and the father of lies. But I speak the truth to you, yet you don't believe me. Which one of you can prove me guilty of any sin? And if I'm telling you the truth then why don't you believe me? Whoever belongs to God listens to God's word; it's because you don't belong to God that you can't hear it.

The Jews then replied, Aren't we right in saying that you're a demon possessed Samaritan? I'm not demon possessed, said Jesus. I revere my Father just as you insult me. I'm not seeking my own glory or justification—that's God's business. I tell you the truth: whoever heeds my message will never die. The Jews said, Now we know that you're demonic! Abraham died and so did the prophets and yet you say that whoever follows your teaching will never die. Do you have the effrontery to claim that you're greater than Abraham who died, as did the prophets? Who do you think you are? Jesus replied, If I glorify myself then my glory means nothing. My Father, who you say is your God, is the one who glorifies me. You don't know him—but I do. If I were to say, I don't know him I would be like you, a liar. But I do know him and I keep his word. Your father Abraham was overjoyed at the prospect of seeing my day; he saw it and rejoiced. But you're not yet fifty, said the Jews, and yet you've seen Abraham, have you? Jesus answered, I tell you the truth: before Abraham was, I am. At this they took up rocks to throw at him, but Jesus hid himself and then slipped out of the temple.

Chapter Nine

A blind man cured vv1–41

As Jesus was passing by he a saw a man who had been blind from birth. And his disciples asked him, Teacher, who sinned this man or his parents so that he was blind from birth? Neither this man sinned, said Jesus, nor his parents, but rather that the power of God might be displayed in his life! We too must continue to display God's power while it's still day; for night's on its way and then it'll be too late. So long as I'm in the world I am the light of the world.

After saying this he spat on the ground and made mud with the spit and smeared the mud on the man's eyes and said to him, Off you go—wash in the pool of Siloam (which means Sent). So he went off and washed and came back with his sight restored.

Then his neighbours and those who were used to seeing him begging were saying, Wait, isn't this the man who used to sit and beg?

Some said, Yes it's him; others insisted, No, it just looks like him. The blind man kept saying, It *is* me! But they kept pressing him, Tell us, how were your eyes opened? He said, A man called Jesus made mud and smeared it on my eyes and told me to go to Siloam and wash there. So I went and after I'd washed I received my sight.

So they said to him, Where is this man? I've no idea, he replied. So they brought the man who had been blind to the Pharisees. Now it was the Sabbath when Jesus made the mud and opened his eyes. The Pharisees again kept asking him how he received his sight. So he said, He smeared mud on my eyes and I washed and now I see. Then some of the Pharisees were saying, This individual isn't from God or else he would keep the Sabbath. Others began to ask, How can a sinful man perform miraculous signs like this? And a dispute broke out among them. They spoke to the blind man yet again, What do you yourself say about this fellow, after all it was your eyes he opened? He replied, He must be a prophet. But the Jews did not believe that he had been blind but could now see, until they fetched his parents. And they quizzed them, Is this your son that you claim was blind from birth? So how is he able to see? His parents replied, We know it's our son and that he was blind from birth, but how he now sees or who opened his eyes, we don't know. Ask him yourselves, he's an adult, he can speak for himself. His parents answered in this way because they were afraid of the Jews who had already determined that if anyone acknowledged that Jesus was the Christ they would be put out of the synagogue. This is why his parents said, He's an adult, ask him.

So they summoned the blind man a second time and said to him, Give God the glory, we know very well that this man is a sinner. He replied, I've no idea if he's a sinner or not, but I know this much, I used to be blind but now I see! They continued to question him, What did he do to you? How did he open your eyes? So he answered them, I've already told you but you wouldn't listen; do you want me to repeat myself? Do you want to become his disciples too? Then they heaped abuse on him, You're a follower of that man! But we're followers of Moses. We know that God has spoken to Moses but we don't even know where this person comes from. The man responded, How amazing! You don't even know where he comes from, yet he opened my eyes. We know that God doesn't listen to sinful people, but if anyone's God fearing and does whatever he asks he hears him. Not since time began has it been heard that anyone opened the eyes of a man blind from birth. If this man wasn't from God he could do nothing. You, they replied, were born a complete and utter sinner! Do you presume to lecture us? So they threw him out of the synagogue.

When Jesus heard that he had been thrown out of the synagogue he found him and said, Do you believe in the Son of Man? He replied, Who's he, sir? Tell me so that I may believe in him. Jesus said to him, You've already seen him; he's looking you in the eye. The man said, I believe, Lord, and fell down at his feet and worshipped him. Jesus said, I came into the world for judgment so that those who cannot see may have their sight restored, and those who think that they see may be struck blind. Now some of the Pharisees who happened to be nearby and heard him said, You're not suggesting we're blind, are you? Jesus answered, If you were blind you would not be guilty of sin; but since you say, We can see, your sin remains.

Chapter Ten

The good shepherd vv1–21

Be warned, I tell you, whoever doesn't use the gate to enter the sheepfold, but climbs in some other way, is a thief and a robber. But the real shepherd will enter through the gate. The gatekeeper opens it for him and the sheep recognise the shepherd's voice and he calls his own sheep by name and leads them out.

Whenever he brings out the whole flock he walks on ahead of them and the sheep follow him because they recognise his voice. But they'll never follow a stranger, in fact they'll run a mile from him because they don't recognise the voice of strangers.

Jesus was speaking figuratively, but they failed to grasp what he was saying. So Jesus told them once again, Listen, I am the gate for the sheep. All who preceded me were nothing more than thieves and robbers; however, the sheep didn't recognise them.

I am the gate; if anyone enters through me he'll be saved, and he'll come in and go out and find pasture. The thief comes only to steal, slaughter and destroy. I've come that they might have life—life in all its fullness!

I am the good shepherd; the good shepherd sacrifices his life for his sheep. The hired hand, who's not a shepherd and doesn't own sheep, flees for his life when he sees a wolf coming. The wolf then attacks the flock and scatters them. He flees because he's merely a hired hand and has no concern for the sheep.

But I am the good shepherd and I recognise my own and they recognise me. I know the Father just as the Father knows me, and I sacrifice my life for the sheep.

I've also other sheep, not of this fold. These too I must gather and they'll listen to my voice so that there'll be a single flock with one shepherd.

It's because I sacrifice my life that the Father loves me; however, I do this so that I may take it back again. No one takes it away from me but I sacrifice it of my own free will. I've been given the authority to sacrifice my life and take it back again because it's what the Father commanded me to do.

Again, these words caused discord among the Jews. Many of them were saying, He's crazed and demonic, why are you listening to him? Others added, But surely these aren't the words of one possessed by a demon, are they? A man with a demon cannot open the eyes of the blind, can he?

The Jews persistently question Jesus vv22–42

The Festival of Dedication was taking place in Jerusalem. It was winter. Jesus was walking in the temple, in Solomon's portico. The Jews encircled him, For how much longer will you keep us on edge? If you're the Christ then tell us plainly! Jesus replied, I've already told you, but you don't believe. The work that I'm doing in my Father's name speaks volumes about me. But you don't believe because you don't belong to my flock. My sheep listen to my voice; I know them and they follow me. And I give them eternal life and they'll never perish and no one will ever snatch them from my hand. My Father, who's given them to me, is greater than all; there's no one who can pluck them from my Father's hand. I and the Father are one.

Then the Jews picked up stones to stone him. I've shown you many good deeds from the Father, said Jesus, for which of them do you stone me? We're not stoning you for any good work, said the Jews, but for blasphemy, because you, a mere mortal, make yourself out to be God.

Jesus replied, Isn't it written in your law, ***I said you are gods?*** If scripture called them gods, to whom the word of God came (and scripture cannot be annulled), are you now saying of me, the one the Father appointed and sent into the world, You're blaspheming, because I said, I'm the Son of God? If I'm not doing my Father's work, don't believe me. But if I'm doing it, even if you don't believe me at least believe for the sake of the miracles, so that you may know that the Father's in me and I in the Father.

Once more they set about finding a way to arrest him, but he escaped their clutches. He went away again across the Jordan, to where John had previously baptised, and remained there. Many people came to him and were saying, John himself didn't perform any miraculous signs, but all that he said about this man was true. And many folk there came to have faith in him.

Chapter Eleven

Jesus restores Lazarus to life vv1–44

Now it happened that a man called Lazarus became ill. He lived at Bethany, the village of Martha and her sister Mary. This was the same Mary who anointed the Lord with ointment and wiped his feet with her hair; it was her brother, Lazarus, who was ill. Then the sisters sent a message to him, Lord, please help us, your dear friend is sick. When he heard this he said, This isn't a fatal illness, but one through which God will reveal his glory, so that through it the Son of God may be exalted. Now Jesus loved Martha, her sister and Lazarus. So when he heard that Lazarus was sick he stayed put two more days.

He then says to his disciples, Come on, let's return to Judea. They reply, Master, are you sure you want to return—the Jews there were only recently trying to stone you? There are twelve hours in the day aren't there? said Jesus. If anyone walks in daylight he doesn't stumble because he sees the light of this world. But if anyone walks at night he stumbles because he doesn't have any light. He said all this, and afterwards told them, Our friend Lazarus has fallen asleep, so I'm going to wake him up. Master, said his disciples, if he's just having a nap what's the problem? But Jesus had spoken about his death; his disciples, however, thought he was talking about sleep. Jesus then told them plainly, Lazarus is dead. I'm glad for your sakes that I wasn't there so that you may have faith; but let's go to him. Then Thomas (nicknamed the Twin) said to the others, Let's go as well so that we may die with him.

When Jesus arrived he found that Lazarus had already been entombed four days earlier. Now Bethany was near Jerusalem, about two miles away. Many of the Jews had travelled to Martha and Mary to offer their condolences for their brother. When Martha heard that Jesus was on his way she went out to meet him while Mary remained at home. Martha then said, Master, if only you'd been here my brother wouldn't have died, but I know that even now God will give you whatever you ask of him. Jesus says to her, Your brother will be raised up. I know, says, Martha, that he'll be raised in the resurrection on the last day. Jesus said to her, I am the resurrection and the life; whoever believes in me, even though they should die, will live. And whoever lives and believes in me will never die. Do you believe this? Yes, master, she says to him, I truly believe that you're the Christ, the Son of God, the one destined to come into the world.

When she had said this she went back and spoke privately to her sister and said, The teacher's here and is asking for you. When she heard this Mary got up quickly and went to him. Now Jesus had not arrived at the village, but was still at the place where Martha had met him. When the Jews, who had been in the house with Mary offering their condolences saw that she had got up quickly and gone out, they followed her assuming that she was going to the tomb to weep there.

So when Mary came to the spot where Jesus was and saw him she fell at his feet saying, Master, if only you'd been here my brother wouldn't have died. When Jesus saw her weeping, along with the Jews who accompanied her, he snorted in indignation, deeply distressed. He said, Where have you placed him? They replied, Master, come and see. Jesus broke down in tears. The Jews were saying, See how much he loved him! But some of them said, Couldn't the man who opened the eyes of the blind have done something to prevent Lazarus from dying?

Then Jesus, again seething with rage, came to the tomb. It was in fact a cave and there was a stone lying across it. Take away the stone, says Jesus. Master, replies Martha, the body will stink because he's been dead four days. Jesus says to her, Didn't I tell you that if you'd believe you'd see the glory of God?

So they took away the stone. Then Jesus lifted up his eyes and said, Father I thank you that you've heard me. I know that you always hear me, but I said this for the sake of the crowd standing here, so that they may believe that it was you who sent me.

After saying this he let out a mighty cry, Lazarus, come out! The dead man came out, his feet and hands bandaged and his face wrapped in cloth. Jesus says to them, Unbind him and let him go. Many of those Jews who had come to Mary and who had seen what he had done believed in him.

Plotting against Jesus vv45–57

However, others went off to the Pharisees and told them all that Jesus had been up to. As a result the chief priests and the Pharisees convened a council and began asking, What are we going to do for this man is performing many miraculous signs? If we leave him to his own devices everyone will believe in him and the Romans will come and destroy our temple and nation. Then one of them, Caiaphas (who was the high priest that year) said, How stupid you are! You know nothing! Don't you realise that it's far better that one man should die for the people than that the whole nation should perish? He did not say this of his own volition, but as high priest for that year he predicted that Jesus would die for the nation, and not only for the nation, but in order that the scattered children of God might be gathered together and made one.

So from that day they plotted to kill Jesus. For this reason he no longer went about openly among the Jews but took himself off to a region near the desert, to Ephraim, and remained there with his disciples.

Now as the Passover approached many Jews went up from the country to Jerusalem in order to purify themselves before the Passover. They kept a lookout for Jesus too, and as they stood around in the temple were saying among themselves, What do you think? Surely he's not going to come to the festival is he? Now the chief priests and the Pharisees gave strict instructions that anyone who knew his whereabouts should report it to them so that they might arrest him.

Chapter Twelve

A loving gesture at Bethany vv1–11

Six days before the Passover festival Jesus came to Bethany, where Lazarus lived who he had raised from the dead. There they prepared a dinner for him with Martha doing the cooking (Lazarus was also among those who ate with him).

Then Mary took a very expensive perfume of pure nard and anointed the feet of Jesus and wiped his feet with her hair, and the fragrance of the perfume filled the house. But Judas Iscariot (one of his disciples who would later betray him) said, Why wasn't this perfume sold for a year's wages and the proceeds given to the poor? He said this, not that he cared a jot for the poor, but because he was a thief and as the treasurer used to help himself to the funds. But Jesus said, Let her be—let her keep it for the day of my burial. You always have the poor with you— but not me.

Meanwhile a large number of the Jews discovered his whereabouts and came not only to see Jesus but also to gawk at Lazarus who he had restored to life. So the chief priests schemed how they might also dispose of Lazarus, because on his account many of the Jews were flocking to Jesus and putting their trust in him.

A ride into Jerusalem where Jesus continues to teach vv12–50

The next day, when a large crowd arrived at the festival they got wind that Jesus was also coming to Jerusalem. So they took palm branches and went out to meet him. They began to cry out, Glory! Glory! Hallelujah! Blessed is the one who comes in the name of the Lord, the King of Israel! When Jesus found a young donkey he got on it, to fulfil what was written, ***Daughter of Zion do not be afraid. See! Your King is coming sitting on a donkey's colt!*** Now at first his disciples totally failed to grasp the significance of all this. But when Jesus was glorified they remembered that these things had been written about him, and done to him.

So those who were with him when he summoned Lazarus out of the tomb and restored him to life continued to brag about Jesus. Indeed, because he had performed this miraculous sign the crowd went out to meet him. Therefore the Pharisees said to each other, Look, we're getting nowhere—the whole world's gone after him!

Now among those who went up to the festival to worship were some Greeks. They came to Philip who hailed from Bethsaida in Galilee and kept pressing him, Sir, we would very much like to meet Jesus. So Philip goes and tells Andrew, and Andrew and Philip go and tell Jesus who says, The hour has come for the Son of Man to be glorified. Listen carefully, unless a kernel of wheat falls to the ground and dies it remains a single kernel whereas if it dies it produces a bountiful harvest. Anyone who loves his life will lose it; anyone who hates his life in this world will preserve it for everlasting life. Whoever would serve me must follow me, and where I am my servant will be there too, and my Father will honour whoever serves me.

But my heart is now in turmoil; what am I to say? Rescue me from this situation? Yet isn't this why I came? O Father, glorify your name! I've glorified it, came a voice from heaven, and I'll glorify it again.

When the people standing nearby heard the voice they began to say, That was thunder; but others said, No, an angel has just spoken to him. Jesus said, The voice spoke for your benefit not mine.

Now is judgment time for this world, when its ruler will be driven out. And I, if I'm lifted up from the earth, will draw everyone to myself.

He was saying this to predict the kind of death he would undergo. The crowd responded, We've heard from the law that the Christ will be with us forever, so why then are you saying that the Son of Man will be lifted up? Who is this Son of Man anyway? Jesus replied, The light will only be with you for a short time, so keep walking while you have the light lest darkness engulfs you. Anyone who walks in the dark doesn't know where he's going. So long as you have the light rely on it, so that you may become children of light.

After he had said this Jesus went away and hid himself from the crowd. Although he had performed many miraculous signs before their very eyes they persisted in their unbelief. This fulfilled the saying of the prophet Isaiah, ***Lord, who has believed our account? And to whom has the arm of the Lord been made known?*** Because of this they could not believe, for Isaiah said elsewhere, ***He has blinded their eyes and made their hearts stubborn, lest they should see with their eyes and understand with their hearts and turn to me and I will heal them.*** Isaiah said all this because he saw Christ's glory and spoke about him.

Despite this many even of the ruling elite began to express faith in Jesus, but they would not acknowledge it openly for fear the Pharisees might expel them from the synagogue (for they craved man's rather than God's glory).

Then Jesus cried out and said, Whoever has faith in me doesn't have faith in me so much as in the one who sent me. Whoever sees me sees God. I've come as light into the world so that all who believe in me shouldn't remain in darkness. If anyone hears my words but doesn't obey them, I won't be his judge, because I've not come to judge the world but to save it. Anyone who rejects me and does not accept what I say already has a judge—the word that I've spoken! This will be his judge on the last day. I've not spoken on my own authority, but the Father who sent me instructed me what to say and speak. And I know that his commandment is the source of eternal life. So whatever I say is exactly what I myself heard from the Father.

Chapter Thirteen

Jesus washes the feet of his disciples vv1–11

It was just before the Passover festival. Jesus knew that his time had come to leave the world and go to the Father. Even so he loved his own, who had to remain in the world, and continued to love them right until the very end.

By supper the devil had already planted in the heart of Judas Iscariot, Simon's son, the idea of betraying Jesus. For his part Jesus knew that the Father had given him authority over all things and that he had come from God and was now returning to him.

So he gets up after supper, takes off his outer garment, and fetching a towel he tied it around his waist. Then he pours water into a washbasin and begins to wash his disciples' feet and to dry them with the towel that was wrapped around him. He comes to Simon Peter who exclaims, Master, surely you're not going to wash my feet are you? Jesus said, You don't grasp what I'm doing now, but you will in time. Absolutely not!

says Peter, on no account will you ever wash my feet! Jesus replied, You'll have no share in my life unless I wash you. In that case master, says Peter, do my hands and my head not just my feet. All who have washed themselves, says Jesus, only need to bathe their feet for they're clean all over. You're clean—but not all of you (because he knew who was going to betray him).

Jesus teaches in the upper room vv12–20

When he had finished washing their feet he took his garments and sat down again. Do you understand what I've just done for you all? You call me teacher and master, and rightly so, for that's what I am. So if I, your master and teacher, have washed your feet you should make a habit of washing each other's feet. I've given you an example to follow so that what I've just done you should do as well.

I tell you, no servant's greater than his master, nor is the messenger greater than the one who sent him. If you know all this and put it into practice you'll be blessed.

I don't speak of you all though, I know who I've chosen. But in order that the scripture might be fulfilled, ***The one who eats my bread has***

kicked me in the teeth. I'm telling you these things now before it happens, so that when it does come about you'll believe that I am who I claim to be. Be assured, whoever receives my messengers receives me and whoever receives me receives the one who sent me.

Jesus reveals the betrayer vv21-32

After he had said these things Jesus was greatly distraught and said, One of you is about to betray me. The disciples began to look at one another bewildered as to who it might be. One of them, Jesus' closest friend, was reclining next to him. So Simon Peter signals to him to ask Jesus who it was he was speaking about. Leaning over to Jesus he asks, Master, who is it? Jesus replies, It's the one I'll give this piece of bread to after I've dipped it in the dish. So after he had dipped the piece of bread he gives it to Judas Iscariot, Simon's son. As Judas took the piece of bread Satan overwhelmed him. Jesus says to him, What you intend to do, do quickly. Nobody at the meal knew why he had said this to him. Since Judas was in control of the funds some of them thought Jesus was telling him to buy provisions for the festival, or to give something to the poor.

The instant Judas took the piece of bread he went out. It was night. When he had gone, Jesus says, The Son of Man's just been glorified and God's been glorified in him! And if God's glorified in him he'll glorify the Son in himself without delay!

Love one another vv33-35

My dear children, I'll only be with you for a short time. You'll look for me and as I told the Jews, so now I say to you, where I'm going you cannot come. So I give you a new commandment that you should love each other, just as I've loved you, so you also should love each other. In this way everyone will know that you're my disciples, if you've love for each other. Simon Peter says, Master, where are you going? Jesus says, Where I'm going you can't follow me right now—but you will later. Peter says, Master, why can't I follow you now? I'll sacrifice my life for you. Says Jesus, Will you really sacrifice your life for me? The truth is the rooster won't crow until you've denied me three times.

Chapter Fourteen

Words of comfort vv1–31

Calm your unsettled hearts. Just as you've faith in God, have faith in me. There are many rooms in my Father's house, if not would I have told you that I'm going there to get everything ready for you? And if I go and prepare a place for you I'll return and take you to be with me so that where I am, there you may be also. And you know where I'm going and how to get there. Thomas blurts out, Master, we've no idea where you're going, so how can we possibly know the way? Jesus replies, I myself am the way, the truth and the life. No one comes to the Father except through me. If you'd known me you'd also have known my Father. From now on you both know and have seen him.

Then Philip says, Master just show us the Father, that's all we ask! O Philip, says Jesus, have I been with you all this time and still you don't know me? Anyone who's seen me has seen the Father, so how can you say, Show us the Father? Don't you believe that I'm in the Father and the Father's in me. The words that I speak to you aren't mine, but the Father who lives in me continues to do his work. Believe me when I say that I'm in the Father and the Father's in me, or else accept the evidence of the mighty works themselves.

Listen, whoever has faith in me will perform the same deeds that I do, and he'll perform greater deeds than these because I'm going to the Father. And I'll do whatever you ask in my name so that the Father may be glorified in the Son. If you love me then you'll obey my commandments. I'll ask the Father and he'll give you another advocate so that he may be with you always. This is the Spirit of truth who the world cannot receive because he's invisible and unknown to the world, but not to you, for you know him, and he's constantly with you and will eventually live in you. I won't abandon you and make you orphans—I'm coming back for you! Soon the world will no longer see me, but you'll see me; because I live, you'll live too. On that day you'll appreciate that I'm in my Father and that you're in me and I in you.

Whoever has my commandments and keeps them is the one who truly loves me. And whoever loves me will be loved by my Father, and I'll love and reveal myself to them as well. Judas (not

Iscariot) says to him, Master, why reveal yourself to us but not to the world? Jesus answered, If anyone loves me he'll keep my word and my Father will love him and we'll come to him and make our home with him.

Anyone who doesn't love me won't obey my teaching, which is not mine but the Father's who sent me. I've told you all this while I'm still with you. But the Comforter, the Holy Spirit, who the Father will send in my name, he will instruct you in everything and cause you to remember all that I've said to you. I'm leaving you peace, I'm giving you my peace; the peace that I'm giving to you isn't the peace the world gives.

Calm your unsettled hearts! Don't be afraid! You've heard me say to you, I'm going away and I'm coming back to you. If you loved me you'd have been glad that I'm going to the Father, because the Father is greater than me. I've told you all this in advance, before it happens, so that when it does happen you might believe. I won't be speaking to you much longer because the ruler of this world is on his way; but he's got no hold on me. The world will learn that I love the Father because I keep his commandments.

Come on, let's go!

Chapter Fifteen

Jesus the true vine speaks further about love
vv1–27

I am the true vine; my Father's the gardener. He lops off every branch of mine that's fruitless and prunes those that are productive, so that they may bear even more fruit. Because of the message I've shared with you, you're already clean. Remain in me and I in you. Just as no branch can bear fruit of its own accord, unless it remains on the vine, so also you cannot bear fruit unless you remain in me.

I am the vine, you're the branches. If you remain one with me and I with you then you'll produce an abundant crop, because without me you can do nothing. If anyone doesn't remain in me he's like a branch that's thrown away and withers; it's then gathered and flung into the fire and burned. If you remain in me and my words remain in you, you need only ask for whatever you wish and it'll be done for you.

In this way my Father's glorified, that you bear much fruit and so truly become my disciples.

Just as the Father's loved me so I've loved you. Remain in my love. If you keep my commandments you'll remain in my love, in the same way that I've kept my Father's commandments and remain in his love. I've said all this so that my joy may be in you, and that your joy may be full. This is my commandment, Love each other just as I've loved you.

This is the greatest love a man can show: to lay down his life for his friends. If you do what I tell you then you're my friends. So I'll no longer call you servants, because a servant has no inkling of his master's affairs; but the reason I've called you friends is because all that I've learned from my Father I've passed on to you.

You didn't choose me; I chose you so that you may go out and bear fruit that lasts, so that whatever you ask in my name the Father may give you. This is my commandment: love each other! If the world hates you remember that it hated me before you. If you belonged to the world, the world would love you as one of its own. But I've chosen you out of the world. It's for this reason that the world hates you.

Remember what I told you, no servant is greater than his master; if they persecuted me they'll persecute you; if they keep my teaching they'll keep yours. They'll do all this to you because of me, for they don't know the one who sent me. If I hadn't come and spoken to them they wouldn't be guilty of sin; but now they've no excuse for their sin.

Whoever hates me hates my Father. If I hadn't done miraculous signs among them they wouldn't be guilty of sin. But of course they've seen my miracles and still they've hated both me and my Father. This fulfils the scripture, ***They hated me without reason.***

Now when the Advocate comes, whom I'll send from the Father (that is to say the Spirit of truth who goes out from the Father), he'll bear witness about me. But it's up to you to bear witness too because you've been with me right from the start.

Chapter Sixteen

Jesus warns his disciples vv1–4

I've told you all this so that you won't lose faith. They'll throw you out of the synagogue, in fact the time's coming when anyone who kills you will think that they're doing God a favour. They'll do these things because they've known neither the Father nor me. I've told you all this so that when the time comes you'll remember the warning I gave you about them. I didn't tell you all this at the outset because there was no need since I was with you.

The Holy Spirit promised vv5–15

But now I'm going away to him who sent me; yet none of you asks, Where are you going? Even so your hearts are grief stricken because I've said these things to you. But in all seriousness, it's much better for you that I'm going away, for if I don't go the Advocate won't come to you; but if I go away I'll send him to you.

When he comes he'll prove the world to be in the wrong about sin, righteousness and judgment. About sin because they don't believe in me; about righteousness because I'm going to the Father and you won't see me any more; and about judgment because the ruler of this world stands condemned.

I've a lot more to tell you, more than you can cope with right now. But when he, the Spirit of truth comes he'll guide you into the whole truth. He won't speak on his own authority, he'll only tell you what he hears and he'll make known to you what's yet to come. He'll glorify me because he'll drive home to you the truth about me. All that belongs to the Father belongs to me. That's why I said he'll tell you all about me.

Grief into joy vv16–22

In a little while you won't see me any more, and then in a little while you'll see me again. At this some of his disciples said to each other, What's he on about, In a little while you won't see me any more, and then in a little while you'll see me again? And, Because I'm going to the Father? They kept asking, What does he mean when he says, A little while? We've not the faintest idea!

Now Jesus saw that they were eager to ask him about this, so he said to them, Are you asking each other what I meant when I said, In a little while you won't see me any more and then in a little while you'll see me again? Listen, you'll weep and wail while the world rejoices. Whenever a woman goes into labour she's in pain because it's her time, but when the baby is born she forgets all about the anguish she went through because she's thrilled that a child's arrived! And it's the same with you, you're sad now, but I'll see you again and then you'll have joy that no one can steal from you.

Promises and warnings vv23–33

When that time comes you won't ask me for anything. Let me assure you that whatever you ask in my name my Father will grant you! Until now you've not asked for anything in my name. Just ask and you'll be granted your request, so that your joy may be overflowing.

I've spoken about these things using figurative language, but soon I won't need to speak like this, but will instead tell you in plain words about the Father. Then you'll ask in my name, but I'm not saying to you that I'll ask the Father on your behalf; because the Father himself loves you for you've loved me, and have come to believe that I've come from God. I came from the Father and entered into the world and now I'm leaving the world and returning to the Father.

Then Jesus' disciples say, Now it's dawned on us that you're speaking plainly not figuratively! Now we realise that you know everything and have no need for anyone to question you. Because of this we believe that you've come from God. Jesus said, So you now believe do you? The time's approaching and indeed has arrived when you'll be scattered, each of you to his own home. You'll desert me and leave me on my own, although I'm not on my own because the Father is with me.

I've shared these things with you so that in me you may have peace. In this world tribulation will be your lot. But be brave. I've conquered the world!

Chapter Seventeen

The high priestly prayer of Jesus Christ vv1–5

When Jesus had finished saying these things he lifted his eyes towards heaven and said, Father the hour's come, glorify your Son that your Son may glorify you, even as you gave him authority over all mankind that he might give them eternal life. This is eternal life, that they might know you the only true God and the one you sent—Jesus Christ. I've brought you glory on earth by completing the task you gave me to do. Now Father, glorify me at your side with the glory that I had with you before the world began.

Jesus prays for his disciples vv6–19

I've revealed your name to those you gave me out of the world. They belonged to you and you entrusted them to me and they've obeyed your word. Now they know that everything you've given me comes from you, because the very words you gave to me I passed on to them. And they've accepted them and know for sure that I came from you, and have believed that you sent me.

I'm praying for them; I'm not praying for the world, but for those you've given to me, because they're yours. All mine are yours and all yours are mine, and it's through them that I have been and I am now glorified. I'm in the world no longer; they remain in the world, but I'm coming to you.

Holy Father, watch over them by the power of your name, which you've given to me so that they may be one, just as we are one. All the time I was with them I was watching over them and kept them safe by the power of your name that you've given to me. Not a single one of them has been lost, except the one consigned to destruction, so that the scripture may be fulfilled.

I'm coming to you now, but I say these things while I'm still in the world, so that they may be filled with my joy. I've given them your message and the world has hated them because they don't belong to the world, any more than I belong to the world. I don't ask that you take them out of the world, but instead that you protect them from the evil one. They don't belong to the world any more than I do. Set them apart in the truth; your word is truth. Just as you've sent me into the world so I've sent them. For their sakes I set myself apart, so that they also might be sanctified by the truth.

Jesus prays for all believers vv20–26

And it's not for them alone that I'm praying, but for those who come to have faith in me through their message, so that all of them may be one just as you're in me and I'm in you, that they also might be in us so that the world may believe that you've sent me. I've given them the same glory that you gave me, so that they may be one just as we're one: I in them and you in me that they may be made perfect in unity, so that the world may know that you sent me and that you love them just as you've loved me.

Father, my wish is that those you've given to me may be with me where I am, that they may revel in my glory—the same glory that you gave me before the creation of the world. Righteous Father, although the world doesn't know you, I know you, and they're convinced that you've sent me. I've revealed your name to them and will continue to reveal it, so that your love for me may be in them, and that I myself might also be in them.

Chapter Eighteen

The arrest and examination of Jesus Christ
vv1–27

After Jesus had prayed this prayer, he left with his disciples and crossed the Kidron Valley. There was an olive grove there that he entered with his disciples. This spot was well known to Judas (who betrayed him) because Jesus often used to go there with his disciples.

So Judas, together with a detachment of soldiers and officers from the chief priest and Pharisees came there, carrying torches, lanterns and weapons.

Jesus, who knew what was about to happen, stepped forward and says to them, Who are you looking for? Jesus of Nazareth, they replied. *EGO EIMI*, Jesus answers. Now Judas, the traitor, was standing there with them. When Jesus uttered the words, *I AM*, they all drew back and fell to the ground.

Jesus asked them once again, Who are you

looking for? And once more they replied, Jesus of Nazareth. Jesus said, I've already told you that's me, so if it's me you're looking for, let these men go. He said this so that what he predicted might come to pass, ***Of those you gave me I have not lost a single soul.***

Then Simon Peter, who happened to have a knife, drew it and took a swipe at the high priest's servant (called Malchus) and cut off his right ear. Jesus said to Peter, Put your knife back in its sheath! Am I not to drink the cup that the Father has given me?

Then the detachment of soldiers with their captain and the Jewish officials arrested and bound Jesus. First they brought him to Annas, the father-in-law of Caiaphas, the high priest that year. It was the same Caiaphas who had advised the Jewish leaders that it was better that one individual should die instead of the whole population.

Now Simon Peter and another disciple were following Jesus. And because that other disciple was known to the high priest he was able to go with Jesus into the high priest's courtyard. But Peter had to wait outside at the door. The other disciple, who was known to the high priest, then came out and spoke to the girl at the door and brought Peter in. She says to Peter, Don't tell me you're one of that man's followers are you? Certainly not, he replies. It was cold and the servants and officials had made a charcoal fire and were standing around warming themselves. Peter also joined them to keep himself warm.

Meanwhile the high priest questioned Jesus about his followers and about his teaching. Jesus responded, I've spoken publicly, I've always taught in the synagogue and in the temple where all the Jews congregate. I've said nothing in secret. Why do you question me? Go and question those who've heard what I said, they know perfectly well what I taught. At this one of the officers standing nearby slapped him, Is that the way to answer the high priest? If I've said anything wrong, replied Jesus, then point it out to me. But if not, why do you hit me? Annas then sent him bound to Caiaphas the high priest.

Meanwhile, Simon Peter was still standing warming himself. They asked him, Surely you're not one of his followers are you? No! said Peter, of course not! One of the high priest's servants, a relative of the man whose ear Peter had cut off, confronted him, Hang on! Didn't I see you in the garden with him? Again Peter denied it and at that instant a rooster began to crow.

They then take Jesus from Caiaphas to the governor's headquarters. It was the crack of dawn, but they did not enter the headquarters, to avoid becoming defiled (because they wanted to eat the Passover meal). So Pilate came out to them and says, What charge are you bringing against this man? They replied, If this man wasn't doing something wrong we wouldn't have handed him over to you. Well take him away yourselves, said Pilate, and judge him by your own law. Ah, the Jews replied, it isn't lawful for us to put anyone to death. (This fulfilled what Jesus had predicted about the kind of death he would die.)

Then Pilate went back again to his headquarters and summoned Jesus and said to him, Tell me, are you the King of the Jews? Is this something you worked out for yourself? Jesus asked, or did others tell you this? Pilate replied, I'm not a Jew, am I? It's your own people and the chief priests who handed you over to me. Just tell me, what have you done? Jesus answered, My kingdom isn't a worldly one, if it were, my subjects would be fighting to stop the Jewish authorities arresting me. No, my kingdom isn't from here. So you are a king then, are you? Pilate inquired. These are your words, said Jesus. I was born and came into the world for this reason to testify to the truth. Everyone who seeks the truth listens to me. Really? says Pilate; what is truth? After he had said this he went out again to the Jews; I can find no evidence to support the charge you make against him, he said. Now, you've a custom that at Passover I should release someone. Who shall it be—the King of the Jews? No! No! they cried, not this man; we want Barabbas!

Barabbas was a terrorist.

Chapter Nineteen

Pilate tries to save Jesus vv1–16

Pilate then took Jesus and had him whipped. The soldiers twisted together some thorns and made them into a crown and put it on his head and put a purple robe on him. They kept coming up to him and saying, All hail, King of the Jews! And they kept slapping his face.

Pilate once again went out and spoke to the Jews gathered there and says, Look, I'm bringing him out to you so that you might know that I can find no evidence to support the charge against him.

So Jesus came out wearing the crown made of thorns and a purple robe; and Pilate says to them, The man himself!

As soon as the chief priests and their staff saw him they roared, Crucify him! Crucify! You take him yourselves and crucify him, says Pilate, I can find no evidence to support the charge against him. The Jews responded, But we have a law, and under this law he must die because he claimed to be the Son of God.

When he heard this Pilate became more fearful. He went back inside his quarters, and again addresses Jesus, Where do you come from? But Jesus remained silent. Pilate says, Look here, aren't you going to speak to me? Don't you get it? I can either release you or have you crucified! Jesus answered, You'd have no power over me unless it was given to you from above. Therefore, the one who handed me over to you has the greater sin.

From this point onwards Pilate was determined to release him, but the Jews kept shouting, If you release this person you're not Caesar's friend, because anyone who claims to be a king is against Caesar!

When he heard this Pilate brought Jesus outside and took a seat on the bench in a place known as The Stone Pavement (called Gabbatha in Hebrew).

Now about noon, as the Jews were getting ready for the Passover, Pilate says to them, Behold your king! But they shouted, String him up! String him up! Crucify him! Says Pilate, are you asking me to crucify your king? The only king we have is Caesar, said the chief priests. Then he handed him over to them to be crucified.

The crucifixion of Jesus Christ vv17–37

So the soldiers took charge of him, and carrying his own cross Jesus went out to the place of the Skull, known in Hebrew as Golgotha. It was there that they crucified him, with two others, one each side and Jesus in the middle. Pilate wrote a notice and had it fastened to the cross. It read, *JESUS OF NAZARETH, KING OF THE JEWS.*

Now quite a few of the Jews read this notice because the place where Jesus was crucified was near the city and it was written in Hebrew, Latin and Greek. So the chief priests of the Jews made a protest to Pilate, Don't write, *The King of the Jews*, but rather, *This one said, I'm the King of the Jews.* Pilate answered, What I've written stands.

When the soldiers crucified Jesus they took his outer clothing, divided it into four, one for each of them, leaving only the tunic. This was seamless, woven from top to bottom in one piece. Let's not rip it up, they said, let's draw lots to see who'll get it. In this way the scripture was fulfilled, ***They divided my clothes among themselves and drew lots for them.*** So this is what the soldiers did.

Now standing at the foot of the cross were his mother, his mother's sister, Mary the wife of Clopas, and Mary Magdalene. When Jesus saw his mother and the beloved disciple, he says to his mother, Lady, this is your son. And to the disciple he says, This is your mother. From then on the disciple made her part of his family.

After this, with full knowledge that everything had been completed, Jesus says, to fulfil scripture, ***I'm thirsty.*** A jar full of sour wine was there, so they soaked a sponge with it, placed the sponge on some hyssop and held it up to his mouth. When he had drunk the sour wine Jesus said, It's finished! Then he bowed his head and gave up his spirit.

The burial of Jesus Christ vv38–42

As it was the day in which the Jews prepared for the Sabbath (and this particular Sabbath was an important one because it occurred at Passover), they asked Pilate that the legs of the crucified might be broken and their bodies removed rather than hang in public. So the soldiers came and broke the legs of the first man, then the other one who had been crucified with him. But when they came to Jesus they saw that he was already dead, so there was no need to break his legs. However, one of the soldiers stabbed his side with his spear and immediately blood and water gushed out.

This is a true and eyewitness account—and the one who saw what happened knows that what he says is true, so that you also may believe.

All this took place so that the scripture might be fulfilled, ***Not a bone of his will be broken.*** And in the words of another passage of scripture, ***They shall look on the one they have pierced.***

Later on, Joseph from Arimathea, a follower of Jesus (though a secret one because of his fear of the Jews) asked Pilate's permission to have custody of Jesus' body. Pilate duly gave permission, so Joseph came and removed the body.

Nicodemus, the man who had first visited Jesus by night, also came bringing a hundred pounds worth of a mixture of myrrh and aloes. They took the body of Jesus and wrapped it in strips of linen with spices, as is the Jewish custom for burial.

Now there was a garden near the place where Jesus was crucified and in that garden there was a new tomb in which no one had yet been interred. Since the tomb was nearby and it was the day of preparation for the Passover, they laid Jesus there.

Chapter Twenty

The resurrection of Jesus Christ vv1–31

Now early Sunday morning, while it was still dark, Mary Magdalene approaches the tomb. She sees that the stone has gone from the entrance. So she goes running to Simon Peter and the beloved disciple and says to them, They've taken away the master from the tomb, and we've no idea what's become of him!

Peter and the other disciple set out and arrived at the tomb. Both were running together, but the other disciple outran Peter and arrived first at the tomb. After he stooped down to look inside he sees the linen wrappings lying there, but he didn't go in. Simon Peter catches up with him. He immediately went into the tomb and beholds the linen wrappings lying there, and the facecloth that had been on Jesus' head lying, not with the linen, but rolled up in a place of its own.

Then the other disciple who had arrived first at the tomb also went inside. He saw and he believed. At that stage, though, they did not grasp that Christ's resurrection had been predicted in scripture. So the disciples went back to their homes.

But Mary stayed outside the tomb in floods of tears. As she wept she stooped to have a look inside the tomb. And she sees there two angels in white sitting where the body of Jesus had been lying, one where his head and the other where his feet had been. They say to her, Woman, why are you in tears? They've taken away my master, and I don't know where they've put him, she replies.

She turned around and who should she see but Jesus standing there; however, she did not realise that it was Jesus. Jesus says to her, Woman, why all these tears? Who are you looking for? Thinking that he was the gardener she says to him, Sir, if you've carried him off somewhere please tell me where, and I'll come and take him away. Jesus says to her, Mary. She swung around and says to him in Hebrew, Rabboni! (which means teacher). Jesus says to her, No, don't cling to me. I've not yet ascended to the Father. Just go to my brothers and tell them, I'm ascending to my Father and your Father, to my God and your God.

Mary Magdalene goes straight to the disciples and declares, I've actually seen the master! And she told them everything he had said to her.

On that Sunday evening the disciples met behind locked doors for fear of the Jews. Jesus came and stood among them. Peace be with you! he says. Then he showed them his hands and his side. The disciples were overjoyed when they saw the master.

Again Jesus said, Peace be with you! Just as the Father has sent me so I'm sending you. He then breathed on them and says, Receive the Holy Spirit! Anyone whose sins you forgive are forgiven; those you don't forgive are unforgiven.

But Thomas, one of the twelve (nicknamed the Twin), was absent when Jesus came. So the other disciples kept telling him, We've seen the master! Unless, he said, I see in his hands the mark of the nails and put my finger into the wound left by the nails, and put my hand into his side, I simply won't believe you.

Eight days later the disciples were indoors again and this time Thomas was with them. Although the doors were locked, Jesus came and stood among them and said, Peace be with you! Then he says to Thomas, Put your finger here and examine my hands, and reach out your hand, put it into my side. Have faith—no more unbelief! Thomas replied, My Lord and my God! Have you believed, says Jesus, because you've seen me? Blessed are those who believe but haven't seen.

Now his disciples were eyewitnesses to many wondrous signs done by Jesus that are not recorded in this book. But those recorded here are written so that you may hold fast to your belief that Jesus is the Messiah, the Son of God, and that by believing you may have life in his name.

Chapter Twenty-One

The risen Jesus at the Sea of Galilee vv1–14

After this Jesus again made himself known to his disciples by the Sea of Tiberias. This is how he revealed himself. Simon Peter, Thomas (the Twin), Nathanael, from Cana in Galilee, Zebedee's sons, and two other disciples were all together. I'm off fishing, says Simon Peter. We'll come with you then, say the others. So off they went and got into the boat; but that night they caught nothing.

At dawn Jesus was standing on the shore, although the disciples didn't realise who it was. So Jesus calls to them, My dear children! Don't tell me you haven't caught any fish? Not a single one, they replied. He said, Cast your net on the right side of the boat and you'll catch some. So they cast the net and were not able to haul it in, for it was brimful of fish!

Then the beloved disciple says to Peter, It's the Lord! As soon as he heard him say, It's the Lord,

Simon Peter wrapped his outer garment around him (because he was naked) and plunged into the sea. But the other disciples came in the little boat, towing the catch because they were not far from the shore, about a hundred yards.

When they had come ashore they see a charcoal fire ready with some smoked fish lying on it, and some bread. Jesus says to them, Bring the fish that you've caught. So Simon Peter went back and dragged the net ashore, heaving with fish, one hundred and fifty three in total—but even with so many the net did not tear. Jesus says to them, Come and have some breakfast! None of the disciples dared ask him, Who are you? Because they knew very well that it was the Lord. Jesus comes and takes both the bread and the fish and gives it to them.

Now this was the third time that Jesus was made known to his disciples after he was raised from the dead.

Jesus tests Peter vv15–23

After breakfast Jesus says to Simon Peter, Simon, son of John, do you love me more than these do? Yes, master, he says, you know that I love you. Then feed my lambs, says Jesus. Again Jesus says a second time, Simon son of John do you love me? Master, he says, you know that I love you. So Jesus says to him, Take care of my sheep. For the third time Jesus asks him, Simon, son of John, do you really love me? Peter was upset that Jesus had asked him for the third time, Do you really love me? So he says to him, Master, you know everything; surely you know that I love you! Jesus says to him, Then feed my sheep. But pay heed, when you were younger you wore what you liked and went about as you pleased; when you're old you will stretch out your hands and someone else will dress you and lead you where you don't want to go. (He said this to show by what death Peter would glorify God.) Then he said to him, Follow me! Peter turned and sees the beloved disciple following them—this was the one who had leaned against the breast of Jesus at supper and had said, Master, who'll betray you? When Peter sees the beloved disciple he says, Master, what about him? Jesus says to him, What about him? If I should want him to stay alive until I return what's that got to do with you? Just follow me! Because of this the word got around to the others that this disciple wouldn't die. But this isn't what Jesus said; rather, If I should want him to remain alive until I return, what business is that of yours?

John's eyewitness account confirmed vv24–25

This is the disciple who testifies about these things and who wrote them down, and we know that his testimony is true. Now Jesus also did many other things, which if they were written down then I suppose even the whole world would not be able to contain the books that would be written!

Amen.

This book is printed on paper from sustainable sources managed under the Forest Stewardship Council (FSC) scheme.

It has been printed in the UK to reduce transportation miles and their impact upon the environment.

For every new title that Matador publishes, we plant a tree to offset CO_2, partnering with the More Trees scheme.

For more about how Matador offsets its environmental impact, see www.troubador.co.uk/about/